NetWarriors in C

Programming 3D Multi-Player Games in C

Joe Gradecki

John Wiley & Sons, Inc.

New York • Chichester • Brisbane • Toronto • Singapore

Dedication:

This book is dedicated to Jesus Christ, my wife Waverly, and our son Matthew.

Acknowledgments:

I have to thank Tim Ryan, my editor, for coming up with the idea of writing this book.
I look forward to working with Tim on many more projects like this.

Publisher: Katherine Schowalter
Editor: Tim Ryan
Managing Editor: Micheline Frederick
Editorial Production & Design: Pronto Design & Production, Inc., New York, NY

Library of Congress Cataloging-in-Publication Data:

Gradecki, Joe, 1967-
     NetWarriors in C: programming 3D multi-player games in C/ Joe Gradecki
        p.   cm.
     Includes index.
     ISBN 0-471-11064-7 (paper/CD-ROM)
        1.C (Computer program language) 2. Computer games. 3. Computer graphics I. Title.
QA76.73.C15G72   1995
794.8 15133--dc20

Printed in the United States of America

10 9 8 7 6 5 4 3 2 1

Table of Contents

▼

INTRODUCTION

There's no doubt that the future of gaming is 3D multi-player games. Games like DOOM, Specter, and Knights of the Sky let players battle it out against each other over modems and networks. This book will show you how to create your own multi-player computer games that work over null modems, modems, ethernet networks, and the Internet.

Not only will we show you how to create the 3D games using a shareware engine called ACK3D, a clone of the Wolfenstein-type graphics, but we will give you complete source code and libraries for serial communications (null modem and modem), ethernet, and Internet.

So you've played DOOM and now want to do ethernet communication. We have included a complete C language ethernet interface. All you need to do is plug in the code and use simple commands like send_pkt and get_from_queue. You can even move up to the Internet which allows you to communicate all over the world with an even simpler interface.

The CD ROM

As you saw on the cover of the book, there is a CD ROM enclosed. This CD ROM contains all of the source code and executables for the Minotaur game that we develop throughout the book and all of the source code and libraries for communications.

We have also included a shareware paint program called MVP Paint that will allow you to easily create the bitmaps for your own game.

In addition, the CD ROM contains over 250 MB of game development code. Here's just a sampler of the directories:

> /LIBS
> /UTILS
> /SOURCE
> /GAMESRC

The /LIBS directory contains graphics libraries for all kinds of different graphics techniques. The /GAMESRC directory includes complete source code to many different games.

What you will find on the CD ROM will amaze you. It will provide you with everything you need to develop your own shareware and commercial games.

What You'll Need

You will need access to a Borland compiler if you want to recompile the code on the CD ROM. You should be familiar with C code and take the time to walk through the development of our Minotaur game.

How This Book is Organized

Chapter 1: The first thing that we need to discuss is what we mean by multi-player network games. This chapter gives you the overview necessary to understand the concepts we will present in the remainder of the book.

Chapter 2: To help you understand the uses of the network in our game programming, we will use a graphics engine based on the technique ray casting. This chapter gives you a background of ray casting and introduces a ray casting engine called ACK3D.

Chapter 3: Before we discuss network concepts, we use the ACK3D engine to develop a skeleton program that shows how to program the basic components of the ACK3D engine.

Chapter 4: One of the more important parts of the ACK3D engine is the graphics. This chapter will show you how to use several shareware programs on the enclosed CD ROM to design and draw the bitmaps necessary for any game.

Chapter 5: This chapter begins our dive into multi-player games. We discuss the concepts of adding graphics and an opponent to our ACK3D skeleton program. We will also discuss the intricacies of moving the opponent.

Chapter 6: We move to adding multi-player communications by putting a NULL modem serial link into our skeleton program. We discuss programming the modem and detail the code necessary for ACK3D.

Chapter 7: This chapter discuss all of the aspects of Ethernet programming. Step-by-step we develop a complete ethernet library that you can use for your own game.

Chapter 8: Once we can communicate on the ethernet, we need to include the interface code into our game. This chapter will give you the further information as well as code for including the ethernet library.

Chapter 9: The Internet. Using a package called WATTCP we are able to add TCP/IP communication to our game. This chapter looks at the WATTCP package, developing a simple communication program, and adding Internet support to our game.

Chapter 10: Adding three or more players to a game is a whole different matter. This chapter covers all of the aspects including graphics and communications.

Chapter 11: We must have monsters in our game in order to give us something to shoot at. This chapter discusses adding a MEDUSA head monster that fires spitballs and the MINOTAUR - a walking, axe chopping monster that literally chases you down.

Chapter 12: What? Oh, yeah. Sound. We look at the support for a popular sound toolkit included on the CD ROM.

Chapter 13: Our last chapter looks at finishing the game. Adding overlays, doors, joystick control, and mouse support, as well as the ability to pick up objects on the floor.

Introduction to Multi-Player Game Programming

You quickly turn your monitor away from the view of the hallway. You tap a few keys and a colorful view into a strange new world appears. You tap another couple of keys and you're instantly in control of a high-powered machine gun. You advance forward, scanning for the enemy and small beads of sweat begin to appear on your forehead.

You step up the pace, turn a corner, and run right into Joan from accounting—but she doesn't look like Joan. She's a soldier like you in the brave new world, but there's no time to swap war stories—five enormous Minotaurs enter the room and charge. You and Joan put your shoulders together and walk slowly backwards, sweeping the entire area with bullets.

As the last monster crumples to the ground, you hear footsteps in the distance—oh no, it's the boss! A quick three-finger salute and the game vanishes from your screen. The spreadsheet you were working on reappears. You breathe a sigh of relief and slump back into your chair. Isn't teamwork great?!

 # Why Network Games?

Team sports have always been much more accepted than solo sports. In fact, about the only major individual sports are bowling and golf. When the computer came along, it in effect forced us to return to individual play. Space Invaders, Asteroids, Battle Zone, and other video games pitted one player against the computer.

You've probably noticed that the computer is usually not the best opponent. How many arcade games have you won? And even if you "win," the machine still keeps your quarter.

It's no challenge to create a computer game that is faster than a human. That's how most arcade-style games work—eventually they wear you down and you can't move that joystick fast enough.

On the other hand, computers are not very smart opponents—you can usually win a computer game by finding the computer's pattern. Most computer opponents are not programmed to think dynamically—they are predictable and eventually boring. They really don't learn from one play of the game to the next. That's why there's no challenge like playing a quick, smart, devious human opponent.

In this book, you'll learn how to create multi-player games that work over:

- Serial cable connections
- Modems
- Ethernet networks
- The Internet

The Classical Foundation

The most popular form of communication via computer is the modem. Every day thousands of people connect to thousands of bulletin board systems around the world. During the connection, data is being exchanged at a furious pace. We can take advantage of the millions of modems in the world by giving the user the ability to connect to another user over ordinary phone lines.

Communication using the modem or a null modem serial line is accomplished using a simple software package that we are including on the enclosed CD ROM. IBMCOM is a public domain interface package that gives you all of the functions necessary to initialize, transmit, and receive through either the modem or the serial port.

With the advent of new high-speed modems operating at speeds up to 28.8k baud, we can successfully create a 3D interactive game that gives each of the players located anywhere in the world an exciting experience.

The Network Foundation

Several years ago, corporate America began to see that its aging mainframe computer systems were simply not going to be able to keep up with the demands of the day. Accounting was getting more complicated, the payroll was being expanded, and all of the employees wanted faster response from their terminals. It appeared that the only option available was to purchase a new multimillion-dollar system.

At about the same time, a company called Novell introduced a package called NetWare that allowed ordinary personal computer systems to be used in a very effective manner. The idea was to give all of the employees in a company their own personal computers. The computers would be used for individual tasks like word processing, and also give employees the ability to communicate and share data with others in the company. The sharing of data and programs was accomplished using Novell NetWare. The software acted as a traffic coordinator for all of the interconnected personal computers.

This arrangement turned out to be much better than using a large mainframe with several hundred terminals. People using their own personal desk computers could accomplish tasks faster because they were using dedicated machines. Only when they needed data from another machine did they experience any delays.

Inexpensive Nets

Once businesses started to use networks, the manufacturers of the hardware and software required to connect the computers together began lowering their prices. In fact, prices are so low that you can easily connect three computers together on a network for under $300 for the hardware and about $200 for the software. A two-person connection via modem is even cheaper, and many people have access to the Internet for free through their businesses. Suddenly there's a huge market for multi-player computer games.

The Software

To use a network, you need software. We will assume that you have a computer and a connection to a network, either a two-computer net or a large net like the Internet. The software used to access the network must link your computer with other computers on the network. The access comes from a coordination of activities between the network communication hardware installed in your computer and an application program. There are several different options; we will only be covering packet drivers in this book.

Novell NetWare

Novell NetWare has a dominate position in the business community. This software has been designed to handle large numbers of computers on a single network. As we've mentioned, its job is to coordinate the activities of these different computers. This coordination includes determining which files can be accessed by individual computers and which applications are available to be executed on the network, as well as providing a high level of security. With everybody on the network and all of their files accessible, there needs to be a level of security that prevents unauthorized access to data.

Windows for Workgroups

Windows for Workgroups appeared on the market several years ago as an alternative to Novell NetWare. This system consists of the Windows environment coupled with networking capabilities. Windows for Workgroups is designed somewhat differently from Novell's software—the network functionality is built right into the application software. When you execute Windows for Workgroups, you are attached to the network by default. There is no outside supervising software controlling your access to the network.

Packet Drivers

The Internet provides us with an interesting assortment of network software. The software available on the Internet is more low-level than either

NetWare or Workgroups. This software, called a packet driver, does not provide security or automatic anything. It is used simply as a link between the hardware and some application code executing on the PC. Its primary job is to take information from the network communication hardware and relay it to your application code.

Creating Network Games

As you can see, there is indeed a foundation for the development of network applications. Millions of computers each day are tapped into either a business network, a personal network, or the Internet. Our goal is to build a 3D graphical computer game that will give users the ability to either play against other humans or team up with them against alien invaders no matter where they are located in the world. Now let's look at the different tools and techniques necessary to build our game.

Programming the Net

Programming for a network is a different process than that normally used to develop software. We have to provide all of the links between our program and the packet driver that will be installed in the individual computer. The link insures that information sent from the computer arrives at the receiving computer without any problems. This can be a real concern, since the user will generally not be able to see the receiving computer, which may be located in another building or even in another country.

Fortunately, a good deal of the work has already been done for us in the way of a *network card*. When you first attach yourself to a network, a network card is installed. This card fits in the back of the computer and has a port that attaches to the network. The card handles the necessary communication timings and the sending and receiving of information.

Communicating with the Card

Since the network card is a piece of hardware, we will require some type of software to access it. We are going to use a packet driver—a small piece of code that has the sole purpose of communicating with the network card. When information arrives at the network card, the card will indicate the situation to the packet driver. The packet driver will take the information from the network card and put it in a buffer. When the packet driver has information to put on the network, it will give the information to the network card and the information will be put on the net.

Because the packet driver must talk directly to the network card and handle information between itself and the card, it is typically written in assembly language—this code is very "tight" and does not waste any time receiving and sending information.

Communicating with the Application

Now we have a network card and the packet driver communicating with the card. To be useful, we need a way of communicating with the packet driver. Communicating with the packet driver is accomplished using two routines built into the packet driver. These routines are SEND and RECEIVE.

When our application program wishes to send information to another computer on the network, it will assemble the appropriate information and call the routine SEND provided by the packet driver. The packet driver will copy the necessary information from the application program and pass it along to the network card when it is ready to receive it.

When our application program needs data from the network, it will call the packet driver's RECEIVE routine. The packet driver will access its internal buffer and give the application program the next available piece of information.

As we will see in a later chapter, the actual communication scheme between computers on the network, between the packet driver and the network card, and between the packet driver and the application are more complex than this simple example, but it should give you a general idea of the process involved in communicating on the network.

Graphics

As we mentioned, we are going to create a *graphical* network game. In determining how to program the graphics for a network game, it becomes clear that we need to focus more on the network communications than on how to draw lines. For this reason we are going to use a graphics engine called ACK3D.

ACK3D is a graphics engine create by Larry Myers and released into the public domain. This engine mimics the very popular Castle Wolfenstein type of graphics. We will discuss more about Wolfenstein and ACK3D in later chapters. By using this engine, we can jump right into our discussion of programming for networks and adding support for networks into our own applications.

Conclusion

You should now have a very broad picture of what we are able to accomplish. Our goal is to bring together the communication networks with

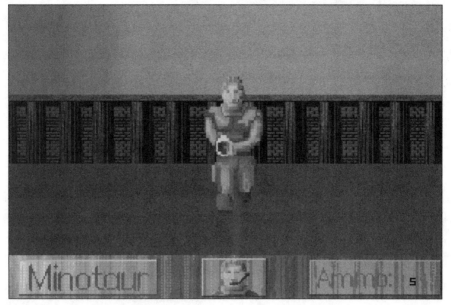

Figure 1.1   Illustration from Minotaur.

computer graphics to create a network-based computer game. No longer will you have to rely on the intelligence of the computer as an adversary. You can now compete head to head with anyone in your company—or the world, for that matter.

It is our goal to give you all of the information and code necessary for you to create network-based computer games. We have included a full sample program complete with firing and monster routines. You will learn how to create your own games. Figure 1.1 shows you just one illustration from the included game.

Even more, we will give you the code for linking your game with others using a serial link, network link, or the Internet. Imagine the fun you and an opponent can have as you communicate over a large distance. Once you become familiar with the network code and the routines necessary to use it, you will be able to use it in other programs. You will have a complete network communication system in both source and executable formats as well as the instructions for using it.

Ray Casting

Since the dawn of computer graphics, programmers have been trying to develop the perfect system for providing realistic, real-time graphics. Many techniques have been developed to meet this challenge; most have been centered around the advancement of the computer hardware as opposed to software algorithms.

Creating Graphics

There are many different ways of creating computer game graphics, including sprites, rendering, ray tracing, and ray casting. Each one of these has its advantages and disadvantages when it comes to realism and speed.

Sprites

The technique called sprites was used quite often during the beginning of the personal computer revolution. The Commodore 64 and Atari personal computers all had routines available for manipulating sprites. A sprite is a specific square area (say 64 x 64 pixels) that contains a graphical image. A sprite can be drawn (and then erased) very quickly over a static background to create the illusion of movement. For instance you can create a "jetfighter" sprite and superimpose it over a background with sky and clouds. By quickly drawing the sprite, erasing it, and redrawing it in a new position, you can make your jetfighter appear to be flying through the sky.

The computer system often provided routines that would detect when one sprite has collided with another sprite. Games could be developed using the sprites and the collision detection. Sprites are still used today in some computer games because it is easy to animate them and develop two-dimensional games with them. However, it is hard to create three-dimensional games with them.

Rendering

To create three-dimensional games, a developer could use a technique called rendering. This is the type of graphics used for most flight simulators and true virtual reality programs. The technique involves drawing three-dimensional objects on the screen in relationship to the player's viewpoint. The objects are given to the system as numbers defining their vertices and lines. The computer must re-create the object according to a viewpoint every time the player moves in the game. The number of views a player can have is nearly infinite, and every object in the game has to be recalculated and redrawn each time the player moves. Even if the player moves a very small step, everything must be redrawn. You can just imagine how the calculations begin to add up very quickly. Suddenly, the computer is spending most of its time doing screen calculations instead of responding to the player's movements and the movements of the opponent, not to mention all of the other housekeeping functions the computer must perform.

This technique creates very good three-dimensional systems and allows the player to have complete movement and interaction with the game, but it suffers from the number of calculations that must be performed for each player movement. Once any sort of detail is given to the objects in the game, the speed declines noticeably.

Ray Tracing

To create a better looking game but keep the speed high, some developers have turned to a technique called ray tracing. The idea behind ray tracing is to define a three-dimensional image using numbers as in the case of rendering, and draw the image using the properties of the objects in the image. For instance, if you had a checkerboard as a floor and a mirrored ball floating above it, the image should be drawn such that the checkerboard floor is reflected in the mirrored ball. To create this image, you have to send a "ray" into the objects for each pixel of the screen. The ray would obey the laws of the objects in the image, and the mirrored ball would reflect rays down to the checkerboard floor. The ray would then end up with an assigned color.

Ray-traced images are very detailed and look outstanding, but just one image can take minutes to hours to complete. To create a game using this technique, the developers would ray-trace all of the images and store them on the player's disk. As you play the game, different images appear on the screen, giving you the idea that you are playing in a realistic world.

Ray Casting

This last technique is sort of a compromise between all of the above techniques. Ray casting is a process whereby a ray is cast into a defined world, but instead of a color for the ray, the height of a wall is determined. The wall is part of a two-dimensional map created when the game was developed. As you move throughout the game, you are constantly looking at the map walls and other objects put into the maze. This technique is very fast and creates some good results visually. It will be the focus for the remainder of this chapter.

How to Cast a Ray

As we have seen from the previous discussion, ray casting can provide a good solution to the problem of creating realistic graphics for our games. In this book, we will be using a freeware ray-casting engine to help us create a multi-player game. Before we discuss how to use the engine, we should look at how ray casting works.

The author of the ray-casting engine we are using set out to create the engine using a simple unoptimized ray-casting technique. To begin ray casting, we need to have a two-dimensional map. This map consists of walls placed in the X,Y plane. Figure 2.1 shows a section of a larger map.

As you can see from the map, the walls are the physical boundaries that keep you within certain areas of the two-dimensional plane. The map should look something like the hunt-and-trace games that you may have played. The purpose of the ray-casting engine is to determine which of the walls should be drawn on the screen and at what height.

Cubes

To cut down on the work that the ray-casting engine has to do, we divide the walls of the map into sections called cubes that are 64 units x 64 units. Our simple map in Figure 2.1 looks like the map in Figure 2.2 when converted to cubes.

The cubes with a black dot in them represent the walls of the map, and the empty cubes are the areas of the map that the player can walk in. Because each of the cubes is 64 x 64 units, the player of the game can only move 64 units in both the X and Y directions.

Player

Once we have our map, we need to place the player in it. For the time being, we will use our simple map and place the player arbitrarily. Our player will be represented by the symbol shown in Figure 2.3.

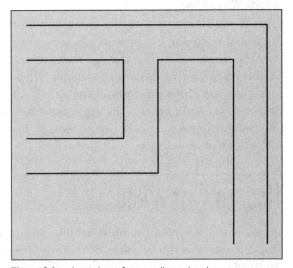

Figure 2.1   A section of a two-dimensional map.

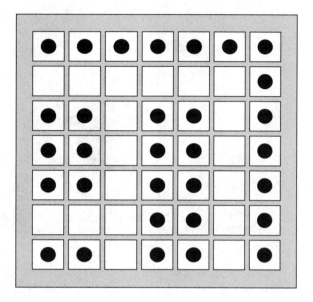

Figure 2.2 Cubed map.

The arrow in the center of the symbol represents the direction that the player is facing. We will always need to know where the player is looking.

Viewport

One of the most important considerations when developing a three-dimensional game is deciding how much of the "world" we are going to allow the player to view. If we give players too much of a viewport into the world they will have to contend with too many features of their surroundings at the same time. In addition, the more we allow the player to see, the more the computer has to keep track of. On the other hand, if we give players too small a viewport, they will spend the majority of their time moving around just to see what's in the world instead of playing the game.

The ACK3D engine we are using for our game uses a 60-degree viewport. This viewport is called the field of view. When players are looking

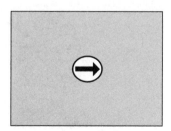

Figure 2.3 Player symbol.

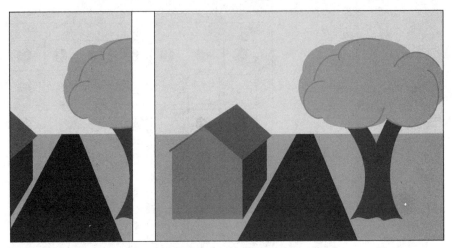

Figure 2.4   Two views of a world: 60 degrees and 180 degrees.

into a "world" they will see 60 degrees of it. We can compare this to our own world, where we have a 180-degree field of view. Figure 2.4 shows the difference between the two.

For ACK3D, the 60-degree field of view is divided evenly according to the direction that the player is looking. This is shown in Figure 2.5.

To see how the 60-degree field of view will look when the player is placed in the map, we can combine Figure 2.5 with Figure 2.2 to get Figure 2.6.

As you can see, the player will see a hallway in front with a wall in the background as well as two walls on each side.

We are now at the point where we can ask how we are going to take the two-dimensional map along with the position of the player and transform it into a three-dimensional maze. From Figure 2.6, it should be clear that the walls on each side of the player are much closer than the wall directly in front. The front wall is considerably farther into the distance and thus must be shown that way. Figure 2.7 shows what Figure 2.6 will look like when drawn in three dimensions.

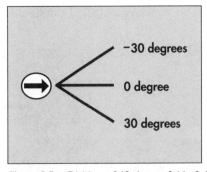

Figure 2.5   Division of 60-degree field of view.

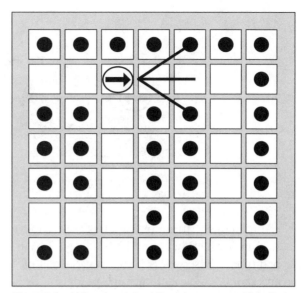

Figure 2.6 What the player will see in our map with a 60-degree field of view.

This figure gives us the answer as to how we are going to transform the two-dimensional map into a three-dimensional maze: by calculating the height of a wall that is visible in the player's field of view according to the distance it is from the player. The farther away a wall is, the smaller it will be drawn on the screen. If the player is pressing his nose right up to one of the walls, then the wall should be drawn very large. In fact, it will be drawn so large that most of the wall will not even fit in the visible part of the screen.

Of course, we will need some way of determining the distance from the player to the wall. This is where trigonometry comes into play. (I sure

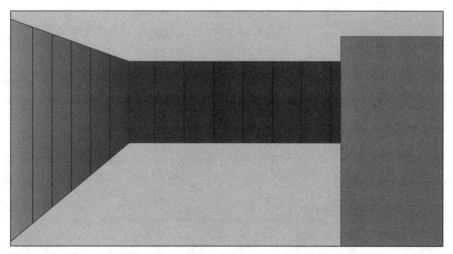

Figure 2.7 Three-dimensional view of Figure 2.6.

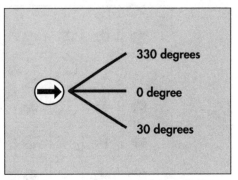

Figure 2.8   Degree positions of the field of view.

can remember sitting in trig class and saying I'm never going to use this stuff in my lifetime. Now I wish I could have a dollar for every time I've had to eat those words.) So, how does all of this work? Let's run through an example to clear things up.

Casting a Ray

We will begin by giving the player's position in the map an X,Y coordinate value. As you can see, the position is in the third cube from the left and second cube from the top. If we consider the upper left corner to be the 0,0 position, this gives us a cube coordinate of 3,2. Since each cube is 64 units by 64 units, we are roughly at the position 160,96—assuming that the player's position is in the center of the cube.

Next, we need to determine the actual angle values of the field of view. The ACK3D engine assumes that angle value 0 is located directly in front. This puts the angle value 30 degrees to the right and 330 degrees to the left, as we see in Figure 2.8.

Since the 330-degree angle is the edge of the player's field of view on the left, we will start with this angle for casting rays. The ray that we cast

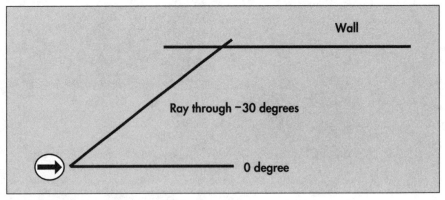

Figure 2.9   First ray, cast through -30 degrees.

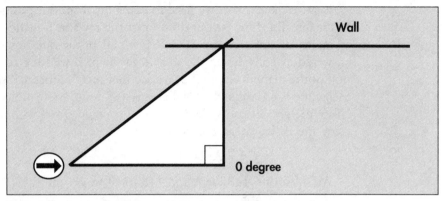

Figure 2.10 A right triangle created between the player and the wall.

will travel from the position of the player, at coordinate (160,96), out 30 degrees to the left until it hits either one of the map walls. Figure 2.9 shows the first ray.

This ray will hit a wall somewhere in the distance. It is the distance from the position of the player to the wall that we want to obtain. We do this by drawing a line extending directly in front of the player, and connecting that line to the point where the ray hits the wall, using a perpendicular line. This creates the right triangle that we see in Figure 2.10.

We can then label the edges that make up the triangle as we see in Figure 2.11.

From the labels and trigonometry, we have the following three equations:

$$\tan(\text{angle}) = \text{Opposite} / \text{Adjacent}$$
$$\cos(\text{angle}) = \text{Adjacent} / \text{Hypotenuse}$$
$$\sin(\text{angle}) = \text{Opposite} / \text{Hypotenuse}$$

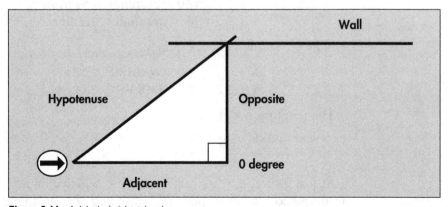

Figure 2.11 A labeled right triangle.

Now, we know that we have to cast a ray from our position 30 degrees to the left. But how far out do we cast the ray and how do we check for an intersection with the wall? The first part of the question can be answered by considering the size of our map. If we look at the small section of the map in Figure 2.2, we see that it is 7 cubes x 7 cubes. Since each cube is 64 units, the total area is 448 units x 448 units. We can calculate the greatest possible distance a ray could travel within this area using the Pythagorean theorem:

$$C^2 = A^2 + B^2$$

We substitute 448 for A and 448 for B to get the value

$$C^2 = 401,408$$
$$C = 633.5676759$$

Note that this is the worst-case value. Many times, the ray will intersect a wall way before the ray gets 634 units from the player; however, we must be prepared for any situation.

With this information, we can find the endpoint of the ray using the equations for a point on a circle. These equations are:

$$X_{circle} = X_{center} + \cos(angle) * radius$$
$$Y_{circle} = Y_{center} + \sin(angle) * radius$$

To see how the equations work, visualize that the player's position is in the center of a large circle. The distance from the center of the circle to any point on the edge of the circle is 634 units. We are just asking the equations to tell us the coordinate values for the point located on the circle moving in a particular direction from the center of the circle.

We already have most of the values for the equations, so we should begin filling things in. Recall that we have estimated the player's position as (160,96). First we can add the center point values:

$$X_{circle} = 160 + \cos(angle) * radius$$
$$Y_{circle} = 96 + \sin(angle) * radius$$

Now the radius and angle values:

$$X_{circle} = 160 + \cos(330) * 634$$
$$Y_{circle} = 96 + \sin(330) * 634$$

The resulting values are:

$$X_{circle} = 709$$
$$Y_{circle} = -221$$

At first glance, it would appear that the negative value for the Y coordinate should actually be positive, but these numbers do not represent the position of the player. They will be used in a line drawing routine that we present in the next section.

Bresenham

At this point we have the coordinate values for the player's position (160,96) and the endpoint of the ray from the player's position (709, -221). Now we need to step along the line connecting these two points and check for an intersection with any of the map walls. Stepping along the ray can be accomplished using the line-drawing technique called Bresenham. This algorithm is very fast and gives us each of the coordinates along the line from the player to its endpoint. As we check each of the points along the ray that has been cast, the x,y value of the point is placed in the equation

$$\text{Map-Position} = (y / 64) * 8 + (x / 64)$$

Recall that the map we are using has 8 squares along the horizontal and each of the squares are 64 units x 64 units. Once a map position value is found, the ACK3D engine looks at the map to see if a wall is in the current position.

If a wall is found, the engine no longer has to check any more points along the ray. It now needs to find the distance from the player to the wall using the following equation

$$C^2 = (\text{xofintersection} - \text{xofplayer})^2 + (\text{yofintersection} - \text{yofplayer})^2$$

The resulting value from this equation is the distance the wall is from the player. The value is used as an index into a table of wall heights. The wall heights are precalculated to show the size they should appear on the screen.

Next Ray

After we have cast the leftmost ray, which is 30 degrees, we need to move slightly to the right to cast the very next ray representing the player's field of view. We don't simply cast the ray that is 29 degrees to the left, since that would only give us 60 of the possible 320 columns of the screen. The correct increment value is 60 degrees/320 columns, or 0.1875 degrees. So the next ray will be at an angle of 29.8125 degrees.

The Algorithm

The resulting algorithm for this type of ray casting is:

```
Loop until the game ends
   Start with ray 30 degrees from the left
   Loop for 320 rays
```

```
    Calculate endpoint of ray using current position of player
        and equation for circle
    Find intersection point with wall
    Calculate distance to wall
    Draw column of wall using height table using distance to
        wall as index
    Increment 0.1875 for next ray.
  End loop
End loop
```

The Problems

Although the preceding technique for ray casting does indeed work, the author of the ACK3D engine notes that it has several problems. The first problem is speed. Casting a ray for each of the 320 points is just plain slow. In fact, the author comments that the screen can be seen updating from left to right.

The second problem is accuracy. The original system was coded using floating point numbers to get the 0.1875 increments and such. As with most accumulations of floating point arithmetic routines, round-off errors begin occurring. The obvious solution to this problem is to move to a fixed point number system.

The third problem is the intersections. When an intersection is found between a ray and a wall, there is no easy way to determine if the wall section is horizontal or vertical. We need to know this information in order to draw the correct wall on the screen.

Ray Casting Version 2.0

Since the author of ACK3D had proven that this method for ray casting was workable, it was time to set out to make it work fast. The first thing done to the system was to eliminate the floating point numbers and switch to fixed point.

The next very important step was to use tables for most of the calculations. If you go back to the section on the player's viewpoint in ACK3D, you will see that each time a new column is to be drawn on the screen, the viewpoint is advanced 0.1875 degrees. At each advancement, we must calculate the sine, cosine, and tangent of the new angle. Obviously it is necessary to calculate the new angles, since, for example, the sine of 30 will be different than that of 29.8125. But what becomes repetitive and clearly a waste of time is that every time the player actually moves and the screen has to be redrawn, we have to go back and recalculate the sine of 30—and of each of the other 320 possible angles. Since trigonometric calculations are time-consuming, the best thing we can do is set up a table of all of the possible sine, cosine, and tangent values for all of the possible angles in our system.

Each of the tables will have 1920 entries, since a circle has 360 degrees and we will advance through the circle at 0.1875 increments. When the ACK3D engine is first executed, it will create all of the tables and store them in main memory. In order to determine which of the table entries holds the correct value for a possible angle, we simple take the angle we are using, say 30, and divide it by the value 0.1875. The resulting value, after truncation, is the lookup table entry.

Line Speedup

After the trig tables have been set up we need to look for even more speedup. The kind of speedup that we are interested in can be found in the Bresenham line-drawing technique of finding an intercept. As things sit right now, we cast a ray from the player's current position out a particular angle and determine where it intersects a wall. We must check each and every point along the ray. If you look at Figure 2.12, you will get a good idea of what we are doing.

As we mentioned earlier, for our simple map, we would have up to 634 points along each ray to check for an intersection. However, if we combine several things that we discussed earlier, we can significantly reduce this number. Recall that when the ACK3D engine begins execution, it places the player at a specific location in the map. When players begin moving in the "world," they are only able to move 64 units per step. Each time they press the Up arrow on the keyboard, the computer will move them 64 units forward.

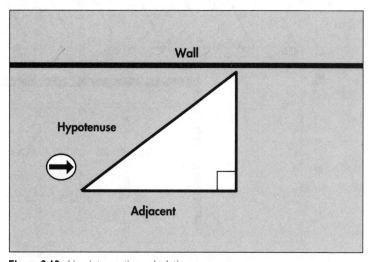

Figure 2.12 Line intersection calculations.

If players are only able to move 64 units at a time, then they cannot intersect the map walls at all of the 634 possible points along a ray. In fact, for every 64 x 64 cube, they can only intersect the wall at one possible location.

Figure 2.13 shows a small section of a map. Using the player symbol, I have plotted a possible course along the top of the map. Since the cubes are all 64 x 64 and our movements are 64 units, these are the only possible positions for the player along the particular path mapped out. This being the case, the first possible intersection with the wall must be at a fixed location. Notice that for all of the points along the ray from the player to the wall, an intersection cannot occur, since the player cannot move in units less than 64. In other words, when a ray is cast from the player, we do not need to make a check for an intersection with all of the points along the line. We only need to check the points at 64 units along the ray. The reason for this is that there is no possible way for the user to move 5 units forward only 64 units.

We can use a little more trig to find the exact location of a possible intersection. To accomplish all of this, we have to break the ray-casting process down to finding any wall intersection on the X side of the player and then any wall intersection on the Y side of the player. The author of the ACK3D engine gives the following algorithm used for ray casting in ACK3D. After the algorithm listing, we will run through an example to show how it works.

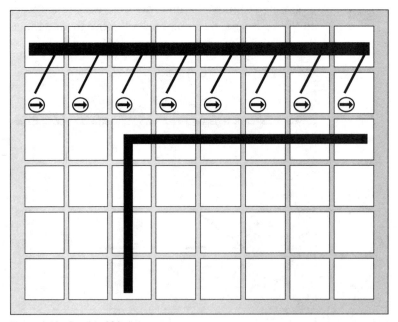

Figure 2.13 Possible 330 degree rays.

```
Loop till game end
   Loop for 320 rays
      Subtract 30 degrees from the player's current position to
         obtain the degree to begin casting rays
      Find the Y intercept of the current cube. We can find the Y
         intercept using the X coordinate and the tangent or
         inverse tangent value of the ray casting angle.
   The resulting X,Y pair is the first possible intersect point for the
current ray
      Increase or decrease the X and Y values by 64 to determine
         the new X,Y coordinate for a possible intersection.
      Continue until a wall is struck.
      After a wall is hit, we know which column or row of the wall to
         draw using the Y value and the X coordinate will tell
         us the distance the wall is from the player. Notice
         that we have the distance without the use of a square
         root.
      Do the process again for the Y walls using the Y coordinate
         and finding the X.
      Compare the X wall ray with the Y wall ray. The smallest
         value is the closest wall
   End Loop
End Loop
```

To see how the algorithm works, let's run through an example using the map in Figure 2.14.

We will start our player out at location (20,236), where (0,0) is located in the upper left-hand corner. The player is facing the 0-degree direction, so we subtract 30 to get the angle 330. Next we need to calculate the Y coordinate of the possible intersection point. Using the fact that a right triangle is formed with the ray cast from 330 degrees and a 0-degree line, we can use the tangent function to find the Y value.

$$\tan(330) = Y / 44$$
$$Y = 44 * \tan(330) = -25.40$$
$$236 - 25 = 211$$

That is, if the Y value of the player's position is 236, that of the point of intersection between the 330-degree ray and the wall is 211. If we draw a line to represent the current position of our ray in Figure 2.14, we get Figure 2.15.

Now that the first point has been calculated and there is no intersection, we increase the X coordinate by 64 units and decrease the Y coordinate by 64 units to get the ray in Figure 2.16.

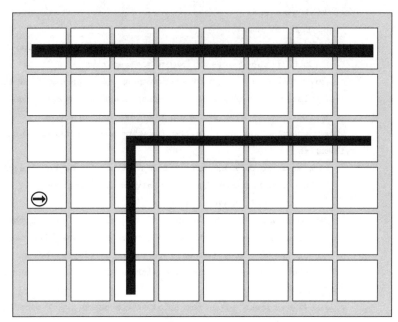

Figure 2.14 Starting map.

There is still no intersection, so we cast the ray again by adding 64 to the X coordinate and subtracting 64 from the Y coordinate. Again there is no intersect, so we do the arithmetic one more time to get the illustration shown in Figure 2.17.

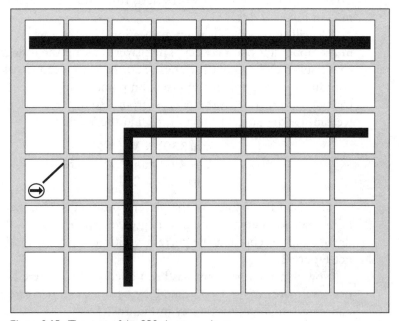

Figure 2.15 The start of the 330-degree angle ray.

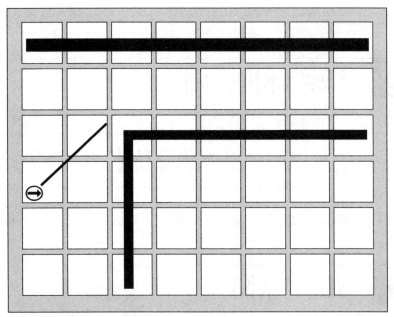

Figure 2.16 The 330-degree ray cast to two cubes.

We now have an intersection. The final intersection coordinate is (256,7). This tells us that the wall is 256 - 20 = 236 units away from us. Once the X wall is found, we can do all of the calculations again to find any Y or vertical wall. After we have the X intersections and the Y intersec-

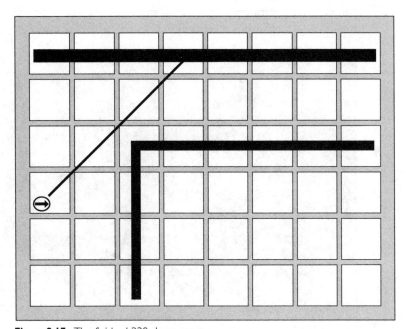

Figure 2.17 The finished 330-degree ray.

tions, we compare the two intersections to see which of them are closest to the player. The closest wall is drawn on the screen.

A Ray-Casting Engine

You have seen and played Castle Wolfenstein and understand how the graphics were accomplished. Now it's time to create your own game using the ray-casting technique. The only problem is that you face actually writing a system that will do the graphics. Even from the description in the previous sections, you can tell that such a system will be quite involved and require a good deal of time to write. Fortunately, someone has already done the work for you. In this section we will explore the ray-casting engine called ACK3D.

What is ACK3D?

ACK3D was developed by Larry Myers and introduced to the general public in late 1992. Its sole purpose is to give those of us without the time and energy to create a ray-casting engine a system that we can immediately use to create Wolfenstein-type games. Figure 2.18 shows a picture of the game we will create in this book.

The system consists of a set of C-callable functions that provide all of the necessary support for creating ray-casting games. Much of the actual ray-casting technique is hidden within the functions and thus not our

Figure 2.18 A screen shot of the Minotaur game.

concern. Most of the work that we have to do to use the engine comes in the form of design. An example of one of the functions is:

$$result = AckInitialize(\&main\_struct);$$

This single function takes care of the majority of tasks involved in initializing the ACK3D engine. We'll discuss ACK's programming functions in more detail later.

Creating a Map of the Game World

Using two additional tools, which will be discussed shortly, we must create a two-dimensional map of our game's world. This map will be similar to the map we used as a demonstration earlier in the chapter. There will be walls and empty spaces that dictate where the player will be allowed to move in the world. In addition to the walls, we are allowed to put in doors. The doors give us the ability to hide things from players such as an enemy who is ready to shoot. The doors can be either visible or invisible. When players come upon a visible door, they simple press the spacebar or other key and the door opens to a new part of the map. An invisible door has to be stumbled upon by the player and then opened.

The first tool that we are going to use is a map-editing program called MEDIT.EXE. The purpose of the program is to allow you to build mazes where the players will do their exploring. Figure 2.19 shows the starting screen for the map editor.

The map editor includes provisions for placing different wall bitmaps as well as different object bitmaps. Walls are placed in the grid part of the map editor simply by clicking the mouse buttons. You have a tremendous

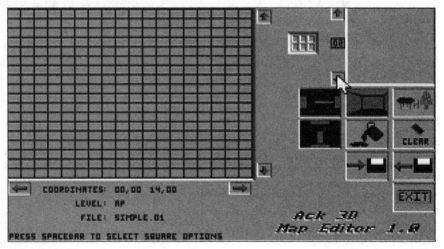

Figure 2.19 Map editor.

amount of space in which to build your game and great flexibility thanks to the map editor. The editor is included on the enclosed CD ROM. For those who want to build even better tools, the complete source code to the editor is enclosed as well.

Creating Walls, Monsters, and Other Objects

Once the map is complete, we come to what is probably the most difficult part of using the ACK3D engine, or any graphics engine, for that matter: creating the graphics. In the ACK3D engine, we create 64-by-64-pixel tiles to represent the walls, doors, monsters, and other objects we place in our map. We will use a versatile paint program called MVP Paint (included on the CD ROM) to draw the tiles. Figure 2.20 shows the main drawing screen of MVP Paint.

Again, using the mouse and various drawing tools, you create the bitmaps that you want to use in your program. In addition to creating your own bitmaps, MVP Paint gives you the ability to bring a GIF, PCX, or BMP image into the program and scale it down to a 64 x 64 bitmap for use in the game. Therefore, if you can get an image into one of the three formats just mentioned, you can use the image as a game object or wall bitmap. The resulting map and colored tiles are fed into an ACK3D program, and suddenly we have a very simple game.

We still have to add characters to our game. This includes giving players the ability to move in the world and perhaps to fire a gun. If our players have the ability to fire a gun, we had better give them something to fire at as well. We can put objects in the world that represent monsters or other creatures

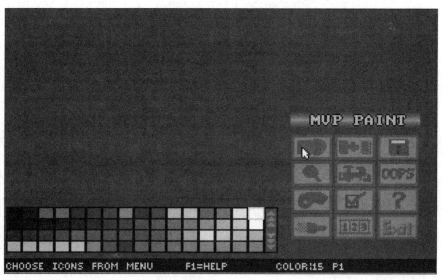

Figure 2.20 Main drawing screen of MVP Paint.

and allow the players to splatter their blood all over our newly created walls.

If all of this discussion has begun to get your creativity flowing, then it's time to discuss the environment necessary to create games using ACK3D.

 # The Environment Necessary to Use ACK3D

Like most computer applications, the ACK3D engine does have several specific software and hardware requirements.

Hardware

When Larry Myers created the ACK3D engine, he tried to get as much speed out of it as possible. This includes using many of the special features of the 386 line of microprocessors. For this reason, the games produced by the engine must be executed on a 386 or better computer. You will also need a 386 machine or better to build the game.

As supplied on the enclosed CD ROM, the engine uses the 320 x 200 x 256 graphics mode of the VGA graphics adapter. This shouldn't be a problem, since most 386 or better computer systems use a VGA display system. Additional devices such as a joystick or a mouse may be required depending on how you create your game using ACK3D. You could also incorporate additional devices such as the head trackers commonly used in the technology of virtual reality.

For the basic ACK3D engine and resulting game, these are the minimum hardware requirements. As you will see, we will take the ACK3D engine beyond its initial state and add support for connecting several machines together to form a multi-player system. On the primitive side, we will connect two computers via the serial port and a null modem cable. For this setup, we will require two computers, two serial ports, and a null modem cable, as well as the minimum hardware requirements given above.

At our most advanced point, we will develop code that will allow the ACK3D system to interconnect with other machines that are part of the Internet. This system will require PCs that have a direct connection to the Internet; each computer being used must have a valid IP address in order to be connected to the Internet.

Software

On the software side of things, the requirements get more complicated. As we noted above, the ACK3D system is a C-callable library. This means that we must be able to write programs that will call the functions of the ACK3D system. Once we have written a program, we will need to compile it and produce an executable file. To perform all of this, we will need a compiler.

The compiler required by ACK3D is Borland C++ 3.1 or higher. Version 3.1 is the compiler that Larry Myers used to create the engine; you can also use Borland's new compiler C++ 4.0 or 4.02.

You will need two pieces of software in addition to the engine and compiler. The first is a map editor—a graphical tool for creating the maps in ACK3D. The second is a paint program to design your graphics.

 ## Conclusion

With that, you are ready to begin building a simple ACK3D game. To create the game, you will need all of the tools on the enclosed CD ROM as well as a Borland C++ compiler, version 3.1 or higher. We will start with a simple, basic program that will be expanded into a multi-player game.

CHAPTER 3

BUILDING ACK3D WORLDS

With all of the introductions out of the way, it's time to begin using the ACK3D engine. This chapter will lead you through the development of MINOSML, a simple skeleton program that will demonstrate how to use the engine. The chapter acts as a springboard for the remaining chapters in the book.

Requirements

In order to make effective use of the following discussions, you will need to install the software from the enclosed CD ROM to your hard drive. Refer to Appendix A for further instructions on how to do this. In addition, you will need access to a Borland C++ compiler. It is recommended that you use either version 3.1 or 4.02. Those using version 4.02 will need to have Microsoft Windows installed on their system.

The code that we are going to build can be found in the \NETWARIO directory on your hard drive after the CD ROM is installed. The name of the file is MINOSML.

The Code

The MINOSML program can read in a map that has been created using a map editor. It then allows you to select a specific viewpoint within an area of the map and give movement to that viewpoint using the arrow keys on the keyboard. The entire code is listed in Listing 3.1.

Listing 3.1

```
#include <stdlib.h>
#include <stdio.h>
#include <dos.h>
#include <mem.h>
#include <alloc.h>
#include <io.h>
#include <fcntl.h>
#include <time.h>
#include <string.h>
#include <conio.h>
#include <sys\stat.h>
#include "ack3d.h"
#include "simple.h"
#define HOME        0x4700
#define END         0x4F00
#define PGUP        0x4900
```

```
#define PGDN        0x5100
#define LEFT        0x4B00
#define RIGHT       0x4D00
#define UP          0x4800
#define DOWN        0x5000
#define SHLEFT      0x4B01
#define SHRIGHT     0x4D01
#define SHUP        0x4801
#define SHDOWN      0x5001
#define SHPGUP      0x4901
#define SHPGDN      0x5101
#define CTRLLEFT    0x7300
#define CTRLRIGHT   0x7400
#define CTRLHOME    0x7700
#define CTRLEND     0x7500
#define CTRLPGUP    0x8400
#define CTRLPGDN    0x7600
#define ESC         0x001B


ACKENG   *ae;
MOUSE  mouse;


char   *MapFileName = "simple.MAP";
char   *PalFile       = "simple.PAL";


BMTABLE bmTable[] = {
    1   ,TYPE_WALL    ,"swall16.pcx",
    -1  ,-1           ,""                  /* End of table */
    };


ColorRange ranges[64] = {
                16,16,
                32,16,
                48,16,
                64,16,
                80,16,
                96,8,
                104,8,
                112,8,
                120,8,
                128,8,
                136,8,
                144,8,
                152,8,
```

```
                    160,8,
                    168,8,
                    176,8,
                    184,8,
                    192,16,
                    208,16,
                    224,8,
                    232,8,
                    0,0
                    };

int shifted;
unsigned getkey(){
  unsigned c;
  union REGS regs;

  regs.h.ah = 2;

  int86(0x16, &regs,&regs );
  shifted = (regs.h.al & 3);

  if ((c=bioskey (0)) & 0xff) c &= 0xff;
  else if ( shifted ) c |= 1;
  return c;
}

int main(void)
{
  int     result,
     done = 0,
     pan = 0;
  int     temp;
  unsigned ch;

  if (result=AppInitialize())
  {
    printf("Error initializing: ErrorCode = %d\n",result);
    return(1);
  }

  if (result=AppSetupEngine())
  {
    printf("Error setting up ACK engine: ErrorCode = %d\n",result);
```

```
        AckWrapUp(ae);
        return(1);
}


if (result=AppLoadBitmaps())
{
    printf("Error loading bitmaps: ErrorCode = %d\n",result);
    AckWrapUp(ae);
    return(1);
}


if (result=AppSetGraphics())
{
    AckSetTextmode();
    printf("Error loading palette: ErrorCode = %d\n",result);
    AckWrapUp(ae);
    return(1);
}
AppSetupPalRanges();
while (!done)
{
    if (pan)
    {
    pan = 0;
    if (ae->PlayerAngle >= INT_ANGLE_360)
        ae->PlayerAngle -= INT_ANGLE_360;
    if (ae->PlayerAngle < 0)
        ae->PlayerAngle += INT_ANGLE_360;
    }
    AppShow3D();

    if (bioskey(1))
    {
    ch = getkey();
    if (ch==ESC) break;

    switch(ch)
    {
        case LEFT : ae->PlayerAngle += (-INT_ANGLE_2 * 5);
                pan = 1;
                break;
        case RIGHT: ae->PlayerAngle += INT_ANGLE_2 * 5;
                pan = 1;
```

```
                    break;
             case UP: AckMovePOV(ae,ae->PlayerAngle,16);
                    break;
             case DOWN: temp= ae->PlayerAngle + INT_ANGLE_180;
                    if (temp >= INT_ANGLE_360)
                     temp -= INT_ANGLE_360;
                    AckMovePOV(ae,temp,16);
                    break;
      }
    }
  }
    AckWrapUp(ae);
    AckSetTextmode();
 return(0);
}
int AppInitialize(void)
{
 if ((ae=malloc(sizeof(ACKENG))) == NULL)
    return(-1);
 memset(ae,0,sizeof(ACKENG));
 return(0);
}
int AppSetupEngine(void)
{
 int result;
 ae->WinStartX = VIEW_X;
 ae->WinStartY = VIEW_Y;
 ae->WinEndX = VIEW_X1;
 ae->WinEndY = VIEW_Y1;
 ae->DoorSpeed  = DOORSPEED;
 ae->xPlayer = PLAYER_X;
 ae->yPlayer = PLAYER_Y;
 ae->PlayerAngle = PLAYER_ANGLE;
 if (result=AckInitialize(ae))
    return(result);
 if (result = AckReadMapFile(ae,MapFileName))
 {
    AckWrapUp(ae);
    return(result);
 }
 ae->TopColor = CEILING_COLOR;
 ae->BottomColor = FLOOR_COLOR;
 ae->LightFlag = SHADING_ON;
```

```c
  return(0);
}
int AppLoadBitmaps(void)
{
 int    result, i=0;
 while (bmTable[i].Number != -1)
 {
    if (result =
AckLoadBitmap(ae,bmTable[i].Number,bmTable[i].Type,bmTable[i].Name))
       break;
    i++;
 }
 return(result);
}
int AppSetGraphics(void)
{
 AckSetVGAmode();
 return(AckLoadAndSetPalette(PalFile));
}
void AppSetupPalRanges(void)
{
 int  i,j,k,found;
 int  rangenos;
 UCHAR     plotcolor;
 for (rangenos = 0; rangenos < 64; rangenos++)
 {
    if (ranges[rangenos].start == 0)
      break;
 }
 for ( i = 0;i<16;i++)
 {
    for (j=0;j<256;j++)
    {
      found = 0;
      for ( k = 0; k < rangenos; k++ )
      {
      if (j >= ranges[k].start && j < ranges[k].start+ranges[k].length)
      {
        found = 1;
        break;
      }
      }
      if (found)
```

```
        {
            if (j+i >= ranges[k].start+ranges[k].length)
                plotcolor = 0;
            else
                plotcolor = j+i;
        }
        else
        {
            plotcolor = j;
        }
        ae->PalTable[j+(i*256)] = plotcolor;
        }
    }
}
void AppShow3D(void)
{
    AckBuildView(ae);
    AckDisplayScreen(ae);
}
```

As you can see, the program is not very long, only 300 lines or so of code. This suggests that a good portion of the work is performed by the ACK3D engine and, furthermore, is located in some other file. In fact, there are several different files that include code for the ACK3D engine besides the program in Listing 3.1. To see where these other files come into play, we should look at how to set up the compiler.

Setting Up the Compiler

As we develop the MINOSML program and other programs in this book, we will need to use the compiler often. For this reason, it would be a good idea to set up a system that makes recompiling easy. This can be done using a project file. A project file is a small file that the compiler uses to keep track of all the code that goes into a single program.

Refer to your compiler's documentation to see how to create and use a project file. Give the project file an appropriate name such as MINOSML or OURGAME and insert the following files into the project file

```
\NETWARIO\MINOSML

    \ACKLIBS\ACKASM.OBJ

    \ACKLIBS\ACKBKGD.OBJ

    \ACKLIBS\ACKDATA.OBJ

    \ACKLIBS\ACKDISP.OBJ

    \ACKLIBS\ACKDOOR.OBJ

    \ACKLIBS\ACKIFF.OBJ
```

```
\ACKLIBS\ACKINIT.OBJ
\ACKLIBS\ACKLDBMP.OBJ
\ACKLIBS\ACKOVER.OBJ
\ACKLIBS\ACKPOV.OBJ
\ACKLIBS\ACKRAY.OBJ
\ACKLIBS\ACKUTIL.OBJ
\ACKLIBS\ACKVIEW.OBJ
\ACKLIBS\ACKWRAP.OBJ
\ACKLIBS\XMSLIB.OBJ
```

All of these files will be used by MINOSML. When you compile MINOSML using the project file, the compiler will link MINOSML's resulting object with all of the object files found in the project file. If you set up your compiler in this fashion, you will be able to make quick changes to program code and recompile very quickly.

Initializing the Application

With the project file setup, we can begin looking at the code that comprises our program. The first thing to do is to initialize any variables or structures needed by the program. The function AppInitialize() has been created for this purpose. The code in this function is:

```
{
 if ((ae=malloc(sizeof(ACKENG)))==NULL)
    return(-1);

 memset(ae,0,sizeof(ACKENG));
 return(0);
}
```

We begin by allocating a part of the computer's memory for the ACK3D engine's main data structure. The pointer to the memory is placed in the global variable **ae**, which is defined as

```
ACKENG   *ae;
```

If the pointer returned by the malloc() function equates to NULL, the malloc() function was unable to get the memory requested. If this is the case, the function returns a value of -1 to the calling routine. It is very important that we test the results of the malloc() function because we will be putting a good amount of information into this main global variable. If the pointer is not NULL, then we have the memory that we need to begin initializing the program.

We continue the AppInitialize() function by initializing the entire ACK3D data structure to 0 and returning to the calling function via the return(0) statement.

If you refer back to Listing 3.1, you will see that the AppInitialize()
function is the very first function called by the program. All it really does
is allocate and initialize memory; no activation of the ACK3D engine is
performed. For this reason, this is the appropriate place to put code for
initializing any code specific to your own program.

An example of this type of program-specific initialization would be to
display programming credits. The code might look something like:

```
int AppInitialize(void)
{
 if ((ae=malloc(sizeof(ACKENG)))==NULL)
 return(-1);
 memset(ae,0, sizeof(ACKENG));
 clrscr();
 printf ( " All of the coding of this application was\n");
 printf ( "performed by myself...\n");
 return(0);
}
```

AppInitialize

The finished code for the AppInitialize() function is:

```
int AppInitialize(void)
{
 if ((ae=malloc(sizeof(ACKENG)))==NULL)
    return(-1);

 memset(ae,0, sizeof(ACKENG));
 return(0);
}
```

The AppInitialize() function is called from the main() function of
Simple. The main function code begins as:

```
int main(void)
{
 int result;
 if (result=AppInitialize())
 {
 printf ( "Error Initializing Application: Code = %d\n",
result);
 exit(1);
 }
}
```

At this point in our development of the MINOSML program, the main() function only has to make a call to the AppInitialize() function. Since the initializing function returns a value to the calling function, it is a good idea to take advantage of the extra information. Recall that the AppInitialize() function returning a value of -1 if the malloc() function was unable to obtain the memory we needed for our ACK engine global variable. The same function returns a value of 0 if everything was initialized fine.

In the main() function, we create a simple test with the statement

```
if (result = AppInitialize())
```

This statement will assign the value returned by AppInitialize to the local variable **result**. The **if** statement will look at the **result** variable and determine if its value is a 0 or some other value. If the value of **result** is 0, then the **true** part of the **if** statement is not executed. If our function AppInitialize() was unable to allocate our memory, it will return a value of -1 which will be assigned to **result** and the **if** statement will evaluate as **true** and the **true** part of the **if** statement will be executed.

The **true** part of the **if** statement simply puts a message on the screen letting the user know there has been an error and then the program is halted.

Setting Up the ACK Engine

Once memory is available for the ACK engine data structure, we need to start filling the engine with information about the application. The function AppSetupEngine() is created for this purpose.

Viewport

The first information that we will fill in is the viewport of the player—the window that the player will look through into the game. In most applications, you will use the entire screen as a viewport, but in 3D maze games like the one we are creating, you sometimes will want to put things like health points, ammunition, and other statistics on the outer edge of the viewport. For the MINOSML program, we will assume that there are no outside graphics—we'll add this stuff later. This means that the ACK3D engine will be able to use all of the screen to display graphics. To give the ACK3D engine this information, we have to set four fields to some value. The four fields are:

        WinStartX—The upper left corner X value

        WinStartY—The upper left corner Y value

        WinEndX—The lower right corner X value

        WinEndY—The lower right corner Y value

Note the capitalization of the field names—this must be followed consistently.

To use all of the screen, we must indicate to the engine the dimensions of the corners of the screen. ACK3D uses the 320 x 200 x 256 mode to display graphics. This means that there are a total of 320 pixels along the X axis and 200 pixels along the Y axis. Using this information, we enter the coordinates of the viewport into the ACK3D data structure as

```
ae->WinStartX = 0;
ae->WinStartY = 0;
ae->WinEndX = 319;
ae->WinEndY = 199;
```

Notice that we are using a C pointer to assign the coordinates of our viewpoint. The reason for this is that the coordinate fields are located within the ACK engine global variable **ae** that the program initialized in the AppInitialize() function. The **ae** variable was declared as ***ae** thus indicating that it is a pointer to some block of memory.

Position

Once the viewport window is set up, we can tell the ACK engine where to place the player when the map is displayed. The position is indicated in two fields of the **ae** global variable:

xPlayer—X position of player
yPlayer—Y position of player

Although it may seem necessary to put a value in each of these fields, it really isn't, and I would simply use the following code:

```
ae->xPlayer = 0;
ae->yPlayer = 0;
```

The reason that we can put zeros into each of these variables is that we will indicate the position of the player when we design the map that will be used in our game. The map editor allows us to do this automatically. However, if during the map-building process we forget to indicate where the player should start, the program will default to the values in these variables. This means that it will be very important that some kind of check list is created when designing maps for a game. Under normal circumstances, you will probably not remember that you did not put coordinates into the xPlayer and yPlayer fields. Thus, if they are forgotten during map development, the game will not begin where you thought it should. This can be a frustrating "bug" during testing.

When we start adding code for the multi-player parts of the game, there will be an additional player location in the map. Since the same map will be used for both players, one of the players will be at location 0,0 or the position created at map development time and the other will be at another location. We will look at this in a later chapter. Because we don't know if the player will be playing the game in single or multi-player mode, we will just assume for now that the player is located at 0,0.

In addition to the position of the player, we must tell the engine in what direction the player is looking. You certainly wouldn't want the player looking into a corner upon starting your game. The name of the field for the player's angle is:

PlayerAngle—Angle of player's view

The value assigned to this field will dictate where the player is looking when the program begins. Now, we cannot put just any value in the field, because the ACK3D engine uses fixed-point numbers (to speed up processing). For those who are not familiar with this technique, it should be explained that software developers will typically find that a large amount of computer processing time is spent in the manipulation (adding, multiplying, etc.) of numbers. If the numbers being manipulated are floating point numbers (used typically when an application deals with measures, angles, and such), the developer will usually try to convert the numbers for fixed point. Fixed point numbers usually allow the developer to continue expressing the information needed without the added computations necessary for floating point numbers. Remember that mathematical coprocessors were developed mostly to handle floating point numbers. Fortunately, there are a number of defines in the file ACK3D.h that simplify specifying the starting angle value. These defines are:

```
#define INT_ANGLE_1       5
#define INT_ANGLE_2       10
#define INT_ANGLE_4       20
#define INT_ANGLE_6       30
#define INT_ANGLE_30      160
#define INT_ANGLE_45      240
#define INT_ANGLE_90      480
#define INT_ANGLE_135     720
#define INT_ANGLE_180     960
#define INT_ANGLE_225     1200
#define INT_ANGLE_270     1440
#define INT_ANGLE_315     1680
#define INT_ANGLE_360     1920
```

So, to start the player looking at 180 degrees, we would use the code

```
ae->PlayerAngle = INT_ANGLE_180;
```

To determine where to place the view angle of the player, just remember that 0 degrees is looking to the south, 90 degrees is looking to the east, etc. These directions will relate to the development of the game's map. Since the map is displayed on the screen, it will have North, South, East, and West directions to it. From looking at the map and the placement of the player, you can determine which direction the player should be looking and place the appropriate value in the **PlayerAngle** field.

DoorSpeed

The last field that we must fill in the ACK3D data structure is

> DoorSpeed—speed at which door opens

This field would be assigned a value of 1 for the slowest speed. A good speed value is 4, assigned as

```
ae->DoorSpeed = 4;
```

Remember that in all cases of the ACK3D data structure, you must follow the capitalization of the field names as shown here or an error will occur during compiling.

Initializing the Engine

After the eight fields of the ACK3D engine are filled, we can tell the engine to officially initialize the data structure. The code to do this is:

```
if (result=AckInitialize(ae))
 return(result);
```

If the function AckInitialize() returns false, then the data structure has been initialized successfully. This is one of the most critical parts of the program, since if the main ACK3D data structure is not initialized correctly by the libraries, the system will not operate. The result of the function is passed to the caller only if the value returned is true.

Reading In the Map File

Now that the ACK3D engine is set up and ready to operate, we can read in the map file that contains the layout of our game. The code for reading the map file is:

```
if (result=AckReadMapFile(ae, MapFileName))
{
 AckWrapUp(ae);
 return (result);
}
```

This first calls the function AckReadMapFile(), giving it the pointer variable to our ACK3D data structure, **ae**, and the name of the map file as it is recorded on our hard drive. The code uses a variable to hold the name of the map file. The variable has been defined as:

```
char *MapFileName = "simple.map";
```

Once the function has been called to read in the map file, the result of the function is analyzed carefully. If the file was corrupted or otherwise unreadable, the code must perform two separate actions. The first action is to return the application to its original state by removing all of the ACK3D structures initialized when the AckInitialize() function was called. This removal is performed by the function AckWrapUp(). The second action returns control back to the caller and indicates an error by returning a non-zero value.

Color
The last task in setting up the ACK3D engine is specifying the ceiling and floor colors and the shading options. The three fields in the ACK3D data structure for these options are:

> TopColor—Color of the ceiling
> BottomColor—Color of the floor
> LightFlag—Shading options

The values available for the TopColor and BottomColor fields are based on the colors that are loaded into the system when the application executes. As you will see shortly, we will load a palette of 256 colors, numbered from 0 to 255. You must make sure to use a value between 0 and 255 for each of the fields. A possible selection could be:

```
ae->TopColor = 5;
ae->BottomColor = 55;
```

The third field, LightFlag, allows us to further affect the color of the sky and ground. If this field is set to the value of SHADING_ON, the sky and ground will be shaded to give an effect of distance. If the field is set to SHADING_OFF, the sky and ground will be colored the solid colors indicated in the TopColor and BottomColor fields. The LightFlag variable is assigned as:

```
ae->LightFlag = SHADING_ON;
```

The two values SHADING_ON and SHADING_OFF are both defined in the header file ACK3D.H, which we will include in our program.

AppSetupEngine Code
The finished code for the AppSetupEngine() function is shown in Listing 3.2.

Listing 3.2

```c
int AppSetupEngine(void)
{
int result;
ae->WinStartX   = VIEW_X;
ae->WinStartY   = VIEW_Y;
ae->WinEndX     = VIEW_X1;
ae->WinEndY     = VIEW_Y1;
ae->DoorSpeed   = DOORSPEED;
ae->xPlayer     = PLAYER_X;
ae->yPlayer     = PLAYER_Y;
ae->PlayerAngle = PLAYER_ANGLE;
if (result=AckInitialize(ae))
   return(result);


if (result = AckReadMapFile(ae,MapFileName))
{
   AckWrapUp(ae);
   return(result);
}
ae->TopColor = CEILING_COLOR;
ae->BottomColor = FLOOR_COLOR;
ae->LightFlag = SHADING_ON;
return(0);
}
```

The AppSetupEngine() function is called in the main() function with
the code

```c
if (result=AppSetupEngine())
{
printf ("Error setting up ACK engine: Error = %d\n"), result);
AckWrapup(ae);
return(1);
}
```

Again we see that the result of the AppSetupEngine() function is
checked for successful completion. If by chance something in the
AppSetupEngine() function went wrong, a value of -1 would be returned
causing the **if** statement to be evaluated as **true**. At this point, the code
prints a message to the user letting them know the situation. All of the
previous initializing previously performed must be cleaned up using the
function AckWrapup(). This function is built into the ACK engine and is
not something we have to construct.

Loading Bitmaps

With the ACK engine initialized and various necessary fields set up, we can begin to bring other components into the application. The main component is the bitmaps. Although we haven't discussed actually drawing the bitmaps yet, we know that all of the walls of our map are created by 64 x 64 bitmaps. In order for the engine to draw the bitmaps, we have to bring them into memory. In our MINOSML program, we have only one bitmap, so loading it can be accomplished with the code

```
return (AckLoadBitmap(ae, 1, TYPE_WALL, "wall.pcx"));
```

The function AckLoadBitmap( ) does the actual work of reading a bitmap from a file and storing it in an appropriate memory location. The first parameter to the function is the familiar pointer to the data structure of the application. The second parameter is the number assigned to the bitmap we want to read in. As you will see shortly, it is possible to use many different bitmaps. The system keeps track of the bitmaps through a simple numbering scheme. In this case, we will only be using a single bitmap, so we will give it the number 1. The third parameter is a type of value that the function uses to determine what type of bitmap it is loading. The parameter is either TYPE_WALL or TYPE_OBJECT. Both TYPE_WALL and TYPE_OBJECT are defined in the ACK3D.H header file. The fourth and last parameter is a character string representing the name of the bitmap as it is stored on the hard drive.

This code is just fine for reading in a couple of bitmaps, but after a time it becomes very repetitive, and we know that repetitive code should be condensed into a loop. We can do exactly that with the code

```
for (i=0;i<TOTAL_BITMAPS;i++)
{
  if(result=AckLoadBitmap(ae, bitmaps[i].Number,
bitmaps[i].Type, bitmaps[i].Name));
  break;
}
return (result);
```

The code loops through a table of bitmaps called—bitmaps. The total number of bitmaps in the table is stored in the variable TOTAL_BITMAPS. The table is defined using a data structure created specifically for the bitmap table. This structure is called BMTABLE and is defined as:

```
typedef struct _BMTABLE {
        int Number;
```

```
        int Type;
        char *Name;
    } BMTABLE;
```

The BMTABLE data structure is used to create the bitmap table.

```
BMTABLE bitmaps[] = {
        1, TYPE_WALL, "wall.pcx"
    };
int TOTAL_BITMAPS = 1;
```

In the MINOSML program being created here, there is only one bitmap to list in the bitmap table. The bitmaps are added to the table using the following format:

```
bitmap #, bitmap TYPE, bitmap filename
```

For each bitmap added to the program, a listing such as this will need to be added.

To add more bitmaps, we simply add a comma at the end of the last bitmaps character string and list the attributes for the rest of the bitmaps. For example, if we had a second bitmap to add, our bitmap table would appear as

```
BMTABLE bitmaps[] = {
        1, TYPE_WALL, "wall.pcx",
        2, TYPE_WALL, "wall2.pcx"
    };
int TOTAL_BITMAPS = 2;
```

Always remember to increment the variable TOTAL_BITMAPS to accurately reflect the addition of another bitmap to the program.

The finished code for the AppLoadBitmaps() function is

```
int AppLoadBitmaps(void)
{
 int result, i;
 for (i=0;i<TOTAL_BITMAPS;i++)
 {
 if(result=AckLoadBitmap(ae, bitmaps[i].Number, bitmaps[i].Type,
bitmaps[i].Name));
  break;
  }
  return (result);
 }
```

The AppLoadBitmaps() function is called from the main() function with the code

```
if (result=AppLoadBitmaps())
{
 printf ( "Error loading bitmaps: Error = %d\n", result);
 AckWrapUp(ae);
 return(1);
}
```

Setting Up Graphics

At this point the ACK3D engine has been loaded and initialized and all of the bitmaps loaded into memory. What we don't have is a graphics screen. Up till now all of our work has been performed with the text mode still activated. We will not be using the text mode for our game. We will be advancing to the graphics mode where we have 320 x 200 pixels which can be any of 256 colors. To get to a graphics mode, the ACK3D library provides the function AckSetVGAmode(). This function performs all of the work necessary to change from text mode into a graphics mode designed to work with the engine.

Once the computer has switched to a graphics screen, it has to be set up to use colors appropriate for the application's bitmaps. The function used to load the palette is called AckLoadAndSetPalette(). This function reads the character string of the name of the palette file, loads the file into memory, and sets the appropriate VGA registers so the palette will be used.

The variable PalFile is defined as

```
char *PalFile = "simple.pal";
```

As we will see in a later chapter, it is very important that we load the palette into the system. When the computer is switched into a graphics mode, a palette is already available called the system palette. The palette contains basic colors that can be used to paint pixels on the screen. In an ACK3D game, the engine will have to automatically change certain colors on the screen depending on our position. If we are far away from a wall, the wall will not be as brightly colored as when we are right up close to it. For this reason, we have to develop and load a specific palette that the ACK engine can use to perform this type of shading.

The finished AppSetGraphics() function is

```
int AppSetGraphics(void)
{
 AckSetVGAmode();
 return(AckLoadAndSetPalette(PalFile));
}
```

The AppSetGraphics() function is called from the main() function with the code:

```
if (result=AppSetGraphics())
{
AckSetTextMode();
printf ("Error loading palette: Error = %d\n", result);
AckWrapUp(ae);
return(1);
}
```

Notice that if an error occurs in the AppSetGraphics() function, the error-handling code must set the system back to text mode, to allow the display of error text.

The Screen Drawing Loop

The ACK3D engine is set up to do nothing until we tell it to do something specific. Therefore, after the engine is set up and initialized, we have to tell it to draw a picture on the screen. We do this with two separate functions, AckBuildView(ae) and AckDisplayScreen(ae). AckBuildView(ae) takes the current position and view angle of the player and determines what the screen will look like. AckDisplayScreen(ae) takes the information from AckBuildView(ae) and displays the current map on the screen. Since the engine must be told constantly to do these two tasks, we should create some type of loop. The following will do:

```
done = 0;
while (!done)
{
AckBuildView(ae);
AckDisplayScreen(ae);
}
```

The code begins by setting a variable, done, equal to a 0. Next, a loop starts displaying the current map on the screen. It continues to do this forever. I think we had better program a way to end the loop! However, we had better place this loop somewhere in our program. The loop should appear in the main() function of our MINOSML program just after all of the function calls we have already documented.

There are a number of input devices that we could use in our game, but the most common and easiest to use at this point is the keyboard. Let's use the Esc key to indicate that the player is finished with the game.

To determine when the player presses a key, we will use the function bioskey(). This function returns a 1 when a key has been pressed. We can see what key the player has pressed by calling the function getkey(), which is a keystroke-handling routine. Once we have the key, we can use a switch() statement to perform a specific action. The code looks like this:

```
while(!done)
{
 AckBuildView(ae);
 AckDisplayScreen(ae);
 if (bioskey(1))
 {
 ch=getkey();
 switch(cd)
 {
   case ESC: done = 1;
       break;
 }
 }
}
```

We now have a complete system with the capability to load a map and display it. However, we are missing one very important thing—the ability to move.

Moving in ACK

Moving in ACK3D is a fairly simple matter, since the engine itself provides the necessary functions. We will look at four different movements: forward, backward, left turn, and right turn.

Forward

Moving forward in ACK is accomplished with the function AckMovePOV(). This function allows the point of view of the player to be moved x steps in the direction the player is currently looking. To add forward movement to our program, we will add the following code in the SWITCH statement of the main loop:

```
case UP: AckMovePOV(ae, ae->PlayerAngle, 16);
        break;
```

The constant UP is defined at the start of our program. It represents the keystroke value for the Up arrow on the keyboard. When the player presses this key, the code will call the AckMovePOV() function and pass it three parameters. The first parameter is the data structure pointer, the second parameter is the direction angle along which the POV should be moved, and the third parameter is the number of units to move forward.

The third parameter determines how quickly or slowly the forward movement occurs. If you put a small number as the step value, many keystrokes will be required to move. On the other hand, if you use a large value, the player will move very quickly through the map. I have found that 16 is a good value; however, you might want to include the ability to change the movement value during game play.

Backward

Moving backward is like moving forward but in the direction 180 degrees from the forward direction. The Down arrow is defined as the key for backward movement. To allow backward movement in the game, add the following code to the SWITCH statement:

```
case DOWN: temp=ae->PlayerAngle + INT_ANGLE_180;
     if (temp>=INT_ANGLE_360)
     temp -= INT_ANGLE_360;
     AckMovePOV (ae, temp, 16);
     break;
```

Backward movement is accomplished simply by adding 180 degrees to the player's current POV and moving forward. There are two important things to note in the code above. The first is that we do not add just any ol' 180 degrees to the PlayerAngle field. We must add the fixed point representation of 180 degrees instead.

The second point follows the code where we add 180 degrees. We must check to make sure that we have not gone over 360 degrees. Note that there are only 360 degrees in a circle. While in some cases, the program is able to compensate for degrees greater than 360, this is not one of them. We can solve this problem by checking the current value in the PlayerAngle field against the fixed point value for 360 degrees and subtract 360 degrees from the total if it is greater than 360.

Turning Left and Right

The player must also have the ability to turn to the left and right. Add the following code to the SWITCH statement to achieve turning:

```
case LEFT: ae->PlayerAngle += (-INT_ANGLE_2 *5);
     pan = 1;
     break;
case RIGHT:  ae->PlayerAngle += (INT_ANGLE_2 *5);
     pan = 1;
     break;
```

Just as we added 180 degrees to the field PlayerAngle to move backward, we can add a negative or positive value to rotate left or right. The

Left and Right arrow keys are defined as causing this rotation. The value that we add to the angle field dictates how fast the player rotates in either direction. The value used here, INT_ANGLE_2 * 5, equates to a rotation of 10 degrees each time the player presses a key. By changing the 5 to some other value, you can slow or speed up the rotation.

Notice that in both CASE statements, we set the variable PAN equal to a 1. The PAN variable is used in the following code, which is placed after the SWITCH statement in the main loop:

```
if (pan)
{
pan = 0;
if (ae->PlayerAngle >= INT_ANGLE_360)
ae->PlayerAngle -= INT_ANGLE_360;

if (ae->PlayerAngle <= INT_ANGLE_360)
ae->PlayerAngle += INT_ANGLE_360;
}
```

This code makes sure that the PlayerAngle field has a value between 0 and 360.

Programming for Other Keystrokes

We have already defined the four arrow keys and Esc. Additional keys can be defined simply by following this scheme:

```
case '<key type>':        code for the key;
                          break;
```

An example is:

```
case 'a':                 code for doing 'a' key;
                          break;
```

Quitting

When players press the Esc key, they are indicating that they wish to quit the program. When this occurs, the ACK3D engine must be cleared from memory. This is accomplished with the commands:

```
AckWrapUp(ae);
AckSetTextmode();
```

These two statements are placed just after our while (!done) loop discussed above. When the user presses the ESC key, the variable DONE is set equal to 1 causing the WHILE loop to be evaluated as false. The computer will skip down to the statements just after the loop, evaluate them and stop execution.

 # Conclusion

That's it. If you look at the code at the beginning of the chapter, you will see the complete ACK3D skeleton program. This is everything code-wise that you need to actually create a simple ACK program. The source and executable for this program are on the CD ROM in the directory \NETWARIO. I would suggest that you now run the program—just type **MINOSML** at the command prompt, and use the arrow keys to run around. Press the Esc key to quit the program. Now go back to the source code and look at how everything works.

BUILDING THE ACK3D GRAPHICS

In Chapter 3, we created the skeleton program for our game using C code and the ACK3D engine. In this chapter, we will discuss the tools MEDIT and MVP Paint, which will be used to build the graphical components of our game.

Creating a Wall Bitmap

As many game developers will attest, creating the graphics for a game is by far the most complex part of the development process. If the graphics aren't put together just right, the application will suffer. Just as a little side note to this, I was once involved with a company that produced VR equipment. In the course of developing the hardware, we paid a visit to a well-known software company which was working on a game that used the advanced DOOM engine even before the DOOM engine had been released to the public. In this company of 15 people, 12 of them were graphic designers, 2 were software developers, and 1 was the president. There was even talk that they needed more graphic designers to get the game finished. Our MINOSML example only needs one graphic component and that is a 64 x 64 bitmap for a wall. Later, we will add wall, door, and other object bitmaps.

A wall bitmap must be exactly 64 pixels by 64 pixels, must subscribe to a specific palette that includes the ability to shade appropriately for the ACK engine, and must have an LBM or BBM format. You may wish to use your favorite paint program, but it must be able to follow the first and second rules. Very few of the good paint programs output the LBM or BBM format—it is the format output from the Deluxe II series of commercial paint programs. Because we wanted to be able to supply you with a paint program on the enclosed CD ROM, we had to come up with a workaround.

The workaround we will describe is not the one originally planned. It had been our hopes that the engine could be changed to use the popular PCX graphics file format directly instead of doing a conversion to LBM. After much work and a good deal of hacking, the direct PCX bitmap never looked like it should, so the work was abandoned (deadlines you know).

The workaround that we have come up with is performed using an additional tool called VPIC. VPIC is a shareware picture-viewing tool with the added capability to convert many different formats into LBM format. This means that you can use just about any paint program and just use VPIC to convert the bitmaps to the LBM format. In developing for the book, the author succesfully converted many different formats such as GIF, PCX and TIF into LBM using the VPIC program. Be sure that you register your copy as well.

We have also included a paint program on the enclosed CD ROM called MVP Paint. This is another shareware program, so if you end up using it beyond a given time frame, you need to register it. I refer you to the documentation that comes with the program for more information.

Using MVP Paint

Using MVP Paint to create bitmaps is very easy. Before running the program, you need to configure MVP Paint for your computer. Run the executable file called Configure and answer the questions appropriately. The only question that needs special attention is the one about screen resolution. MVP Paint will allow you to paint images up to 1024 x 768, but since we will be editing rather small images of 64 x 64 pixels, I would recommend that you select the screen mode 320 x 200. This will allow you to have a very good view of the image being created.

After the program has been configured, you can run it by typing **mvp-paint** and pressing Enter. Once the program has been loaded, you will see the screen image shown in Figure 4.1.

Notice that a good number of the icons in the lower right corner are shaded gray. This indicates that you cannot select them.

To begin creating a new image, click on the diskette icon to bring up the menu shown in Figure 4.2. This menu allows you to either create a new image or load a preexisting image. Move the mouse arrow to any place on top of the "create new image" string and click the left button to bring up the screen in Figure 4.3.

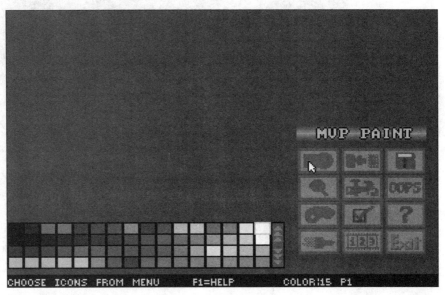

Figure 4.1   MVP Paint start-up screen.

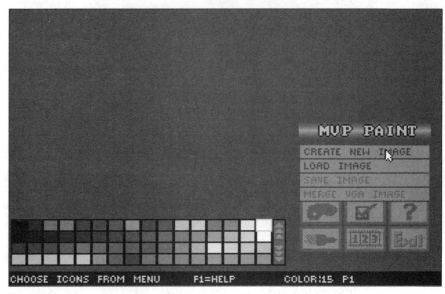

Figure 4.2   Disk icon menu.

This screen shows one of the features that makes MVP Paint such a good paint program. Using the mouse, you can drag the lower right-hand corner of the elastic red box to the exact size of the image you are going to create. The image size given in pixels is shown in the lower right corner of the screen.

For our purposes, you should stretch the box until the image is 64 pixels by 64 pixels and then click (press the left mouse button) to accept the

Figure 4.3   Image size calculation screen.

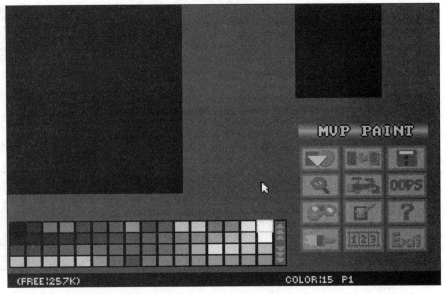

Figure 4.4 Painting screen.

image size. You may notice that the box is very sensitive to your mouse movements. Sometimes when you have the box at the right size and go to click the mouse, the image size will move by one pixel. You will need to scrap the image and try again. The bitmap size must be 64 x 64.

Once you have snapped an image size of 64 by 64, you will see the screen shown in Figure 4.4.

This is the main painting screen for MVP Paint.

Before you begin painting a bitmap, you need to bring in a palette that will work correctly with the ACK3D engine. It is very important that you bring the palette into MVP Paint *before* you begin painting the bitmap, because ACK3D must have a specific palette format. If you forget, you will have to redo your painting.

To load a new palette, click on the icon with the painter's palette. You will see the image in Figure 4.5.

Then click on the "load palette" button. The software will look for all palette files (those with the .PAL extension) and display them in a list. In the list will be a file called MINOTAUR.PAL. This is the palette file we are going to use for our image. Once you click on the name, you will see the palette at the bottom left of the screen change.

Take a moment to look at the structure of the palette. The first row of the palette holds the 16 main EGA colors. The second row starts with white and goes through varying shades all the way to black. The next row down is the color red. If you keep moving down the list, you will see that some colors have 16 transitions and others have only eight. This is just a

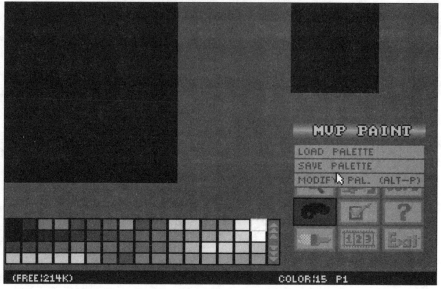

Figure 4.5 Palette menu.

characteristic of this particular palette. You will learn how to change this later in the book.

Now that you have a palette loaded into MVP Paint, you can begin painting an image. Let's run through a simple example to show you how to use the tools. I suggest that you read through the documentation provided with MVP Paint to get a better feel of the power of this program.

Start your painting by drawing a large red box over the entire image area. The first thing that you need to do is select a color to paint with. Because the ACK3D engine allows shading of the walls based on the distance the player is from them, you have to be careful about the color you pick to draw with. Generally, you will want to draw with the brightest color possible. This will give the ACK3D engine a wide number of colors to shade through as the player approaches or backs away from a wall. For the red background, move the arrow over to the leftmost red color in the third row of the palette. Click to select the color. You will notice that a white box appears around the color square.

To draw the rectangle, you need to bring up the menu with the rectangle command in it. Click the mouse on the top left icon with the rectangle, triangle, and circle figures in it. Once you do this, a small menu will appear. Now click on the entry labeled RECTANGLE. In the left part of the screen, a blue rubber-band rectangle will appear. As you move the mouse, the rectangle will grow and shrink. Move the mouse so that the rectangle fills to the bottom right corner and click. You will be prompted with a message asking whether or not the rectangle should be filled. Click

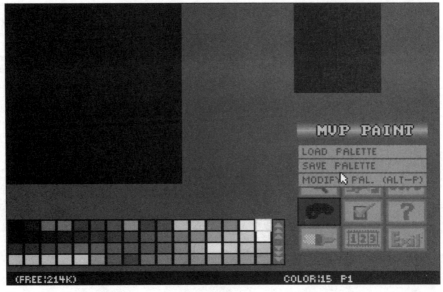

Figure 4.6   Red rectangle.

on Yes. You will have filled the entire bitmap with the color red, as shown in Figure 4.6.

You can now add other things to your image. Figure 4.7 shows lines added to the image, and Figure 4.8 shows a circle added.

Now you have a pretty good image for your bitmap. The last step is to save the image. Click the mouse on the diskette icon in the lower right

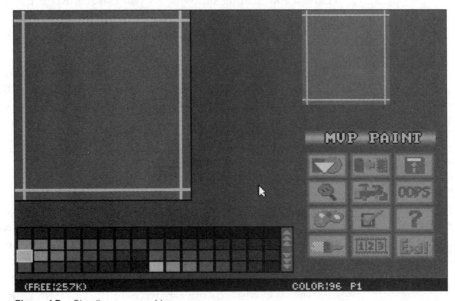

Figure 4.7   Blue lines on a red box.

Building the ACK3D Graphics   **61**

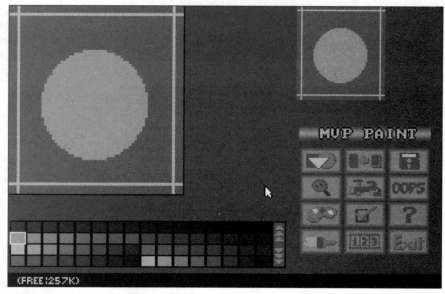

Figure 4.8　Solid green circle on a red box.

part of the screen. This will bring up a menu asking, among other things, if you want to save the image. Click on the "save image" entry. You will be presented with a second message asking what file format to use to save the image. Click on the entry for PCX. The system will now ask for the name of the file to save. You only have to enter the first part of the filename, since the program will automatically attach the .PCX extension.

That's it for creating bitmaps. As you can see, MVP Paint provides many different types of tools for creating the bitmaps. It is highly recommended that you register your copy of MVP Paint in order to take full advantage of the package.

One advantage in registering is the fact that you can bring a PCX image into MVP Paint and scale the image to the 64 x 64 bitmap size that the ACK system uses. If you have a favorite image, you can scale it and use it in a game. Just remember to be careful of copyright infringement.

Creating an LBM Bitmap

Now that you have a bitmap for the ACK3D game, you need to convert it to LBM format. This can be done using the VPIC.EXE program found on the enclosed disk. You should configure the VPIC program for your specific video card using the configuration program supplied with the VPIC program.

To start the VPIC program, copy it to the directory with the PCX bitmaps that you wish to convert. Execute the program with the command **vpic.exe**. A screen like the one shown in Figure 4.9 will appear.

```
FIG3-2.TIF    192K
FIG3-3.TIF    192K
FIG3-4.BMP     65K
FIG3-5.BMP    192K
FIG3-6.BMP     65K
FIG3-7.BMP     65K
FIG3-8.BMP     65K




                                                     Memory=450048
SPACE=Tag/UnTag ENTER=Show ESC=Quit F1=Help F2=Slides F3=Info F4=EGA/VGA  <-  ->
F5/F6=+/-Res F7=Lock/Auto/Norm F8=Wait F9=Path AltF9=DIRS F10=ShowPath PgUp PgDn
```

Figure 4.9 VPIC start-up screen.

The program will list the different graphic files that are in the current directory and can be viewed with VPIC. Highlight the name of the bitmap file you have created and press the Enter key. Once the file appears on the screen, you can press the ? key to find the different options available while viewing a graphics file. The D option creates an LBM file. Press D and you will be asked whether or not you want to convert the file to the LBM format; press Y. You will then be asked if you want an enhanced file; press Y. The last question that you will be asked is if the conversion should be a compressed file. Press Y again. You will now have an LBM file on your disk using the filename of the original graphic file.

Creating a Map

Creating a map for your game is a simple matter of determining where to place walls (and other components, as you will see later) so that the player has a fun time exploring your new world. If you had to create the map by hand, the process might be more complex, but the author of ACK3D has provided a map editor that makes creating maps a breeze.

The map editor, called MEDIT, requires one parameter to operate correctly. The parameter is the name of a description file that lists the different files and filenames that make up your bitmaps. An example of a description file is shown in Listing 4.1.

Listing 4.1

```
; Description file for ACK-3D demo program
```

Building the ACK3D Graphics **63**

```
Walls:
 Files:
 1 , wall.lbm
 EndFiles:
EndWalls:
Objects:
 Files:
 EndFiles:
EndObjects:
MapFile: simple.MAP
PalFile: simple.PAL
; Palette ranges - starting color, number of colors
RANGE: 16,16
RANGE: 32,16
RANGE: 48,16
RANGE: 64,16
RANGE: 80,16
RANGE: 96,8
RANGE: 104,8
RANGE: 112,8
RANGE: 120,8
RANGE: 128,8
RANGE: 136,8
RANGE: 144,8
RANGE: 152,8
RANGE: 160,8
RANGE: 168,8
RANGE: 176,8
RANGE: 184,8
RANGE: 192,16
RANGE: 208,16
RANGE: 224,8
RANGE: 232,8
```

The description file includes places to put the names of the wall and object bitmaps you are using to create your game. As you can see from the listing, one wall bitmap is used in our MINOSML program. We have listed the wall number (1, since it is the first and only wall bitmap), followed by a comma, and then the filename of the bitmap. If you had more wall bitmaps, you would simply list them in order, making sure to include both a wall number and a comma.

The description file for our Simple example is called MINOTAUR.01 and is located in the \NETWARIO directory. Load this file when you exe-

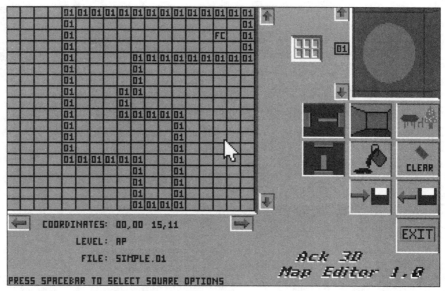

Figure 4.10 Map Editor main screen.

cute the map editor by typing **medit MINOTAUR.01**. Be sure to put a space between medit and MINOTAUR.01. Once you type this command, you will see the screen shown in Figure 4.10.

The maze in the left part of the screen may not look exactly like that in Figure 4.10, but it does not make any difference, as we will be clearing that part of the screen shortly.

Map Editor Features

Before you can use the map editor, you should become familiar with the various parts of it. We will use the screen shot in Figure 4.10 as a guide. The most prominent part of the screen is taken up by the two-dimensional grid. This represents the map and is where we will place the wall bitmap. The arrows below and to the right of this grid allow you to scroll, so that you can build a map larger than what is visible at one time.

In the upper right part of the screen is the wall bitmap. Beside the bitmap is a number indicator and a couple of arrows. These arrows allow you to change from one bitmap to another. Under the bitmap are nine icons. You will learn about each of these icons as they are needed.

Using the Map Editor

Begin creating your own map by first clearing the current map. Click on the Clear icon. You will be asked if you indeed wish to clear the current map. You should answer Yes. Once you do this, you will have the screen shown in Figure 4.11.

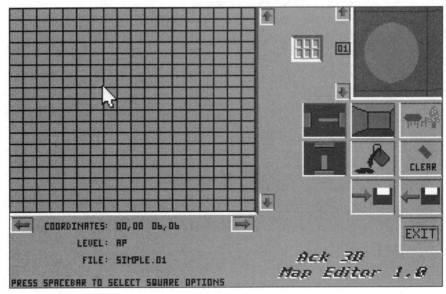

Figure 4.11 A clear map.

Now that you have a clear map, you can start placing bitmaps. First, click on the Up arrow next to the bitmap representation. Notice that the bitmap area goes blank, as in Figure 4.12. The numerical indicator also changes, from 1 to 2. This shows that only one wall bitmap is defined as far as the map editor is concerned. Use the other arrow to bring the number 1 bitmap back up on the screen.

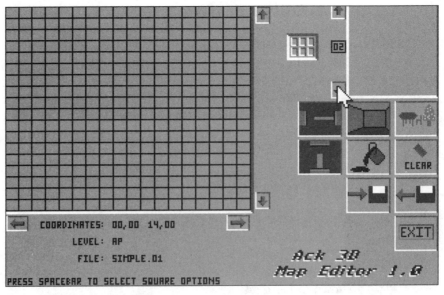

Figure 4.12 Blank bitmap image.

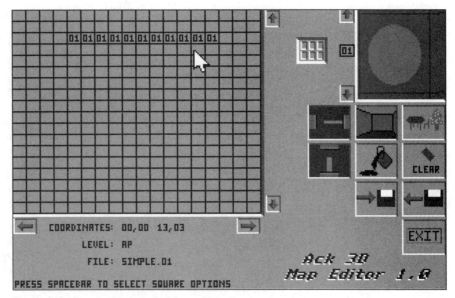

Figure 4.13 Drawing horizontal walls.

Placing Walls

Placing walls using the map editor is very simple. Move the arrow to the grid position at which you want to place the current wall bitmap—the one shown in the upper right-hand corner—and click. You will see the number of the current bitmap appear in the grid position. Figure 4.13 shows several wall bitmaps placed in a horizontal line to create a segment of wall.

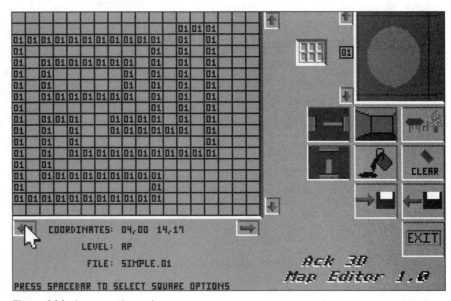

Figure 4.14 A more enhanced maze.

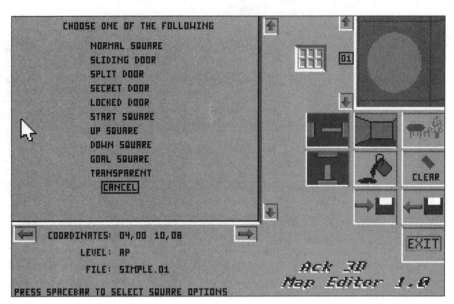

Figure 4.15 Grid options.

You are now free to build your map any way that you wish. To allow someone to go through your maze, you should leave at least one blank square of the grid between any two walls. You can see this in Figure 4.14, a small but complete map that you can use as an example.

The last thing that needs to be done is to place a starting position into the grid. To do this, move the cursor arrow to one of the empty grid squares and press the Spacebar. This will bring up the menu shown in Figure 4.15.

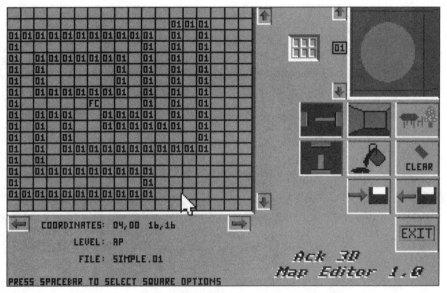

Figure 4.16 A starting location added to the maze.

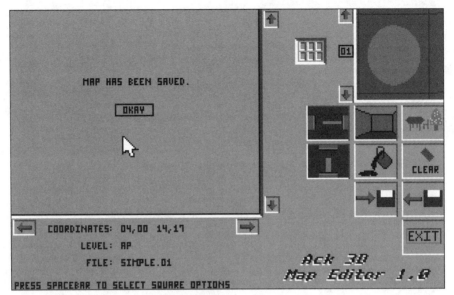

Figure 4.17 Map editor showing that a map has been saved.

The menu includes many different things that can be placed in the current grid. We will cover more of them in a later chapter. The only one that we are interested in now is the one for the starting position. Move the cursor arrow to "start square" and click. When you do this, the map will put the letters FC in the appropriate square, as shown in Figure 4.16.

With the starting position selected, you are ready to save the map. Click on the icon that has an arrow pointing toward the diskette. The map editor will indicate that a file of this name already exists. You can click on Yes to overwrite the file. The program will indicate that the map has been saved, as shown in Figure 4.17.

 # Running It

That's it. You now have a complete ACK3D program and bitmap ready to run. Just type **MINOSML** at the command prompt while in the \NETWARIO directory and you will see the fruits of your labor. You can use the arrow keys to move around the world and the Esc key to quit the program. Use the map editor to change your map and get a feel for different types of situations.

CHAPTER 5

ADDING TWO-PLAYER SUPPORT TO ACK3D

Now that you have a basic understanding of how the ACK3D engine works and how to integrate the different library function calls into a working game, let's begin looking at adding more players to the game. Our first step will be the addition of one player; we will discuss adding other additional players in a later chapter. The theory and code in this chapter are designed to be used for serial, network, and Internet connections.

Two-Player Connections

If our game consists of a square playing field and we put two players into the world, we have the view shown in Figure 5.1. Player A is located at position 2,2 and Player B is located at position 7,7. What we have here is the overhead view of the game. To bring the position of the players into better focus, let's look at the game from the point of view of each player. Assume that when we play the game, from my point of view I am Player A. This means that I am at position 2,2 and you, my opponent, are at position 7,7. At the same time, from your point of view you are Player A at position 2,2 and I, your opponent, am at position 7,7.

Obviously, we can't both be Player A at location 2,2 as well as Player B at 7,7. Thus, we must set things up in a manner so that one of us is Player A and the other is Player B. Figure 5.2 shows the view according to Player A and Figure 5.3 shows the view according to Player B. You can see that each of us is at a single specific position, as we should be.

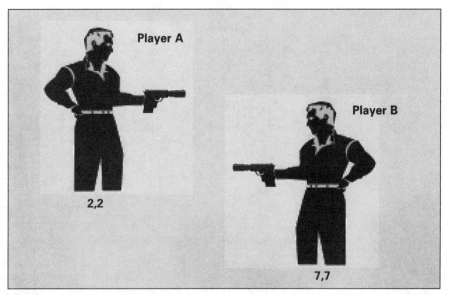

Figure 5.1   Player locations.

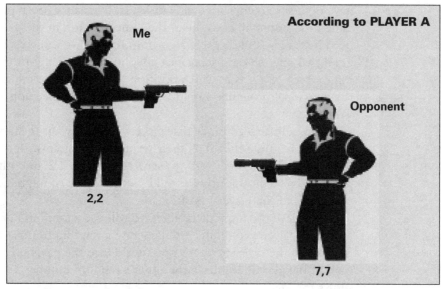

Figure 5.2 View according to Player A.

Determining the Position

Now we need to come up with a way of letting each of the players know who is who. By far the simplest way to do this is to create one program that has its main point of view at position 2,2 and another program that has its main point of view at position 7,7.

This is quite unacceptable though, since it only works if the players

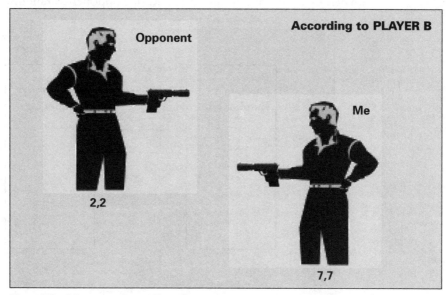

Figure 5.3 View according to Player B.

have opposite (complementary) disks. If, by chance, both players get the same disk, both will again be at the same position in the game. What we need instead is some type of algorithm so that we can create a single program that anyone can use against anyone else. The algorithm would determine which player is in which position. Once the determination is made, the individual programs would be informed of the decision and the game would begin.

We should also consider that players will not want to start in the same position each time they start their respective programs. In other words, Player A will sometimes want to start at position 2,2 and other times at position 7,7. The algorithm should give a degree of unpredictability in its placement of the players' positions.

To achieve the unpredictability, we will use a random number generator. Each player's computer will generate a random number and pass this number to the other player's computer. Once the passing is accomplished, each of the players will have the other's random number. Figure 5.4 shows the idea.

Once each player has both random numbers, the players make a simple comparison. The player with the larger random number is Player A located at position 2,2, and the other player is Player B at position 7,7. If we consider the case in Figure 5.4, we see that this makes "us" Player B at position 7,7 and "them" Player A at position 2,2.

What would happen if the two computers picked the same number? The answer is that both of the players would be assigned to "no player" and the game would probably crash. The solution is to add a condition whereby if our random number and our opponent's random number are

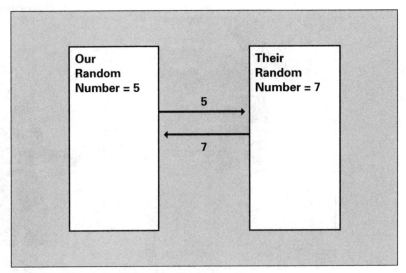

Figure 5.4   Number exchange algorithm.

equal, then both machines pick new random numbers. The complete algorithm can be described as:

```
DO
    get Our random number
    transmit Our random number to other machine
    receive Their random number from other machine
    IF Our > Their THEN
        our_position = 2,2
        their_position = 7,7
        match = 1
    ENDIF
    IF Our < Their THEN
        our_position = 7,7
        their_position = 2,2
        match = 1
    ENDIF
UNTIL match
```

Notice that the equality case falls through the cracks only to be picked up by the loop condition. *In other words, if both of the values in the variables OUR and THEIR are the same, neither of the IF statements will be executed. Since the IF statements are not executed, the value of MATCH will remain such that the code generates new random numbers and starts the process over again.*

Once the position algorithm is translated into C code, it will be placed in our game code. Since we are checking on the initial locations of the game players, we will assume that a communication link has been established. It is only after the link has been established that we want to converse with the other computer.

Making the Opponent Move

At this point, we have determined which player is Player A and which is Player B. The programs know the exact location of each player. These locations are programmed into the system during the development process. Once game play begins, the initial locations are meaningless, since both players will be moving their viewpoints. We now must consider how each computer shows the movements of both players. One aspect of this is that in order to see our opponent's movements, we will need to give our opponent an actual graphical figure in our game. This will be accomplished using an ACK3D object and will be discussed in the next section.

How are one player's movements communicated to the other? When Player A moves forward, the graphical figure that is representing Player A in Player B's game must move in an appropriate direction. There are basi-

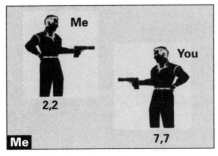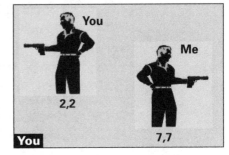

Figure 5.5   Starting position.

cally two different techniques for conveying the movement information: position and movement value.

Position

The first technique for communicating movement information to the opponent's computer involves sending the position. Let's assume that I am located at position 2,2 and you are at position 7,7. I will move forward one step to position 3,2. My new position will be sent to your computer.

Once your computer receives this new position data, it will change the location of the graphical figure representing me so that it looks like I am moving. Figure 5.5 shows the starting position of the game. Figure 5.6 indicates the movement of my viewpoint forward one step and the transmitting of the new position to your computer.

Once your computer receives the information, its graphical representation of me is moved appropriately as shown in Figure 5.7. As you can see, this is a very effective movement operation.

What if information is lost by the connection link? Let's say that I made the move forward one step and passed the new position 3,2 to your computer. Your computer does not, however, receive the information, so my graphical figure is not updated correctly. Now I make a move to the right by one step, which gives me the location 3,3. This new location is transmitted to the other computer so that it can update my figure.

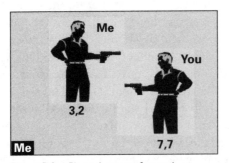

Figure 5.6   Player A moves forward.

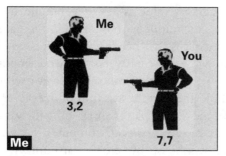

Figure 5.7   Player A's movement is reflected on Player B's screen.

Although the movement to position 3,2 was lost, both of the computers will have my correct location at 3,3. We can be sure that the two computers will not be out of step more than a few movements. And even if the computers are out of step, they will come back together on the next successful communication.

The only problem with the position technique is that with ACK3D, the graphical figure is moved by relative values based on the current location of the player. The relative values, not the positions, are transmitted between the computers.

Movement Values

Using movement values to communicate the current position of one player's viewpoint to the other computer involves passing single values. In the example above, I moved from position 2,2 to position 3,2. This was a forward movement of length 1. Therefore, my movement value was 1 in the forward direction. This is the information that will be transmitted to the other computer. The other computer will take the information and move my graphical figure in the appropriate direction. In order to illustrate how this technique works, consider the following table of characters and meanings:

character	movement representation
A	move forward one unit
B	move backward one unit
C	turn to the right one unit angle
D	turn to the left one unit angle

Using the information in this table, my movement can be accurately represented by simply sending a single character to your computer. If I press the UP arrow on my keyboard to move forward three times, the computer will send three "A" values to your computer. Your computer will receive the three "A" values and move my graphical representation forward a total of three units, one for every "A" value received.

This technique is very useful because it cuts down on the amount of information that needs to be transmitted between the two computers.

Instead of sending an x and a y value as in the technique above, we just send one character. If this technique is to be used in the game, there is a problem with lost transmissions that needs to be addressed. There are times when information will be lost between the two computers. With the technique described earlier, the system can self-correct itself since successive transmissions will hold the current location of my player. This is not self-correction. If I have moved by player three units forward and only two of the "A" values are received by your computer, my graphical representation on your screen will be off by one forward unit. If this happens several times, the two machines will be seriously out of sync.

We are going to solve this problem by counting the number of moves each person makes and periodically sync the two machines by sending the exact locations of all of the objects in the game to the other computer. This way, if my graphical representation is off on your machine, my machine will let your machine know my true current location and everything will be synced again. While it may take some time to do the syncing, this way of doing things make a good trade off between speed and accuracy of the game.

A Graphical Figure for the Opponent

We mentioned that each of the players of the game must have a representation of the other player so that they know what each other is doing. We will be using a graphical representation that is created as an ACK3D object.

ACK3D objects are designed as a collection of bitmaps just like the bitmaps we created for the walls of the game. In order to create objects for the ACK3D system, we have to make several decisions. The first decision concerns the number of views the graphical object will consist of.

We can look at an object in the real world from an unlimited number of viewpoints. We can look at its front or back, or any angle we wish. This gives us the ability to move around the object and see that it is a three-dimensional structure. In ACK3D, since we are creating a three-dimensional game, we will probably want to create the graphical figure for our opponent so that we can move around it and also see it is as a three-dimensional object. We would certainly want to be able to look at the front and back of the figure, since there may be times when we sneak up behind or run into our opponent face to face.

At a minimum then, we want to have two views of our graphical figure: front and back. How many additional views should we have? As you think about the answer to this question, keep in mind that each view will require 4 KB of main memory and, probably more important, you will have to draw each of the views by hand (using MVP Paint).

In order to make the objects seem realistic but not consume large amounts of memory or artistic time, they should consist of either four

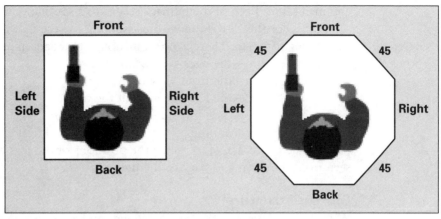

Figure 5.8   Four- and eight-view objects.

or eight different views. An object with four views will have front, back, left side, and right side views. An object with eight views will have these four views as well as views at 45 degrees off each of them. Figure 5.8 shows the four- and eight-view objects. For all of the demonstrations in this and the remaining chapters, we will be using only four views of all objects.

Using MVP Paint, each of the views should be created as a separate 64 x 64 pixel bitmap and saved under an appropriate name. Once the four views are created, it's time to put the object into our game by adding it to the code from the last chapter.

When creating the bitmaps for the graphical representation of your opponent as well as any other object that you are going to put in your game, you will want to keep in mind the way that the object in going to be moving. As you will see when you run our final game, we add movement to our graphical representation. When I move forward on my machine, my graphical representaion on your machine will actually have legs that look like they are running. Simply by adding the effect of running, the bitmap count for the graphical figure rose from 4 to 12. Thus, this one figure requires 48k of memory. If we have chosen the 8 view option, this figure will required 24 bitmaps and 96k of memory. In addition to the memory requirements, someone has to draw all of the bitmaps. My thanks goes to Tim Ryan, a wonderful graphic artist and editor, for taking the time to create the different bitmaps for our game. He spent countless hours designing the bitmaps. You can expect to pay some good money to have nice looking bitmaps designed.

Adding an ACK3D Object

To illustrate adding an object to our MINOSML program, assume that we have four 64 x 64 pixel bitmaps called man1.lbm, man2.lbm, man3.lbm, and man4.lbm. Each of the bitmaps relates to a specific view of the graphical figure. For this discussion we are assuming the the figure will look the same when it moves. There is no animation. The relations are:

> man1.lbm—the back view of the figure
> man2.lbm—the front view of the figure
> man3.lbm—the left side view of the figure
> man4.lbm—the right side view of the figure

You will notice from the pictures of the graphical figure, that each of the side views are drawn to mimic the positions of the legs and arms as seen from the front and back of the figure.

Bitmap Structure

With the four views of the figure defined, we are ready to tell the Simple program to read the bitmaps into the engine. If you recall from our original discussion of the Simple program, we have an array at the start of the program that holds all of the filenames of the bitmaps that will be used in the program. The array is:

```
BMTABLE bmTable[] = {
  1   ,TYPE_WALL        ,"wall.lbm",
  -1 ,-1         ,""              /* End of table */
  };
```

The first number in the array structure is the index into an array of bitmaps. There are two bitmap arrays: one for wall bitmaps and one for object bitmaps. Each of the arrays can hold up to 256 bitmaps. The second value in the array structure is the type of the bitmap being described. There are two types of bitmaps: wall bitmaps defined by the constant TYPE_WALL, and object bitmaps defined by the constant TYPE_ OBJECT. The third value in the array structure is the actual filename of the bitmap.

We are ready to add the four views of the graphical figure object to the array structure. We will begin adding the bitmaps at index value 1 and type TYPE_OBJECT:

```
BMTABLE bmTable[] = {
  1   ,TYPE_WALL          ,"wall.lbm",
  1 ,TYPE_OBJECT  ,"man1.lbm",
  2 ,TYPE_OBJECT  ,"man2.lbm",
  3 ,TYPE_OBJECT  ,"man3.lbm",
  4 ,TYPE_OBJECT  ,"man4.lbm",
  -1 ,-1         ,""              /* End of table */
  };
```

You don't need to worry about the order that you place the bitmaps into the bitmap structure. This structure is only used to read the bitmaps into the engine. The actual order of the bitmaps will come into play when we define the object. What is important about this array structure is the bitmap number given to each of the views. In order to keep things straight, it might be a good idea to create several #define statements like these:

> #define opponent_back 1
> #define opponent_front 2
> #define opponent_left 3
> #define opponent_right 4

Creating the #defines will allow us to use a descriptive word instead of a number to refer to a bitmap. The last thing we have to do is set the global variable TOTAL_BITMAPS equal to the correct value like:

> **int TOTAL_BITMAPS=5;**

Setting this variable equal to the correct number of bitmaps in our array will allow the routine reading the bitmaps to read the correct number of them.

The AppSetObject Function

Now that the engine is able to read in the bitmaps that make up the graphical figure object, we need to actually create the object. We will create the object in the function AppSetObject(). The function is declared as:

```
int AppSetObject(void)
{
 UCHAR bitmaps[4];
 int result;
 bitmaps[0] = opponent_back;
 bitmaps[1] = opponent_left;
 bitmaps[2] = opponent_front;
 bitmaps[3] = opponent_right;

 ae->ObjList[1].Flags |= OF_PASSABLE;
 ae->ObjList[1].Speed = 1;
 ae->ObjList[1].Dir = 0;

 AckCreateObject (ae, 1, 4, bitmaps);
 return(0);
}
```

The process used to create the graphical figure object is a generic process, although you must keep track of the specific characteristics of your object. There are four different characteristics that we must set up before we tell the ACK3D engine to create the object.

First is an array structure of bitmaps indices. We will be using a function called AckCreateObject() to ultimately create our graphical figure object as well as any other objects that we might want to create later on. One of the parameters of this function is an array that contains the bitmaps a particular object will use. Each of the array locations will have an object bitmap index. Recall that when the bitmaps are read into the system, they are placed into either a wall or object bitmap array. The bitmap number assigned to a bitmap is the index into the particular array where this bitmap is located. The array we are passing to the AckCreateObject() function is just a list of the indices into the main object bitmap array. The array is defined as:

```
UCHAR bitmaps[4];
```

We have set the bounds of the bitmap array to 4 because four bitmaps make up this object.

Next, we need to assign bitmap indices to each of the locations of our new array structure. We need to be cautious here, because the order in which the bitmap indices are assigned must follow a specific pattern. Assume that we have a four-view object as we see in Figure 5.9.

We want to apply our bitmaps to the figure so that the front bitmap is located at the front of the object. In order to do this, we must follow the numbering of the positions shown in Figure 5.10.

When we developed our bitmaps and read the bitmaps into the system, we assigned each of the bitmaps a number:

Number 1—man1.lbm—the back view of the figure
Number 2—man2.lbm—the front view of the figure
Number 3—man3.lbm—the left side view of the figure
Number 4—man4.lbm—the right side view of the figure

However, we did not want to memorize the particular numbers so we assigned character strings to represent the numbers. Using these strings

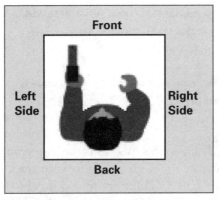

Figure 5.9 Views of the graphical figure.

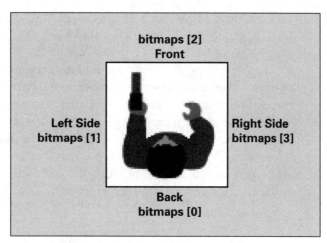

Figure 5.10 Views of the figure in relation to array positions.

and the diagram in Figure 5.10, the bitmap array can be assigned the appropriate values.

```
bitmaps[0] = opponent_back;
bitmaps[1] = opponent_left;
bitmaps[2] = opponent_front;
bitmaps[3] = opponent_right;
```

Now that we have a list of the bitmaps and their respective positions in the object, we will fill in other necessary parts of the developing object. All of the objects in our application are kept in an array called ObjList, which is attached to the main ACK3D variable. The array is declared as:

```
typedef struct {
    char    Active;
    UCHAR   bmNum[MAX_VIEWS];
    int     Sides;
    int     Dir;
    UCHAR   Flags;
    UCHAR   CurNum;
    UCHAR   MaxNum;
    char    Speed;
    int     VidRow;
    int     x;
    int     y;
    int     mPos;
} OBJECTS;
```

Only three of the fields in the OBJECT data structure are going to be directly manipulated by us. These fields are Dir, Flags, and Speed. The other parts of the OBJECT data structure can basically be ignored as they will be filled in by the ACK engine. However, notice that this structure contains all of the important details about a particular object such as its place in the map, its x and y coordinates, etc. Some of this information will become useful when our game begins to unfold more.

We just mentioned that all of the objects in our application are stored in one array. We will need to keep track of what position in the object array corresponds to which object. We will do this by defining a constant at the top of our program—for example:

```
#define    other_guy  0
```

Now whenever we want to access the graphical figure object for our opponent, we just use the code

```
ae->ObjList[other_guy].Dir;
```

followed by a field name such as Dir.

The first field that we are going to fill is Dir. This field relates to the angle of movement for the object we are defining. The appropriate values for this field are any of the constants defined in a previous chapter called

```
#define INT_ANGLE_1      5
#define INT_ANGLE_2      10
#define INT_ANGLE_4      20
#define INT_ANGLE_6      30
#define INT_ANGLE_30     160
#define INT_ANGLE_45     240
#define INT_ANGLE_90     480
#define INT_ANGLE_135    720
#define INT_ANGLE_180    960
#define INT_ANGLE_225    1200
#define INT_ANGLE_270    1440
#define INT_ANGLE_315    1680
#define INT_ANGLE_360    1920
```

We will assume that our object is facing forward by assigning the value of 0 to the Dir field:

```
ae->ObjList[other_guy].Dir = 0;
```

After the Dir field is assigned, we can move to the Flags field. This field can be assigned one of two values: OF_PASSABLE and OF_

ANIMATE. The value OF_PASSABLE is used when the object is movable. The value OF_ANIMATE is used when the object is going to be stationary but will be animated. The animation comes about by the ACK3D engine rotating through all of the bitmaps assigned to this object in succession. *As an example of why you might wish to create an object like this, let's assume that you are creating an Egyptian type game. In this game, you will walk into a palace where you come upon several statues. These statues are deadly however. Every once in a while, a large tongue comes out of their mouth and if it touches you, you are dead. To create this type of object, you would have a bitmap of the stationary statue with its mouth closed. The next bitmap would be the mouth slightly open and the tongue starting to come out. The third bitmap is the mouth fully open and the tongue fully stretched out. The fourth and final bitmap is the same as the second bitmap. If the ACK engine rotated through these four bitmaps, it would look like the statue was moving its mouth and tongue toward you.*

This field can also be assigned a value of 0 to indicate that the object is going to be stationary and not be animated. Because we are defining the object for our opponent, we will want the object to be moveable, so we will use the code

```
ae->ObjList[1].Flags |= OF_PASSABLE;
```

The last field that we need to assign is Speed. This field determines the speed at which the system animates an object. The field must be set to a value of at least 1 for an object to be activated in the system. A value of 2 gives the object about average speed.

Once all of the bitmaps are assigned and the fields of our developing object are filled, we make a call to the function AckCreateObject(). This function is designed to take all of the bitmaps and object fields and initialize internal structures for the new object. The format of the function is:

```
int AckCreateObject (ACKENG *, int Object_number, int
Num_bitmaps, UCHAR *);
```

The first parameter to the function is our ACK3D engine variable. The second parameter is the object number of the object that we are creating. To avoid any confusion, you should make sure that you use the defined constants created for each of the objects like the #define constant we used for this object: other_guy. The third parameter is the total number of bitmaps used in the object. The fourth parameter is the bitmap array that we defined that contains all the indices to our bitmaps for this object. For our figure object, the function call is

```
AckCreateObject (ae, 1, 4, bitmaps);
```

That's all there is to creating an ACK3D object, except that we need to put the object in our game's map. To do this, we will use the map editor.

Setting the Object Using the Map Editor

Before we can add the object to our game's map, we need to include a description of the new object in the ASCII description file for our game. Recall that the description file for our game is called MINOSML.01.

Using a DOS editor, open this file and add the following lines of code:

```
Objects:
 Files:
    1, man1.lbm
 EndFiles:
Number: 1
Direction: 0
Speed: 1
Bitmaps: 4
EndObjects:
```

The object description code begins with the type word OBJECTS:. This keyword indicates that the descriptions to follow are those of the objects that will be placed in the ACK3D game. Immediately following is the keyword FILES:. This keyword tells the map editor the object number and associated lbm files for the object. After all of the bitmap files have been listed, the keyword EndFiles: is put into the file.

Now we must put a small description for each of the objects, consisting of Number, Direction, Speed, and Bitmaps. Number specifies the object number. Direction is the direction value for the object. Speed is the speed value for the object. Bitmaps is the total number of bitmaps that make up this object. All of the values for these four keywords must be identical to the values assigned in our application program.

We are now ready to actually add the object to our map. To do this, execute the map editor, using **MINOSML.01** as the only command-line parameter. Once you do this, you will get the familiar working screen of the map editor. When the map editor first executes, it is set up to use the different wall bitmaps. To change this so that you can place objects in the map, click on the map editor icon that shows a table and chair, representing objects. You will see the bitmap for the first object appear in the upper right-hand corner of the start-up screen. Next to the bitmap will be the number 1 highlighted with a blue box around it. You can now use the mouse to place the object anywhere on the map just by clicking one of the map locations. Figure 5.11 shows a sample map with a starting location and an object marked.

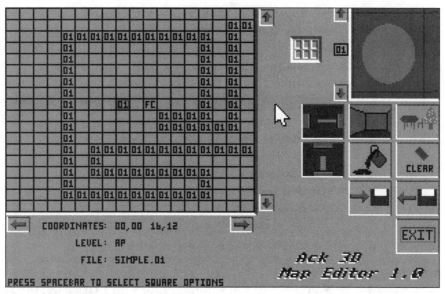

Figure 5.11 Placing an Object in the Maze

Once the object is placed, save the new map and exit the map editor. To see the results of adding the figure object, execute the program MINOSML.exe in directory \NETWARIO.

Setting Up Movement Values

With the opponent's figure loaded, we are ready to program movement into the system. We want to be sure and set things up so that adding serial, network, and Internet support is easy. In addition, we need to set things up so that we can acknowledge the receipt of movement values sent from the other computer. To do this, we will look at adding code for forward movement of the object.

The function that we are going to add is process_communications( ). This function has a single parameter that accepts a CHAR variable. The CHAR variable will be one of many different movement values from the opponent. The initial format of the function is:

```
void process_communications(char value)
{
   switch (value)
   {
   }
}
```

As soon as the function receives a character from some type of communication medium, it immediately tries to determine what character has been received by evaluating the switch statement. In order for the function to interpret characters, we need to have characters for it to interpret. Let us assume that we are going to assign the character A as representing a forward movement of the opponent. We need to add a case statement to our function:

```
void process_communications(char value)
{
    switch (value)
    {
        case 'a':
            break;
    }
}
```

Now when this function is called with a character, the switch statement can determine if the contents of the VALUE local variable is an A or not. With the case statement in place, we can begin to add code for making the opponent's figure object move forward. The ACK3D engine includes a single function for moving any object. The function is called AckMoveObjectPOV() and has a format of

```
int AckMoveObjectPOV (ACKENG *, int Object_number, int ANGLE, int DISTANCE);
```

The function returns an int value that can be of any of the following values:

```
#define POV_NOTHING         0
#define POV_XWALL           1
#define POV_YWALL           2
#define POV_OBJECT          3
#define POV_PLAYER          4
```

These values can be used by the application program to determine if any reaction has occurred from the movement of the object. It should be obvious that if the value returned by the move object function is POV_PLAYER, then the object being moved has hit the player. This could be especially useful if our opponent has fired a gun at us and the bullet object has to hit us.

For now, though, we just need to use the function to move our opponent's object forward. We will do this using one single statement:

```
AckMoveObjectPOV (ae, other_guy, ae->ObjList[other_guy].Dir, MOVE_VALUE);
```

The first and second parameters of the function call should be obvious.

The third parameter is the direction of the object's motion. The Dir field of the object array is used to indicate the appropriate direction. This is a convenient place to keep track of the angle of movement. The fourth parameter of the function is the distance to move the object. We have defined a constant called MOVE_VALUE to indicate the distance to move the object. This constant is defined as

#define MOVE_VALUE 16

With the addition of code to actually move the opponent's object forward, we now have the following:

```
void process_communications(char value)
{
   switch (value)
   {
      case 'a': AckMoveObjectPOV (ae, other_guy, ae->ObjList[other_guy],
MOVE_VALUE);
           break;
   }
}
```

This function should be added to the Simple program we have been developing.

We should also test the function to make sure that everything is working correctly. To do this, we can use the keyboard as a communication device. Instead of having to write code that allows us to communicate between two different computers in order to just test this one function, we will rely on ourselves for the test.

In our program, we have the code for processing the keystroke from the player. In this code, we need to add the following case statement:

```
    case 'a': process_communications ('a');
               break;
```

This code has the effect of passing the character "a" to the movement function whenever the player presses the A key on the keyboard. So what we are doing is allowing our machine, just for the moment, to move the graphical figure representation of our opponent. We are ONLY doing this for the moment to test out the code that we have put in the process_communications() routine. When we add code for creating a communication link between our computer and another, we will take this code out since everything will be working correctly. Once the code is added, the keyboard handling appears as

```
if (bioskey(1))
{
```

```
ch = getkey();
if (ch==ESC) break;
switch(ch)
{
  case LEFT : ae->PlayerAngle += (-INT_ANGLE_2 * 5);
      pan = 1;
      break;
  case RIGHT: ae->PlayerAngle += INT_ANGLE_2 * 5;
      pan = 1;
      break;
  case UP:  AckMovePOV(ae,ae->PlayerAngle,16);
      break;
  case DOWN: temp= ae->PlayerAngle + INT_ANGLE_180;
      if (temp >= INT_ANGLE_360)
       temp -= INT_ANGLE_360;
      AckMovePOV(ae,temp,16);
      break;
  case 'a': process_communications('a');
        break;
  }
}
```

To test the results of adding this code, make the changes and compile the
MINOSML program using the steps documented in earlier chapters. If you

Figure 5.12 Front view of the opponent.

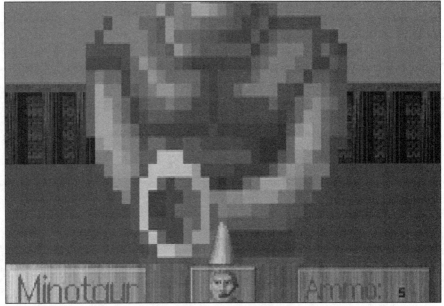

Figure 5.13 The opponent steps towards us.

run the program, you should get the progression shown in Figures 5.12 through 5.15. Figure 5.12 shows the figure upon execution of the program. Figure 5.13 shows the effect of pressing the A key once. Figure 5.14 shows the effect of pressing the A key until the opponent's figure moves through us.

Figure 5.14 The opponent walks through us.

Figure 5.15 Back view of the opponent.

Figure 5.15 shows the back of the opponent's figure when we turn our viewpoint around 180 degrees—that is, when the opponent has walked through us and we turn around to look.

Now that we have the forward movement working, we can do the backward movement with just a bit more effort. The code for the backward movement is:

```
temp_angle = ae->ObjList[other_guy].Dir + INT_ANGLE_180;
if (temp_angle >=360) temp_angle -= INT_ANGLE_360;
if (temp_angle <=0) temp_angle += INT_ANGLE_360;
ae->ObjList[other_guy].Dir = temp_angle;

ae->ObjList[other_guy].bmNum[0] = opponent_front;
ae->ObjList[other_guy].bmNum[1] = opponent_right;
ae->ObjList[other_guy].bmNum[2] = opponent_back;
ae->ObjList[other_guy].bmNum[3] = opponent_left;
AckMoveObjectPOV (ae, other_guy, ae->ObjList[other_guy].Dir, 16);
```

At first glance, everything should look somewhat familiar since we used basically the same code when we wrote the code for our own viewpoint to walk backwards. The first four lines of code are used to turn the viewpoint of the object around 180 degrees. The reason for this is that the object is supposed to represent a human being. Humans normally turn around to move in the opposite direction—rarely do we walk backwards. Such is the case for our graphical figure object. Once we have the object pointing in the correct direction, we have to change the order of the object's bitmaps to show that the player has turned around. This is just a matter of changing the object's bitmap numbers to reflect different bitmaps in different locations. After the bitmaps are switched, we can make the object move.

We will put the backward code into the process_communications() function under the character of "b" and add a second case statement to the keyboard handling code. Figure 5.16 shows the effect of pressing the B key one time. Note that we are still testing this code, so there is no link between your computer and another machine. When pressing the B key, you are only testing the movements of the graphical figure.

Notice that the object has turned its back to us and moved away as well. If we continue to press the B key, the figure will move further away from us as we see in Figure 5.17. For the image shown in Figure 5.17, we pressed the B key as many times as we could until the object ran into the wall. Notice that the object cannot go beyond the wall.

What do you expect will happen when we press the A key to bring our opponent closer to us? Well, the object will certainly move closer, but it will have its back to us instead of looking at us. The reason for this is that when we wrote the forward movement code, we didn't know that we would have to rearrange the bitmaps when the object moved backwards. To get the object to respond correctly to the forward movement key, we need to add the following code to the "a" code in the process_communications() function:

Figure 5.16 Object moving away from us.

Figure 5.17 Object running into a wall.

```
ae->ObjList[other_guy].bmNums[0] = opponent_back;
ae->ObjList[other_guy].bmNums[1] = opponent_left;
ae->ObjList[other_guy].bmNums[2] = opponent_front;
ae->ObjList[other_guy].bmNums[3] = opponent_right;
```

Once the new code is added to the "a" movement value, the object moves
in the correct fashion. When we press the A key, the object moves forward
with its appropriate face turned toward us, and when we press the B key, the
object turns around and moves in the other direction. Now if we press the A
key again, the object should turn around and move toward us again.

But if we run the program with the above code added, we find that
although the object does turn around toward us when we press the A key
a second time, it does not move toward us but away from us. This is
because we have not turned the direction of the object around 180
degrees in the other direction.

Unfortunately, if we were to add the code to change the direction of
the object toward us, we would have a real problem on our hands. Every
time we press either the A or B key, we turn the direction of the object by
180 degrees. But if we press any of the keys twice, we in fact turn the
object completely around in a circle, which is not the intended action.
Although I won't show the code for it, we have an additional problem
when we put in code to turn the object. Each time we pressed either the
A or B key, we would move forward according to the object's original
position and not forward in the direction that we had turned the object.

This all means that we have to come up with a different scheme for the movement of the object. The scheme must be such that we actually move the object in its intended direction and the bitmap of the object changes to reflect the direction we are moving it.

A New Movement Scheme

The simple solution to our problem is illustrated in the diagram in Figure 5.18. The diagram shows the different bitmap types that are assigned to our four-sided object. Since there are only four bitmaps, we can divide the 360 degrees around our object into four different areas. The frontal area is defined from 315 to 45 degrees. The right area is defined from 45 to 135 degrees. The back area is defined from 135 to 225 degrees, and the left area is defined from 225 to 315.

Forward Movement

When moving forward, we must always have the front bitmap assigned to the part of the object facing forward. We can achieve this only by reassigning the bitmaps of the object on two separate occasions—when the object is moving forward or backward. When we tell the object to move forward, the code should look at the current object Direction angle and rotate the bitmaps so that the side within our defined area is assigned the frontal bitmap and the other sides of the object get the appropriate bitmaps.

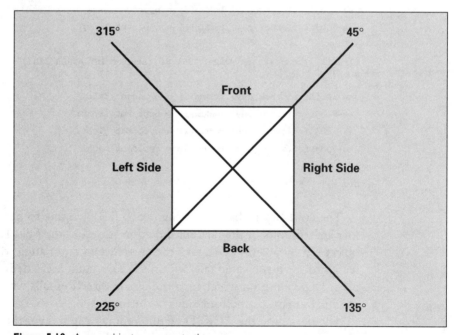

Figure 5.18 A new object movement scheme.

The code for doing this type of algorithm is shown in Listing 5.1.

Listing 5.1

```
AckMoveObjectPOV (ae, other_guy, ae->ObjList[other_guy].Dir, 16);
temp = ae->ObjList[other_guy].Dir;
if ((temp < INT_ANGLE_45) && (temp > INT_ANGLE_315))
{
 ae->ObjList[other_guy].bmNum[0] = opponent_back;
 ae->ObjList[other_guy].bmNum[1] = opponent_left;
 ae->ObjList[other_guy].bmNum[2] = opponent_front;
 ae->ObjList[other_guy].bmNum[3] = opponent_right;
}
else if ((temp >= INT_ANGLE_45) && (temp < INT_ANGLE_135))
{
 ae->ObjList[other_guy].bmNum[0] = opponent_right;
 ae->ObjList[other_guy].bmNum[1] = opponent_back;
 ae->ObjList[other_guy].bmNum[2] = opponent_left;
 ae->ObjList[other_guy].bmNum[3] = opponent_front;
}
else if ((temp >= INT_ANGLE_135) && (temp < INT_ANGLE_225))
{
 ae->ObjList[other_guy].bmNum[0] = opponent_front;
 ae->ObjList[other_guy].bmNum[1] = opponent_right;
 ae->ObjList[other_guy].bmNum[2] = opponent_back;
 ae->ObjList[other_guy].bmNum[3] = opponent_left;
}
else if ((temp >= INT_ANGLE_225) && (temp < INT_ANGLE_315))
{
 ae->ObjList[other_guy].bmNum[0] = opponent_left;
 ae->ObjList[other_guy].bmNum[1] = opponent_front;
 ae->ObjList[other_guy].bmNum[2] = opponent_right;
 ae->ObjList[other_guy].bmNum[3] = opponent_back;
}
break;
```

The code begins by instructing the ACK3D engine to move the object forward 16 units in the current direction stored in the field Dir of the object's array position. We take the current Direction angle value and search to see if the value falls within the four main areas defined in Figure 5.18. Depending on which area the object direction falls within, we assign specific bitmaps to the four sides of our object.

The next time the ACK3D engine redraws the screen, the object will change its view and move 16 units in that direction.

Backward Movement

The other case where we need to change the bitmaps of the object is when the object is moving backward. In this case, we turn the object completely around and move it several units "forward." In order to keep things syncing correctly, we will change the bitmaps of the object and move the object backward. After these steps, we make a quick call to the function AppShow3D(). This function does a very fast redraw of the screen to move the object backward and returns the bitmap of the object to its original position. The reason that we must do this is because if we change the direction of the object permanently, we will not be able to move the object forward.

The code that does the backward movement is shown in Listing 5.2.

Listing 5.2

```
AckMoveObjectPOV (ae, other_guy, ae->ObjList[other_guy].Dir, 16);
temp = ae->ObjList[other_guy].Dir;

if ((temp < INT_ANGLE_45) && (temp > INT_ANGLE_315))
{
 ae->ObjList[other_guy].bmNum[0] = opponent_back;
 ae->ObjList[other_guy].bmNum[1] = opponent_left;
 ae->ObjList[other_guy].bmNum[2] = opponent_front;
 ae->ObjList[other_guy].bmNum[3] = opponent_right;
}
else if ((temp >= INT_ANGLE_45) && (temp < INT_ANGLE_135))
{
 ae->ObjList[other_guy].bmNum[0] = opponent_right;
 ae->ObjList[other_guy].bmNum[1] = opponent_back;
 ae->ObjList[other_guy].bmNum[2] = opponent_left;
 ae->ObjList[other_guy].bmNum[3] = opponent_front;
}
else if ((temp >= INT_ANGLE_135) && (temp < INT_ANGLE_225))
{
 ae->ObjList[other_guy].bmNum[0] = opponent_front;
 ae->ObjList[other_guy].bmNum[1] = opponent_right;
 ae->ObjList[other_guy].bmNum[2] = opponent_back;
 ae->ObjList[other_guy].bmNum[3] = opponent_left;
}
else if ((temp >= INT_ANGLE_225) && (temp < INT_ANGLE_315))
{
 ae->ObjList[other_guy].bmNum[0] = opponent_left;
 ae->ObjList[other_guy].bmNum[1] = opponent_front;
 ae->ObjList[other_guy].bmNum[2] = opponent_right;
```

```
ae->ObjList[other_guy].bmNum[3] = opponent_back;
}
break;
```

As you can see, we save the current position of the bitmaps and assign them back to the object after we have moved the object backward. The only thing left for us to do is create the code for the left and right panning of the object.

Panning

The panning of the object will be accomplished using two additional character values, "c" and "d." The actual panning of the object must be identical to the panning of the opponent. We pan our own viewpoint using the angle value of INT_ANGLE_2 * 5. This will be the value that we use for the panning of the object. The code looks like

```
case 'c':
 temp = ae->ObjList[other_guy].Dir + INT_ANGLE_2 * 5;
 if (temp >= INT_ANGLE_360) temp -= INT_ANGLE_360;
 if (temp <= 0) temp += INT_ANGLE_360;

 ae->ObjList[other_guy].Dir = temp;
 break;
case 'd':
 temp = ae->ObjList[other_guy].Dir - INT_ANGLE_2 * 5;
 if (temp >= INT_ANGLE_360) temp -= INT_ANGLE_360;
 if (temp <= 0) temp += INT_ANGLE_360;

 ae->ObjList[other_guy].Dir = temp;
 break;
```

Each of the panning functions gets the current value of the Dir field of the object and adds or subtracts INT_ANGLE_2 * 5 to the field. After the panning value is added or subtracted to the field, we must check the result to the value INT_ANGLE_360 to determine if we need to get the value into the range 0 to INT_ANGLE_360.

After we have the correct panning result, we assign the value to the Dir field of the object. Now when our opponent moves forward or backward, the object will move appropriately.

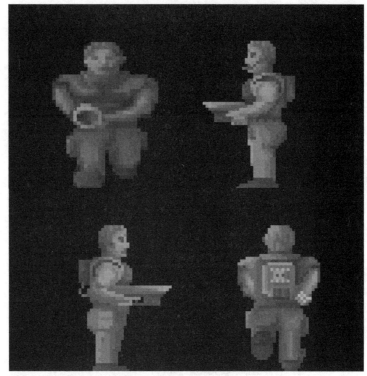

Figure 5.19 Four views of the opponent's player.

Conclusion

As you can see from this chapter, there is quite a bit of work involved in getting a graphical representation to act appropriately when our opponent makes any moves. We will now spend the next couple of chapters establishing three different links to our game: serial, ethernet, and Internet. After we have the appropriate connections, we will fill in the missing pieces to our game.

At this point we have the following code, reflecting the changes we made in this chapter

Main Code

```
#define other_guy 1
#define opponent_back 1
#define opponent_front 2
#define opponent_left 3
#define opponent_right 4
```

```
ACKEN    *ae;
MOUSE    mouse;
char     *MapFileName = "simple.MAP";
char     *PalFile = "simple.PAL";
BMTABLE bmTable[] = {
  1  ,TYPE_WALL  ,"swall16.lbm",
  1  ,TYPE_OBJECT  ,"man1.lbm",
  2  ,TYPE_OBJECT  ,"man2.lbm",
  3  ,TYPE_OBJECT  ,"man3.lbm",
  4  ,TYPE_OBJECT  ,"man4.lbm",
  -1 ,-1          ,""                    /* End of table */
};
```

Main Function

```
int main(void)
{
  int   result,
     done = 0,
     pan = 0;
  int   temp;
  unsigned ch;
  if (result=AppInitialize())
  {
   printf("Error initializing: ErrorCode = %d\n",result);
   return(1);
  }
  if (result=AppSetupEngine())
  {
   printf("Error setting up ACK engine: ErrorCode = %d\n",result);
   AckWrapUp(ae);
   return(1);
  }
  if (result=AppLoadBitmaps())
  {
   printf("Error loading bitmaps: ErrorCode = %d\n",result);
   AckWrapUp(ae);
   return(1);
  }
  if (result=AppSetGraphics())
  {
   AckSetTextmode();
   printf("Error loading palette: ErrorCode = %d\n",result);
   AckWrapUp(ae);
```

```
   return(1);
 }
 if (result=AppSetObject())
 {
  AckSetTextmode();
  printf("Error loading palette: ErrorCode = %d\n",result);
  AckWrapUp(ae);
  return(1);
 }
 AppSetupPalRanges();
 while (!done)
 {
  AckCheckObjectMovement(ae);
  if (pan)
  {
 pan = 0;
 if (ae->PlayerAngle >= INT_ANGLE_360)
    ae->PlayerAngle -= INT_ANGLE_360;
 if (ae->PlayerAngle < 0)
    ae->PlayerAngle += INT_ANGLE_360;
  }
  AppShow3D();
  if (bioskey(1))
  {
 ch = getkey();
 if (ch==ESC) break;
 switch(ch)
 {
  case LEFT : ae->PlayerAngle += (-INT_ANGLE_2 * 5);
      pan = 1;
      break;
  case RIGHT: ae->PlayerAngle += INT_ANGLE_2 * 5;
      pan = 1;
      break;
  case UP:  AckMovePOV(ae,ae->PlayerAngle,16);
      break;
  case DOWN: temp= ae->PlayerAngle + INT_ANGLE_180;
      if (temp >= INT_ANGLE_360)
       temp -= INT_ANGLE_360;
      AckMovePOV(ae,temp,16);
      break;
  case 'a': process_communications('a');
    break;
```

```
    case 'b': process_communications('b');
      break;
    case 'c': process_communications('c');
      break;
    case 'd': process_communications('d');
      break;
  }
 }
}
```

AppSetObject Function

```
int AppSetObject(void)
{
 UCHAR bitmaps[3];
 int result;
 bitmaps[0] = opponent_back;
 bitmaps[1] = opponent_left;
 bitmaps[2] = opponent_front;
 bitmaps[3] = opponent_right;
 ae->ObjList[other_guy].Speed = 1;
 ae->ObjList[other_guy].Dir = 0;
 AckCreateObject (ae, other_guy, 4, bitmaps);
 return(0);
}
```

Process_communication Function

```
void process_communications(char value)
{
  int temp, num1, num2, num3, num4;
  switch(value)
  {
   case 'a': AckMoveObjectPOV (ae, other_guy, ae-
>ObjList[other_guy].Dir, 16);
       temp = ae->ObjList[other_guy].Dir;
       if ((temp < INT_ANGLE_45) && (temp > INT_ANGLE_315))
       {
        ae->ObjList[other_guy].bmNum[0] = opponent_back;
        ae->ObjList[other_guy].bmNum[1] = opponent_left;
        ae->ObjList[other_guy].bmNum[2] = opponent_front;
        ae->ObjList[other_guy].bmNum[3] = opponent_right;
       }
       else if ((temp >= INT_ANGLE_45) && (temp < INT_ANGLE_135))
```

```
        {
         ae->ObjList[other_guy].bmNum[0] = opponent_right;
         ae->ObjList[other_guy].bmNum[1] = opponent_back;
         ae->ObjList[other_guy].bmNum[2] = opponent_left;
         ae->ObjList[other_guy].bmNum[3] = opponent_front;
        }
        else if ((temp >= INT_ANGLE_135) && (temp < INT_ANGLE_225))
        {
         ae->ObjList[other_guy].bmNum[0] = opponent_front;
         ae->ObjList[other_guy].bmNum[1] = opponent_right;
         ae->ObjList[other_guy].bmNum[2] = opponent_back;
         ae->ObjList[other_guy].bmNum[3] = opponent_left;
        }
        else if ((temp >= INT_ANGLE_225) && (temp < INT_ANGLE_315))
        {
         ae->ObjList[other_guy].bmNum[0] = opponent_left;
         ae->ObjList[other_guy].bmNum[1] = opponent_front;
         ae->ObjList[other_guy].bmNum[2] = opponent_right;
         ae->ObjList[other_guy].bmNum[3] = opponent_back;
        }
        break;
  case 'b': temp = ae->ObjList[other_guy].Dir + INT_ANGLE_180;
        if (temp >= INT_ANGLE_360) temp -= INT_ANGLE_360;
        if (temp <= 0) temp += INT_ANGLE_360;
        num1=ae->ObjList[other_guy].bmNum[0];
        num2=ae->ObjList[other_guy].bmNum[1];
        num3=ae->ObjList[other_guy].bmNum[2];
        num4=ae->ObjList[other_guy].bmNum[3];
        ae->ObjList[other_guy].bmNum[0] = opponent_front;
        ae->ObjList[other_guy].bmNum[1] = opponent_right;
        ae->ObjList[other_guy].bmNum[2] = opponent_back;
        ae->ObjList[other_guy].bmNum[3] = opponent_left;
        AckMoveObjectPOV (ae, other_guy, temp, 16);
        AppShow3D();
        ae->ObjList[other_guy].bmNum[0] = num1;
        ae->ObjList[other_guy].bmNum[1] = num2;
        ae->ObjList[other_guy].bmNum[2] = num3;
        ae->ObjList[other_guy].bmNum[3] = num4;
        break;
  case 'c': temp = ae->ObjList[other_guy].Dir + INT_ANGLE_2 * 5;
        if (temp >= INT_ANGLE_360) temp -= INT_ANGLE_360;
        if (temp <= 0) temp += INT_ANGLE_360;
        ae->ObjList[other_guy].Dir = temp;
```

```
                break;
        case 'd': temp = ae->ObjList[other_guy].Dir - INT_ANGLE_2 * 5;
            if (temp >= INT_ANGLE_360) temp -= INT_ANGLE_360;
            if (temp <= 0) temp += INT_ANGLE_360;
            ae->ObjList[other_guy].Dir = temp;
            break;
    }
}
```

Adding Serial Communication Support

In Chapter 5, we looked at the techniques necessary to add a graphical figure object to our ACK3D world. This object was to be used as a representation for the opponent when two computers are linked in a two-player game. As we developed the object, we created a simple function called process_communications( ), which has the task of figuring out what to do with the data that comes across some communication link. To test the system, we used a link between ourselves and the keyboard. Each time we pressed a particular key, a handling routine would pass the character of the key we pressed to the process_communications( ) routine.

This type of system is hardly a two-player system. We need to have a way of connecting two different computers, regardless of whether the machines are in the same room next to each other or across the world.

The simplest type of connection that we can make is through the serial port. Using a NULL modem cable, we can connect two machines that are near each other just by plugging the cable into the serial port of each machine. If the machines are located across the city, state, or world, we can connect them using a modem and a telephone line.

In this chapter, we have the task of learning about the serial port and how to program it. We will extend the discussion to include programming the modem and adding the necessary code to our ACK3D game to provide a direct link between two different computers, each running the game program.

The IBM PC Serial Port

The serial port on the IBM PC is designed to transmit information one bit at a time. When a character or a byte is sent to the serial port, the byte is split up into the eight separate bits that form the byte. These data bits are sent out the serial port one at a time or "serially."There are several additional bits sent along with the data bits. The first bit is called the *start bit* and indicates the beginning of a unit of data. After the start bit, there are the eight data bits. Once the eight data bits have been sent, one or two *stop bits* are sent to indicate the end of the data.

If you have ever connected to an on-line service, you know that the service will typically indicate how many stop and data bits are used by its system. Sometimes there is an additional bit called the *parity bit*. The parity bit was developed as a simple but really ineffective form of protection against transmission errors. Because most of the transmission protocols used today use their own form of error detection and correction, the parity information is not used. If the parity bit was used, it would be located between the data bits and the stop bit. The following shows the sequence of bits:

Start Bit — Data Bits —[Parity Bit] — Stop Bit

When using this type of start, data, stop bit transmission, it is imperative that both machines connected have their serial ports transmitting and receiving information at the same *baud rate*. The baud rate is the total number of signal changes per second that are allowed to occur at the serial port. For the IBM PC, the baud rate translates into the number of bits per second or bps that can be transmitted or received. The bps must include the start, data, and stop bits.

RS-232C

The serial port of the PC follows a protocol called the RS-232C standard, developed by the Electronic Industries Association (EIA). This standard is equivalent to the V.24 standard of the European committee CCITT. The purpose of the standard is to define certain aspects of the serial port and the interface between machines equipped with serial ports. When transferring information from one machine to another, the RS-232C standard assumes that there is a DTE (data terminal equipment) device and a DCE (data carrier equipment) device. When a modem is in use, the computer is the DTE device and the modem is the DCE device. When using two different machines connected by a serial cable, we have to fake one of the serial ports into thinking that it is a DCE device. We will see how to do this later.

For the PC, the serial port uses 11 out of a total of 25 data lines. If you look at the back of your computer, you will see a port that appears like the one in Figure 6.1.

If you do not see a connector with 25 pins, you may see one with nine pins. The nine-pin connector is a serial port that was defined by IBM for some of its later computer systems. Both types of ports perform the same functions.

Table 6.1 lists the pins of importance to us. As you will notice, only two of the pins are used to transfer information from one machine to another. All of the other pins are used for the following control purposes:

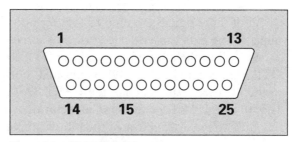

Figure 6.1   RS-232C Serial port.

Table 6.1 Serial port pins and signal descriptions.

Signal Type	Description	25 pin Port	9 pin Port
GND	protective ground	1	N/A
TD	transmitted data	2	3
RD	received data	3	2
RTS	Request to send	4	7
CTS	clear to send	5	8
DSR	data set ready	6	6
N/A	signal ground	7	5
DCD	data carrier detect	8	1
DTR	data terminal ready	20	4
RI	ring indicator	22	9
DSRD	data signal rate detector	23	N/A

RTS– The request-to-send signal tells the DCE device that the DTE device is going to send it some data. The DCE device must prepared itself to accept the data. DTE -> DCE

CTS– The clear-to-send signal tells the DTE that the DCE is ready to accept the data. This signal is usually in response to the RTS signal from the DTE. DCE->DTE

DCD– The data carrier detect signal is activated when the DCE detects a carrier from another CDE device, like a modem, that it has connected with. DCE->DTE

DSR– The data set ready signal is activated by the DCE when it has been turned on, initialized, and is ready for operation. DCE->DTE

DTR– The data terminal ready signal is activated by the DTE upon power-up of the data terminal. DTE->DCE

RI– The ring indicator is activated by the DCE when a ring has occurred. DCE->DTE

DSDR– The data signal rate detector is used to indicate that the data terminal and the data carrier should select a different baud rate. DCE->DTE

All of these signals are used to transfer information from the data terminal to the data carrier device, which is usually a modem.

With all of the lines going from the DTE to the DCE and back to the DTE, things could get pretty complicated. For this reason, the developer of the PC used a special chip: the UART 8250, or UART 16450 or 16550. The UART, or universal asynchronous receiver and transmitter, is designed to take over most of the job of timing and synchronization and allow us to do our transmitting and receiving of data. Accessing the UART and, subsequently, the serial port and the modem can be accomplished in three different ways: through DOS, BIOS, and register access.

The Software

In order to determine which way to access the UART, we need to determine at what speed we wish to communicate with other machines. The UART 8250 is designed to be used at a maximum rate of 9600 baud. For this reason, the DOS and BIOS routines are only designed to accept and transmit data up to this speed limit. In fact, if you are going to use DOS as your software interface, you will probably be limited to 2400 to 4800 baud because of the tremendous amount of overhead in the DOS routines. If you need to go beyond the 9600 limit and have a UART 16450 or 16550, then you will have to do some direct register manipulation of the UART chip.

DOS

Communicating with the serial port using a DOS interrupt is fairly simple. The DOS interrupt 21h has two function handlers:

> function 03h—read character from the serial interface
> function 04h—output character from the serial interface

The only problem with these function numbers is that there is no direct way of setting up the serial port as far as baud rate and other settings are concerned. In addition, you will only be able to achieve a pretty slow connection. So the next thing to do is to look at the system BIOS.

BIOS

The BIOS is the system of basic input/output routines of the computer. Within these routines is interrupt 14h, which is designed to control the serial port. There are six different functions within this one interrupt:

> function 00h—initialization of the serial port
> function 01h—output a character
> function 02h—receive a character
> function 03h—obtain status of serial port
> function 04h, 05h—extended initialization

Initialization

Before we can begin using the serial port, we have to initialize it. The initialization is done using function 00h of interrupt 14h and a parameter byte. The parameter byte is defined as:

```
Bit:    1  2  3  4  5  6  7  8
        |  |  |  |  |  |  |  |
        |  |  |  |  |  |  +  +---Data Bits - 10= 7 bits, 11= 8
bits
        |  |  |  |  |  +---Stop Bits - 0= 1 stop bit, 1= 2
stop bits
        |  |  |  +  +---Parity - 00=none, 01=odd, 10=none,
11=even +  +  + --- Baud Rate - 000=110 baud
                  001 = 150 baud
                  010 = 300 baud
                  011 = 600 baud
                  100 = 1200 baud
                  101 = 2400 baud
                  110 = 4800 baud
                  111 = 9600 baud
```

By filling in the correct values of the byte, we can initialize the serial port correctly. With the addition of a second function 04h, we can extend the baud rate up to 115,200. The assembly code for actually using the function is:

```
mov ah, 00h
mov al, 11100011b
mov dx, 00h
INT 14h
```

The first line of the code, mov ah, 00h, puts the function number that we want to access into the AH register. The second line of code, mov al, 11100011b, assigns our parameter byte to the AL register. The third line of code, mov dx, 00h, tells the system which of the COM ports is going to be used by the interrupt. A value of 00 indicates COM1, and 01 indicates COM2.

Transmitting a Character

To transmit a character out the serial port, we will use function 01h of interrupt 14h. This function can be used as follows:

```
mov ah, 01h
mov al, 'a'
INT 14h
```

We put the function handler number that we want to use in the AH register. We then put the character or byte value that we want to send out the serial port into the AL register. After these steps, we call the interrupt number 14h.

Receiving a Character

To receive a character from the serial port, we use function number 02h of interrupt 14h. Sample code looks like:

```
mov ah, 02h
mov dx, 00h
INT 14h
```

The function waits for a character to arrive at the serial port. Once the function returns, a character will be available in the AL register.

If you look at the two routines above, you can see that we may have a problem. We cannot possibly call a function that waits for a character to arrive at the serial port. What if it takes several milliseconds or even a second to get a character? We will not be able to move in our own game, since it will be waiting for a character to arrive. What we need is a scheme that will buffer information coming from the serial port and still allow us to play our game. In addition, the code must be able to transmit characters as well as allow us to connect machines through a NULL modem cable or a modem.

The way to do this is using code that directly accesses the registers of the UART. The UART has ten control and status registers. Each of the registers controls a different part of the UART. Because of the enormous amount of code involved in programming the UART, I would recommend that you consult a hardware book on the PC. We will skip the details and present you with some code that performs all of the functions you need. The code is called IBMCOM.C.

IBMCOM

The freeware package called IBMCOM allows us to proceed without having to write our own software. This package was placed in the public domain several years ago by someone, whose name never appeared on the release, and converts PASCAL code to C form. The package was further enhanced by Jerry Isdale to support all four COM ports and by me to support dynamic buffers instead of static ones.

This package includes all of the functions necessary for controlling the serial port. It will allow us to send and receive data between two computers. Before we actually begin using the package to create a simple test program, let's look at the functions we are going to use.

```
int com_install(int portnum);
void com_deinstall(int portnum);
void com_set_speed(int portnum, long speed);
void com_set_parity(int portnum, enum par_code parity, int stop_bits);
void com_tx(int portnum, char c);
char com_rx(int portnum);
void com_flush_tx(int portnum);
void com_flush_rx(int portnum);
int com_rx_empty (int portnum);
```

int com_install(int portnum); This function is used to install the software interface for the serial port. It must be called before any of the other functions. The parameter is the COM port number that the interface should control. If you ever need to run two serial ports at the same time, this function can handle it, as it allows you to call each of the functions with a specific COM port number. When this function is called, it will try to create two dynamic queues, one for transmitting and one for receiving. The queues are currently set at 4 K and 8 K respectively. The function will return a value of 0 if the install failed or 1 for a successful installation.

void com_deinstall(int portnum); This function is used to deinstall the software interface for the serial ports. It should be called at the end of your program. Besides its own housekeeping duties, this function will deallocate the memory reserved for the transmit and receive queues.

void com_set_speed(int portnum, long speed); This function is used to set the speed of the serial port. The function should be called after the software driver has been installed. The available speeds are 110, 300, 1200, 2400, 4800, 7200, 9600, 19200, 38400, and 119000.

void com_set_parity(int portnum, enum par_code parity, int stop_bits); This function is used to set the communication parameters for the indicated COM port. The parity values available are COM_NONE, COM_EVEN, COM_ODD, COM_ZERO, and COM_ONE. The available stop bits are 1 and 2.

void com_tx(int portnum, char c); This function appends a single character to the transmit queue. Note that the character is not immediately sent by the serial port to the awaiting computer system. The character is queued and will be sent automatically by the system when it is able to send.

char com_rx(int portnum); This function returns a character from the receive queue of the indicated COM port. If a character is not available on the receive queue, the function blocks or waits until a character is available.

void com_flush_tx(int portnum); This function clears the transmit queue of all waiting characters. The function is specific to the indicated COM port.

void com_flush_rx(int portnum); This function clears the receive queue of all waiting characters. The function is specific to the indicated COM port.

int com_rx_empty (int portnum); This function is used to look at the receive queue. If the function returns a value of 0, there are no characters in the receive queue of the indicated COM port. If the function returns a value of 1, there is a character in the receive queue. Note that the function does not remove any characters from the queue. It just looks to see if characters are available.

These are all of the functions that we need to add communication to our ACK3D system Before we take that step, we need to build a NULL modem cable and create two simple programs that will test its operation.

Creating a NULL Modem Cable

Once you have serial ports installed in both computer systems, you need to create the cable that will connect both machines. The cable is called a NULL modem cable. You can either purchase one of these cables or build one yourself. If you are going to build one, you will need:

> 2 - MALE DB25 connectors
> 2 - Hood
> 1 - 3 connector wire—25 feet or the length you need

Once you have the parts (available from Radio Shack), the connectors should be attached to each other using the wire as shown in Figure 6.2. Just plug the cable into both of the computer's serial ports and you are ready to begin communicating data.

Test Programs

What we want the test programs to do is pass data between themselves in order to show us that the NULL modem cable is operating as it should. If we do not get an indication of data flowing between the computers, then we know something isn't working correctly. We will create a single program that will handle both sending and receiving information. The program will consist of a single main function that begins:

```
#include <stdio.h>
#include "serial.h"
void main()
{
    char selection, data;
```

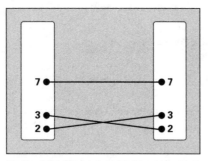

Figure 6.2   Serial port NULL modem connector.

```
int PORT;
clrscr();
printf ( "Enter the COM port to use: (1,2,3,4): ");1
scanf ("%d\n", PORT);
if ((PORT < 1) || (PORT > 4))
{
   printf ( "The selection %d is not a valid COM port\n", PORT);
   exit(1);
}

if (com_install(PORT) == 0)
{
   printf ( "Unable to installed com driver at COM port %d\n", PORT);
   exit(1);
}
else
{
   printf ( "Com driver installed correctly at COM port %d\n", PORT):
   delay(3000);
}
com_set_parity (PORT, COM_NONE, 1);
com_set_speed (PORT, 2400);
}
```

At this point in the code, we have asked for the COM port to install the software interface and made an attempt at installing the driver. If the driver was successfully installed, this is indicated and we delay for a moment. We then set the parity and speed of the serial port. If either the PORT value or the COM driver was not successfully installed, the program indicates such and exits.

We will now determine which computer is the sender, which is the receiver, and begin transferring information. The code continues:

```
printf ("(R)eceiver or (S)ender: ");
scanf ("%c\n", selection);

while (!kbhit())
{
   if (toupper(selection) == 'R')
   {
      printf ( "%c\n", com_rx(PORT));
      com_tx(PORT, 'B");
   }
   else if (toupper(selection) == 'S')
```

```
    {
        com_tx(PORT, 'A');
        printf ( "%c\n", com_rx(PORT));
    }
}
```

Once you select which computer is the sender and which is the receiver, the program will enter a loop. The WHILE loop will continue to execute until you press any key. Once inside the loop, the computer tests to see if this computer is the receiver. If it is, the program will make a call to the function com_rx() and wait for a character to come across the serial port. Once a character arrives, it is printed on the screen. The computer will then send out the character "B" to the other computer.

At the same time, the other computer will be executing the code for the sender. This code begins by sending the character "A" to the other computer using the function com_tx(). After it sends the character, it will wait to receive a character of its own and display it on the computer's screen.

That's it. You should enter this program into a file using a DOS editor or get it from the CD ROM in the directory \CHAPT06 in the file Comtest.c. To compile the program, use the command **tcc -c comtest.c serial.obj** if using Turbo C or C++, or **bcc -c comtest.c serial.obj** if using Borland C++.

Copy the program to each of the computers linked by the NULL modem cable and execute it on both. Select the appropriate COM port and press R on one machine and then S on the other. You will see the letter A running down the screen of one machine and the letter B running down the screen of the other machine.

If you do not get this result, check the connections on your NULL modem cable and make sure that you have put it into the correct serial ports on the machines.

Coding

Most of the foundation work has already been done for adding modem support to our game. All modems, whether internal or external, interface to the computer through a serial port. Internal modems have a serial port built into their electronics, and external modems attach directly to a serial port card inside your computer. We just need to add a couple of things to get information moving.

Hayes AT Command Set

Programming your modem would be very difficult if it weren't for the Hayes AT command set. Early in the development of the modem, Hayes was the leader in technology. Their modems were designed to be communicated with using a series of simple commands shown in Table 6.2.

Table 6.2 Hayes AT command set.

AT Command	Purpose
A	Manual Answer
A/	Execute the last command
AT	Required command prefix
Bn	US/CCITT Answer Sequence
	0 = CCITT
	1 = US
Dn	Dial, n=
	P = pulse
	T = tone
	, = two-second pause
	; = return to command mode
	and others
En	Local Echo
	0 = Echo OFF
	1 = Echo ON
Hn	hook control
	0 = Hang up - go on hook
	1 = go off hook
Ln	Speaker volume
	0 = low
	1 = low
	2 = medium
	3 = high
Mn	Speaker Operation
	0 = speaker always off
	1 = speaker on until connect
	2 = speaker always on
	3 = speaker on after dial through connect
On	return online
	0 = return online
	1 = return online and refrain
Qn	result codes
	0 = display result codes
	1 = no result codes
	2 = result code only in originate mode
Sr=n	set register R to N
Vn	Result code types
	0 = numeric codes
	1 = verbal codes
Xn	result code set
Z	reset to software defaults

There are commands for every option that a modem is capable of performing. As modems have advanced, so has the Hayes command set. The extended command set (in which the commands are preceded by an & sign) continues to grow as more advanced modems and standards become commonplace.

Talking to the Modem

A modem is given commands using one of the commands in Table 6.2. In order for the modem to understand that you are trying to communicate with it directly, the commands must be preceded at the command prefix "AT." There are four rules that should be followed when talking with the modem:

1. Commands should be in uppercase or lowercase, not both; since there are some modems that will only accept AT commands in uppercase, it's safer to use only uppercase.
2. If a command requires a numerical option and you don't include a number, the modem will assume that the number is 0.
3. All commands except A/ and +++ must begin with "AT" and end with a carriage return.
4. Command strings must be 40 characters or less. The "AT" prefix, carriage return, and spaces do not count in the 40-character limit.

To really see how to communicate with the modem, we will build a simple test program. Most of the code is the same as for the serial port communication we discussed in the last section. Our test program appears in Listing 6.1.

Listing 6.1

```
#include <stdio.h>
#include <conio.h>
#include "serial.h"
void main()
{
        int PORT = 2;
    char ch;

    com_install(PORT);
    com_set_speed(PORT, 2400);

    com_raise_dtr(PORT);
    com_tx_string (PORT, 'AT');
    com_tx(PORT, 13);

    while (!kbhit())
```

```
{
    if (!com_rx_empty(PORT))   printf ( "%c\n", com_rx(PORT));
    ch = getkey();
    com_tx(PORT, ch);
}

com_lower_dtr(PORT);
com_tx_string (PORT, '+++');
com_tx(PORT, 13);
}
```

The program begins by installing the COM driver at the PORT you enter, which must be the port the modem is attached to. After the driver is installed and the speed of the modem is set, we raise the data terminal ready line. This tells the modem that we are ready to begin communicating with it. The next two commands

```
com_tx_string (PORT, 'AT');
com_tx(PORT, 13);
```

send the character string "AT" and a carriage return to the modem. Sending just "AT" to the modem is like saying Hi.

Getting a Response Back

Not only are we able to communicate with the modem, but it communicates back to us. In the remainder of the test program, you will see a simple loop that reads the COM port the modem is attached to and prints the results to the screen. If you run the test program and give your modem port, the program will print "OK" on your screen.

What has happened is that you have asked the modem if it is available and it has responded that it is available and ready for work. We call this a verbal response from the modem. We could have given the modem a command that instructed it to respond with a numerical value instead. If we had done this, the modem would have given back a value of 0. The result codes that the modem is able to give are shown in Table 6.3.

Table 6.3   Modem result codes.

Result Code	Purpose
0	OK
1	connect
2	ring
3	no carrier
4	error
5	connect 1200

6	no dial tone
7	busy
8	no answer
10	connect 2400
13	connect 9600
18	connect 4800
20	connect 7200
21	connect 12000
25	connect 14400

Setup

With that simple introduction to communicating with the modem, we can continue adding modem support to our application program. The first change we need to make to add modem support is to add the line

```
com_lower_dtr(PORT);
```

to the initialization function of the serial line. Unlike NULL modem serial lines, a modem must be instructed whether or not to listen to information that we are going to pass to it and whether or not to pass information down the telephone line.

The data terminal ready signal, which, with the above statement, we are turning off, tells the modem that we are not ready to communicate with it at this time. Since we are in a setup phase, we just want to make sure that the modem knows what we are doing. After the modem and serial port are initialized, we can begin using the modem.

Origination

Modems are able to communicate with each other by either originating or answering a connection. If you have ever called a BBS and listened to the tone, you heard a modem answering a phone call. The originating modem waits to hear the answering modem's tone before establishing a connection. When modems are used with our ACK3D application, one user will have to be an originator and the other an answerer. There are two ways that you can originate a modem connection: by making a voice call to the answering modem, or by letting the modem dial the number for us.

Voice

When you make a voice call to the answering modem, you will have to give control to the modem once you hear the answering modem's tone. To do this, you would use the AT command D. D stands for dial. In fact, you will also use this command when the modem does the dialing. The command looks like

```
com_raise_dtr(PORT);
```

```
com_tx_string (PORT, 'ATD');
com_tx (PORT, 13);
```

The modem will connect to the phone line and begin listening for the answering modem's tone. At this point, you would hang up your voice telephone.

Dial

Since the modem can dial the phone automatically, you might as well let it. Letting the modem dial uses the same commands as above but adding a telephone number. You also need to give the D command the letter T or P, indicating tone or pulse dialing. If you want the modem to using touch-tone dialing, the dialing command is DT; for pulse dialing, the command is DP. The entire dialing sequence would look something like this:

```
com_raise_dtr(PORT);
com_tx_string (PORT, 'ATDT16088771017');
com_tx (PORT);
```

The modem would pick up the telephone line and touch-tone dial the number to the PCVR Magazine BBS. It's pretty simple.

Once the code has finished originating the call, it will continue with whatever code follows the three lines above. But all the modem has done is made the telephone call. What if the answering modem does not pick up, or the modems begin to connect and the line is cut? The software has made the assumption that the connection between the modems was established with no problems.

Verifying a Connection

What we need to do is verify that a good connection was established between the modems. We do this by waiting for the modem to tell us that a connection has been made. If you look back at Table 6.3, you will see that there are result codes for many different situations that the modem can find itself in. For instance, if your modem dials a number and the other modem is busy, your modem will respond with the result code 7. Again looking back at Table 6.3, you will see that in order for result code 7 to be sent by the modem, we have to be in the x3 code area. Most modems default to the x1 area, which means we are going to have to tell the modem to go into a new area. Since we want to catch most of the results, we might as well go into result code area x4 and get all of them.

In addition to telling the modem about the result code areas, we need to instruct the modem to send us numerical results instead of verbal ones. Both of these can be done in the same command string used to tell the modem to dial a number. The new dialing command is:

```
com_tx_string (PORT, "ATX4V1DT16088771017');
```

As you can see, we put the two new commands between the AT and the DT so that the last thing the modem does is dial the telephone number.

Once the modem has dialed, we will listen for a response using the code

```
delay(3500)
a=0;

while ((!bioskey(1))&&(a==0)))
 if(!com_rx_empty(PORT)) a = com_rx(PORT);
if (!bioskey(1))
{
 b = com_rx(PORT);
 if(b!=13) d = com_rx(PORT);
}
if ( b == 13 ) result = a - 48;
else if ( d == 13 ) result = (a-48)*10 + (b-48);
```

This code might seem a bit much, but it gets the job done. It first delays a few seconds to give the telephone company time to switch the telephone number we have dialed. After that we sit in a loop and wait for the modem to send us a value. When the modem responds with a result, it sends the value as a character. If the result is a 0, it will be sent as a 0 followed by a carriage return. If the result code is 12, then the modem will send a 1 character followed by a 2 character and then a carriage return.

The loop waits for a character to arrive in the receive buffer or for the user to press a key to cancel the dialing. Once either of these things has happened, the loop ends and the code determines which situation ended the loop. If the user didn't press a key, the loop returns to the receive buffer and grabs a second character. If this new character is a carriage return, then we know that the result code is a single digit. If not, the code grabs a third character from the receive buffer.

After we have the result code, we convert it into a true numerical value and put the result in the variable **result**. We can now handle any of the results in the x4 areas. For instance,

```
switch (result)
{
   case 0: //OK from modem
   case 1: //Connection established
   case 2: //Ring- only when answering a call
   case 3: // NO carrier
}
```

Answering

On the other end, the modem connection is answering a call. Answering a call is very much like dialing except that we have to tell the modem when to pick up the phone. We do this by putting a number in one of the modem's registers. Register S0 is used by the modem to set the number of rings before the modem automatically picks up the telephone. A value of 0 in this register tells the modem that it should never automatically pick up when the telephone is ringing. A value of 1 tells the modem to pick up on the first ring. So the code to answer a call is

```
com_raise_dtr(PORT);
com_tx_string (PORT, 'ATV0X4S0=1');
com_tx(PORT, 13);
```

Just as for the dialing code, we have to be aware of what the modem communicates back to us after issuing the command. In addition, we have to be able to tell when a connection has been established. The first thing that happens is that the modem returns the value of 0 after we send the answer string; then we need to wait for a connection to be established. The code looks just like the dialing code. You can see the entire code in the file Simple.c under the keyboard handling routine and the 'a' case statement.

Transmitting and Receiving

Once a connection has been established by the modems, we will be able to send and receive information. Thankfully, we don't have to make any changes to applications that are already set up to use the serial line interface. Since all modems work through serial ports, we already have transmission support in our application.

Hanging Up

When we are finished with our modem connection, we have to disconnect the connection. The code used to hang up is

```
com_lower_dtr(PORT);
delay(1100);
if (com_carrier(PORT))
{
  com_tx_string(PORT, "+++");
  com_tx(PORT, 13);

  delay(1100);

  com_tx_string(PORT, "ATH");
  com_tx(PORT, 13);
}
```

We begin by lowering the DTR line. This will hang up most modems. To verify that the connection has been cut, we use the function com_carrier. This function will return a value of 1 if a modem connection is still available. If there is no connection, we are finished. If there is a connection, we send the command +++ to our modem, followed by the ATH command. After this sequence of commands, the modem connection will be terminated.

Adding Serial Support to Our Game

The last step in creating a two-player game is taking all of the information about serial ports and modems and putting it in the ACK3D game.

Connection Menu

When our game is executed we need a way for the players to select how they wish to connect with their opponent. We want to include all of the different connection options, including the NULL modem, modem, and ethernet as well as single-user mode. By far the easiest way to provide the connection option is through a text-based menu. The menu that we are going to display to the user is:

```
(E)thernet connection
(I)nternet connection
(N)ull Modem connection
(M)odem connection
(S)ingle User
```

Our code will be set up so that when the user presses any of the highlighted characters, the selection is recorded and the user progresses to the next part of the game. The code will be contained in a function called select_communication_device(), shown in Listing 6.2.

Listing 6.2

```
int select_communication_device()
{
 char ch;
 int result;
 while (!com_device)
 {
    clrscr();
    printf ("\n\n\n");
    printf ("Please select the communication medium that you
would like to use:\n\n");
```

```
            printf ("(E)thernet connection\n");
            printf ("(I)nternet connection\n");
            printf ("(N)ull Modem connection\n");
            printf ("(M)odem connection\n");
            printf ("(S)ingle User\n");
            printf (":");
            ch = getkey();
            printf ("%c\n", ch);
            switch (toupper(ch))
            {
                case 'E': com_device = 'e';
                  break;
                case 'I': com_device = 'i';
                  break;
                case 'N': com_device = 'n';
                  result = setup_com();
                  break;
                case 'M': com_device = 'm';
                  result = setup_com();
                  break;
                case 'S': com_device = 's';
                  result = 0;
                  break;
            }
    }
 return(result);
}
```

As you can see, the code begins with a loop. The loop is used so that the user must press one of the five available options. We cannot continue with the game until we know their connection intentions. Once a key is pressed, the code uses a SWITCH statement to determine which of the keys were pressed. When an appropriate key is pressed, the global variable com_device is set to the character value. We will be using the variable com_device later in the ACK3D code. In addition to setting the com_device variable, we do some initialization depending upon which connection option was selected. Since we are only working on the serial port connection options, we make a call to the function setup_com(), which does the initialization. This function will be discussed shortly.

In order to call the select_communicaton_device() function, we must insert the following code in the main() function of our game. The code must be the very first thing that the application executes:

```
if (select_communication_device())
```

```
    {
        printf ( "Error setting up communication device\n");
        return(1);
    }
```

Creating the Link

Once the user has entered the appropriate connection option, we have to actually create the link to the opponent. The link is created using the function create_link(), which is shown in Listing 6.3.

Listing 6.3

```
int create_link()
{
    int got_one = 0;
    char ch;
    switch(com_device)
    {
        case 'e': break;
        case 'i': break;
        case 'n': while (!got_one)
                {
                clrscr();
                printf ("Is this machine the originating or answering
machine?\n");
                printf (":");
                ch = toupper(getkey());
                printf ("%c\n", ch);
                if (ch == 'O')
                {
                    null_dial();
                    got_one = 0;
                }
                if (ch == 'A')
                {
                    null_answer();
                    got_one = 0;
                }
            }
            return(1);
            break;
    case 'm': while (!got_one)
            {
            clrscr();
            printf ("Is this machine the originating or answering
```

```
machine?\n");
        printf (":");

        ch = toupper(getkey());
        printf ("%c\n", ch);

        if (ch == 'O')
        {
           dial();
           got_one = 0;
        }

        if (ch == 'A')
        {
           answer();
           got_one = 0;
        }
        }
        return(1);
        break;
    }
}
```

The create_link() code looks at the current value of the global variable com_device and selects an appropriate course of action. Since we are still only working on the serial port link, we only have the n and m options filled in with code.

The n option is used to create a NULL modem link and the m option is used for the modem link. In both cases, one user must select a dialing option, the other an answering option. One user has to be at each option. From this point, the code calls the code dialing/answering code for either the NULL modem or modem link. Each of these functions will be discussed later.

To call the create_link() function we add the following code to the main() function right after the calling code for the select_communication_device() function:

```
if (com_device != 's')
   if (create_link())
   {
   printf ("Error creating communication link\n");
   return(1);
   }
```

Notice that we only call the create_link() function if we are actually using a connection link. If we are going to play the game in single-user mode, then we don't need to create a link.

Setup_com Function

Let's back up a bit and look at some of the functions that the select_communication_device() and create_link() functions call. The first function is called setup_com() and loads the IBMCOM/serial handling code into the computer. The function appears in Listing 6.4.

Listing 6.4

```
int setup_com()
{
    int com, ok = 0;
    char ch;
    // get COM port of serial device
    clrscr();
    printf ( "\n");
    printf ( "Select the COM port to which your modem or NULL
modem connection");
    printf ( "\n");
    printf ( "is attached.");printf ( "\n\n");
    printf ( "Enter COM port number ( 1,2,3, or 4):");
    ch = getkey();
    while ( (ch<49) || (ch>52))
    {
        printf ( "\n");
        printf ( "Enter COM port number ( 1,2,3, or 4):");
        ch = getkey();
    }
    {
        return(1);
    }
}
SPEED=0;
while (!SPEED)
{
    clrscr();
    printf ( "\n");
    printf ("Please select the appropriate baud rate\n\n");
    printf (" 2400\n");
    printf (" 4800\n");
    printf (" 9600\n");
    printf (" 14400\n");
    printf ("(E) 28800\n");
```

```c
    ch = toupper(getkey());
    switch (cn)
{

  case 'A': SPEED = 2400; break;
  case 'B': SPEED = 4800; break;
  case 'C': SPEED = 9600; break;
  case 'D': SPEED = 14400; break;
  case 'E': SPEED = 28800; break;
    }
}
com_set_speed(PORT, SPEED );
com_set_parity(PORT, COM_NONE, 1);
com_lower_dtr(PORT);
com_raise_dtr(PORT);
com_lower_dtr(PORT);
if (com_device=='m')
{
  printf ( "\n");
  printf ( "\nChecking Modem at COM Port %d...\n", PORT );
  if (check_port())
    {
  com_raise_dtr(PORT);
  com_tx_string ( PORT, "ATV0E0S0=0");
  com_tx(PORT,13);
  com_lower_dtr(PORT);
  ok = 1;
    }
  if ((!ok)&&check_port())
    {
  com_raise_dtr(PORT);
  com_tx_string ( PORT, "ATV0E0S0=0");
  com_tx(PORT,13);
  com_lower_dtr(PORT);
  ok = 1;
    }
  if ((!ok)&&check_port())
    {
  com_raise_dtr(PORT);
  com_tx_string ( PORT, "ATV0E0S0=0");
  com_tx(PORT,13);
  com_lower_dtr(PORT);
  ok = 1;
    }
```

```c
    if (!ok)
    {
  clrscr();
  printf ( "\n\n\n The system was unable to locate a modem at
the COM port specified" );
  printf ( "\n\n Please check the connection and COM port.
It is imperative that" );
  printf ( "\nthe modem has a dedicated IRQ line. Check the
following chart to");
  printf ( "\ndetermine if you have a possible conflict");
  printf ( "\n\n\n");
  printf ( "                Modem COM Port          COM Ports
Not to Use");
  printf ( "\n\n");
  printf ( "                COM Port 1
Ports - 3\n");
  printf ( "                COM Port 2
Ports - 4\n");
  printf ( "                COM Port 3
Ports - 1\n");
  printf ( "                COM Port 4
Ports - 2\n");
  printf ( "\n\n\n\n\n\n\n");
  exit(1);
    }
 }
 else
 {
    printf ( "\n\nBypassing Modem setup...\n");
    delay(1000);
 }
 return(0);
}
```

The setup_com() code begins by asking the user where his or her
NULL modem serial port or modem is located. The appropriate answer is
one of the COM numbers 1-4. These are the official serial port addresses
that the IBM PC uses to keep track of the serial ports. After the user
selects a COM port, the system tries to install the serial port interrupt driver code as the recorded COM port. If the system is unable to find a serial
port at the recorded COM port, an error will be displayed and the program will terminate. If the system is successful in installing the serial driver,
the code will ask for the desired baud rate of the serial device. The allowed

options are 2400, 4800, 9600, 14400, and 28800. After the baud rate is entered, the code sets the speed, parity, and DTR signal of the serial port.

If the user selected the modem link option, the code does a verification of the modem at the recorded COM port. It does this by giving the modem a single acknowledgment code called AT. If a modem is attached, it will respond with the numerical code 48. The setup_com() function tries three times to connect with the modem. If it is unable to make a connection with the modem, the program displays an error message and terminates. Once a connection has been established with the modem, the program ends the function.

NULL Modem Dialing

When the user selects a connection link of NULL modem, one of the computers is the dialer and one is the answerer. There really isn't any dialing involved with a NULL modem, but the link must be created. The code for the dialer of the NULL modem connection is shown in Listing 6.5.

Listing 6.5

```
void null_dial()
{
 clrscr();
 printf ("This machine will begin the NULL modem communication link.\n\n");
 printf ("Be sure that the cable connects both of the machines.\n\n\n");
 printf ("Initializing serial port for link...\n");
 com_flush_rx(PORT);
 com_flush_tx(PORT);
 com_raise_dtr(PORT);
 delay(1500);
 null_modem = connected = 1;
 printf ("Exchanging initial data...\n");
 delay(1500);
 do_link();
}
```

The code begins by clearing the user's screen and displaying its intentions in text. Next, the transmission and reception character buffers are cleared and the DTR signal is raised indicating that this computer is ready to communicate with another system. At this point, a connection will soon be availble, so we set two global variables, null_modem and connected, equal to the value of 1. One additional message is displayed to the user and the function do_link() is called. This function performs the code for establishing one of the users in one part of the game and the other user in another part of the game. At this point a NULL modem connection has been established and we are ready to begin game play.

NULL Modem Answering

The NULL modem answer code located in the null_answer() function is very much like the null_dial() function just described. The only change is the messaged displayed to the user. The code is shown in Listing 6.6.

Listing 6.6

```
void null_answer()
{
 clrscr();
 printf ("This machine will receive the NULL modem communication
link.\n\n");
 printf ("Be sure that the cable connects both of the machines.\n\n\n\n");
 printf ("Initializing serial port for link...\n");
 com_flush_rx(PORT);
 com_flush_tx(PORT);
 com_raise_dtr(PORT);
 delay(1500);
 null_modem = connected = 1;
 printf ( "Exchanging initial data...\n");
 delay(1500);
 do_link();
}
```

Modem Answering

Just as is the case for the NULL modem connection, if the user selected the modem connection option, they have to dial or answer the modem depending upon which action the user wishes to accomplish. Since we have already looked at how to answer the modem, we won't go into details about this function. This function is called answer() and is given in Listing 6.7.

Listing 6.7

```
void answer()
{
    char a, b, d, result;
    clrscr();
    if (!connected)
    {
       com_raise_dtr(PORT);
       com_flush_rx(PORT);
       delay(1100);
```

```c
        com_tx_string_with_delay(PORT, "ATE0X4V0AS0=1", 10, 10 );
        com_tx(PORT, 13); delay(10);
        printf ( "Waiting to answer modem...\n\n");
        delay(3500);
        a=b=d=0;
        while((!bioskey(1))&&(a==0)&&(!com_carrier(PORT)))
          if(!com_rx_empty(PORT))
          {
          a = com_rx(PORT);
          if ( a == 50 )
          {
            b = com_rx(PORT);
            if (b==13)
            {
              a = com_rx(PORT);
              b = 0;
            }
          }
          }
delay(2000);
if (!bioskey(1))
{
   if(b==0)  b = com_rx(PORT);
   if(b!=13)  d = com_rx(PORT);
}
if ( b == 13 ) result = a - 48;
else if ( d == 13 ) result = (a-48)*10 + (b-48);
if (bioskey(1))
{
   getkey();
   if (!com_carrier(PORT))
  com_tx(PORT,13);
   else
  hangup();
   return;
}
 if ((com_carrier(PORT))&&(result!=ERROR)&&(result!=
NODIALTONE)&&(result!=NOCARRIER))
 {
    printf ("Waiting to connect...\n\n");
    com_flush_rx(PORT);
    connected = 1;
    delay(5000);
```

```
      do_link();
   }
   else if ( result == NODIALTONE )
   {
      busy = 1;
      printf ( "No Dial Tone...\n");
      delay(5000);
   }
   else if ( result == NOCARRIER )
   {
      busy = 1;
      printf ( "No Carrier...\n\n");
      delay(5000);
   }
   else
   {
      hangup();
      printf ( "Unable to connect. Please Try Again...\n");
      delay(5000);
      busy = 1;
     }
   }
}
```

Modem Dialing

The user on the other end of the modem connection will have to dial the
modem. The code for dialing the modem is in the function dial() and is
given in Listing 6.8.

Listing 6.8

```
void dial()
{
   char a, b, d, result, inbuff[15];
   clrscr();
   if (!connected)
   {
     if ( busy && num_stored )
     {
        printf ("Redial previous number? (y/n)");
        a = getkey();
        while ( (a!='y') && (a!='n'))
        a = getkey();
        if ( a == 'y' )
```

```c
            {
            com_raise_dtr(PORT);
            com_flush_rx(PORT);
            delay(1100);
            com_tx_string_with_delay(PORT, "A/", 10, 10);
            com_tx(PORT,13);
             }
    }
    if ( (!busy) || (a == 'n') )
    {
        printf ("Number: ");
        scanf ("%s", inbuff);
        com_flush_rx(PORT);
        com_raise_dtr(PORT);
        printf ("Dialing...\n\n");
        num_stored = 1;
        delay(1100);
        com_tx_string_with_delay(PORT, "ATE0X4V0DT", 10, 10 );
        com_tx_string_with_delay(PORT, inbuff, 10, 10);
        com_tx(PORT, 13);
    }
    delay(3500);
    a=0;
    while ((!bioskey(1))&&((!com_carrier(PORT)&&(a==0)))
       if(!com_rx_empty(PORT)) a = com_rx(PORT);
    delay(2000);
    if (!bioskey(1))
    {
       b = com_rx(PORT);
       if(b!=13) d = com_rx(PORT);
    }
    if ( b == 13 ) result = a - 48;
    else if ( d == 13 ) result = (a-48)*10 + (b-48);
    if (bioskey(1))
    {
       getkey();
       if (!com_carrier(PORT))
      com_tx(PORT,13);
       else
      hangup();
       return;
    }
    if ((com_carrier(PORT))&&(result!=ERROR)&&(result!=NODIALTONE)&&(re
```

```
sult!=NOCARRIER)&&(result!=BUSY))
    {
        busy = num_stored = 0;
        printf ("Waiting to connect...\n\n");
        com_flush_rx(PORT);
        connected = busy = 1;
        delay(5000);
        do_link();
    }
    else if ( result == NODIALTONE )
    {
        busy = 1;
        printf ( "No Dialtone...\n\n");
        delay(5000);
    }
    else if ( result == BUSY )
    {
        busy = 1;
        printf ( "Busy...\n\n");
        delay(5000);
    }
    else if ( result == NOCARRIER )
    {
        busy = 1;
        printf ( "No carrier...\n\n");
        delay(5000);
    }
    else
    {
        hangup();
        printf ("Unable to connect..Please try again...\n\n");
        delay(5000);
        busy = 1;
    }
    }
}
```

The dialing code follows the same basic format of the dialing description given earlier in the chapter.

Transmitting Our Movements

Now that we have a communication link established over the serial NULL modem line or the modem, we need to begin communicating information back and forth between the two games. Since we are trying to get our graphical figure object on our opponent's computer to mimic our movements, we had better tell the other computer when we move our viewpoint. We move our viewpoint in the keyboard handling routine of the MINOSIM program.

At this point, we only have four keys defined for movement, so we only have to transmit four different characters. Recall that we have set up the four characters, a, b, c, and d as the movement values for forward, backward, right pan, and left pan respectively. Every time that we press the Up arrow on our keyboard to move forward, we need to transmit the character "a" to the other computer, and so on for the other keyboard movement keys. The new keyboard handling code is shown in Listing 6.9.

Listing 6.9

```
switch(ch)
{
 case LEFT : if ((com_device =='n') || (com_device=='m'))
com_tx(PORT, 'd');
        ae->PlayerAngle += (-INT_ANGLE_2 * 5);
        pan = 1;
        break;
 case RIGHT: if ((com_device =='n') || (com_device=='m'))com_tx(PORT, 'c');
        ae->PlayerAngle += INT_ANGLE_2 * 5;
        pan = 1;
        break;
 case UP: if ((com_device =='n') || (com_device=='m'))com_tx(PORT, 'a');
        AckMovePOV(ae,ae->PlayerAngle,16);
        break;
 case DOWN: if ((com_device =='n') || (com_device=='m'))com_tx(PORT, 'b');
        temp= ae->PlayerAngle + INT_ANGLE_180;
        if (temp >= INT_ANGLE_360)
      temp -= INT_ANGLE_360;
        AckMovePOV(ae,temp,16);
        break;
  }
```

The only thing that has changed in the case statements is the addition of the code:

```
if ((com_device=='n') || (com_device=='m') com_tx(PORT, character);
```

We have to use an IF statement, since we will have other communication links and they don't all use the serial port. This is all the code necessary to transmit our movements to the other computer.

Receiving Movements

Now that we can transmit information to the other computer, we must be able to receive the same type of information. Recall that we already created the function process_communications() to react to the movement values coming from the other computer. We have set up four keys on the keyboard to act as test values. The first thing we need to do is remove the code for these keys. After these key case statements are removed from the keyboard handling code, we add the following code to the main() function just above the keyboard handling code:

```
if ((com_device == 'n') || (com_device == 'm'))
{
  if ((!null_modem) && (!com_carrier(PORT)))
  {
      hangup();
      AckSetTextmode();
      printf("Lost communication link");
      AckWrapUp(ae);
      delay(5000);
      exit(1);
  }
  if (!com_rx_empty(PORT))
process_communications(com_rx(PORT));
}
```

The purpose of this new code is to receive characters from the other computer. However, it must do more than that. The code begins by making sure that we are using a serial line communication link. If we are not using such a link, we certainly don't want to go into this code. The code will be using the serial line communication and if no link is established, the code will not function correctly. The next line, the IF statement, is very important. Since we are using a serial link, we must always make sure that the link has been established. This is especially important for the modem link but not so much for the NULL modem connection. The IF statement must first make sure that we are not a NULL modem connection. If we are, the IF statement is false and we continue in the code.

If we are not a NULL modem connection, a call is made to the function com_carrier(). This function goes to the modem and asks it if it is still connected with another modem. A value of 1 indicates that the connection is still good. If the connection is no longer good, the code terminates the game and displays an error message.

Once all of the link determination is finished, a final IF statement makes a call to the function com_rx_empty(). This function looks at the IBMCOM receive buffer. If there are no characters in the function, we don't want to make a call to com_rx() to get the character, since com_rx() waits for a character and there won't be one available.

If a character is available, we call the function process_communications() with a parameter of com_rx(). Com_rx() will get the character and send it automatically to the process_communications() function.

Hanging Up

Since we are able to establish a connection, we had better be able to end the connection. The function hangup() is the function to use. The code is:

```
void hangup()
{
    com_lower_dtr(PORT);
    delay(1100);
    if (com_carrier(PORT))
    {
        com_tx_string_with_delay(PORT, "+++", 10, 10);
        delay(1100);
        com_tx(PORT, 13); delay(10);
        com_tx_string_with_delay(PORT, "ATH", 10, 10);
        com_tx(PORT, 13); delay(10);
    }
    com_flush_rx(PORT);
    com_flush_tx(PORT);
    busy = num_stored = null_modem = connected = 0;
}
```

We have already seen several places where this function is called if an error has occurred, but we also need a place where we can voluntarily disconnect the connection. We will add a key handler for the character "h" which will call the hangup() function. The code to add to the function handler is:

```
        case 'h': hangup();
        return();
```

Do_link()

The last function that we will discuss for the serial communication link is do_link(). This function is one of the most important because it determines which user is Player A and which is Player B. No matter which communication link we have, NULL modem or modem, both computers will call the function do_link(). This function begins by picking a random number. The random number is transmitted to the other computer. Once the number is sent to the other computer, the code must receive the opponent's random number. The two random numbers are compared to each other. An IF statement determines if our random number is less than our opponent's. If this is the case, then the global variable **person** is assigned the value 0, otherwise **person** is assigned the value 1. If by chance the random numbers are the same, each computer will pick another random number and the process starts over again.

```c
void do_link()
{
 char ours, theirs, do_again = 1;
 randomize();
 while ( do_again )
 {
    do_again = 0;
    randomize();
    ours = random(50);
    com_tx(PORT, ours);
    theirs = com_rx(PORT);
    if (ours<theirs) person = 0;
    else person = 1;
    if (ours==theirs) do_again = 1;
 }
}
```

The global variable person, once set by the do_link() function, will be used in the main() function as well. The following code is used to place the two players in the single world:

```c
if (person)
{
    temp = ae->ObjList[other_guy].x;
    ae->ObjList[other_guy].x = ae->xPlayer;
    ae->xPlayer = temp;
    temp = ae->ObjList[other_guy].y;
    ae->ObjList[other_guy].y = ae->yPlayer;
    ae->yPlayer = temp;
}
```

Basically, if the global variable is the value 0, then we don't make any changes to the initial placement of the viewpoint and the graphical figure object. Since only one computer will have the person variable set to 0, the other computer will have to change the position of the viewpoint and graphical figure object. This is done by exchanging the X and Y position fields of the user's viewpoint.

Conclusion

That's it for the serial link code and setup. All of the code that we discussed in this chapter is in the file MINOTAUR.c in the \NETWARIO directory. You can learn how to execute this latest version by looking at Appendix A.

The code changes to minotaur.c are listed here.

Global Variables

```c
//Communication variables
int SPEED, PORT;
int busy = 0,
  null_modem = 0,
  connected = 0,
  num_stored = 0,
  person = 0;
int com_device = 0;
```

Main Function

```c
int main(void)
{
int     result,
      done = 0,
      pan = 0;
int     temp,
      packet_length;
unsigned ch;
if (select_communication_device())
{
   printf ( "Error setting up communication device\n");
   return(1);
}
if (com_device != 's')
   if (create_link())
   {
  printf ("Error creating communication link\n");
  return(1);
   }
if (result==AppInitialize())
{
   printf("Error initializing: ErrorCode = %d\n",result);
```

```
      return(1);
   }
   if (result==AppSetupEngine())
   {
      printf("Error setting up ACK engine: ErrorCode =
%d\n",result);
      AckWrapUp(ae);
      return(1);
   }
   if (result==AppLoadBitmaps())
   {
      printf("Error loading bitmaps: ErrorCode = %d\n",result);
      AckWrapUp(ae);
      return(1);
   }
   if (result==AppSetGraphics())
   {
      AckSetTextmode();
      printf("Error loading palette: ErrorCode = %d\n",result);
      AckWrapUp(ae);
      return(1);
   }
   if (result==AppSetObject())
   {
      AckSetTextmode();
      printf("Error loading palette: ErrorCode = %d\n",result);
      AckWrapUp(ae);
      return(1);
   }
   AppSetupPalRanges();
   //if person == 1 then we need to switch locations of us and
opponent
   if (person)
   {
      temp = ae->ObjList[other_guy].x;
      ae->ObjList[other_guy].x = ae->xPlayer;
      ae->xPlayer = temp;
      temp = ae->ObjList[other_guy].y;
      ae->ObjList[other_guy].y = ae->yPlayer;
      ae->yPlayer = temp;
   }
   while (!done)
   {
```

```
        AckCheckObjectMovement(ae);
        if (pan)
        {
    pan = 0;
    if (ae->PlayerAngle >= INT_ANGLE_360)
        ae->PlayerAngle -= INT_ANGLE_360;
    if (ae->PlayerAngle < 0)
        ae->PlayerAngle += INT_ANGLE_360;
        }
        AppShow3D();
        if ((com_device == 'n') || (com_device == 'm'))
        {
    if ((!com_carrier(PORT)) && (!null_modem))
    {
        hangup();
        AckSetTextmode();
        printf("Lost communication link");
        AckWrapUp(ae);
        delay(5000);
        exit(1);
    }
    if (!com_rx_empty(PORT))
process_communications(com_rx(PORT));
        }
        if (bioskey(1))
        {
    ch = getkey();
    if (ch==ESC) break;
    switch(ch)
    {
      case LEFT : if ((com_device == 'n') || (com_device ==
'm'))com_tx(PORT, 'd');
                ae->PlayerAngle += (-INT_ANGLE_2 * 5);
                pan = 1;
                break;
      case RIGHT: if ((com_device == 'n') || (com_device ==
'm'))com_tx(PORT, 'c');
                ae->PlayerAngle += INT_ANGLE_2 * 5;
                pan = 1;
                break;
      case UP: if ((com_device == 'n') || (com_device ==
'm'))com_tx(PORT, 'a');
                AckMovePOV(ae,ae->PlayerAngle,16);
```

```
                break;
    case DOWN: if ((com_device == 'n') || (com_device == 'm'))com_tx(PORT,
'b');
                temp= ae->PlayerAngle + INT_ANGLE_180;
                if (temp >= INT_ANGLE_360)
               temp -= INT_ANGLE_360;
                AckMovePOV(ae,temp,16);
                break;
   }
 }
}
```

Hangup Function

```
void hangup()
{
 com_lower_dtr(PORT);
 delay(1100);
 if (com_carrier(PORT))
 {
    com_tx_string_with_delay(PORT, "+++", 10, 10);
    delay(1100);
    com_tx(PORT, 13); delay(10);
    com_tx_string_with_delay(PORT, "ATH", 10, 10);
    com_tx(PORT, 13); delay(10);
 }
 com_flush_rx(PORT);
 com_flush_tx(PORT);
 busy = num_stored = null_modem = connected = 0;
}
```

Do_link Function

```
void do_link()
{
 char ours, theirs, do_again = 1;
 int packet_length;
 randomize();
 while ( do_again )
 {
    do_again = 0;
    randomize();
    ours = random(50);
    if ((com_device == 'n') || (com_device == 'm')) com_tx(PORT,
```

```
ours);
    if (com_device=='e')
    {
        data_packet[20] = ours;
        send_pkt (interrupt_number,d_packet, 64);
    }
    if ((com_device == 'n') || (com_device == 'm'))theirs=com_rx(PORT);
    if (com_device=='e')
    {
        while (!get_from_queue(data_packet, &packet_length, 0))
        NULL;
        theirs = data_packet[20];
    }
    if (ours<theirs) person = 0;
    else person = 1;
    if (ours==theirs) do_again = 1;
 }
}
```

Answer Function

```
void answer()
{
 char a, b, d, result;
 clrscr();
 if (!connected)
 {
    com_raise_dtr(PORT);
    com_flush_rx(PORT);
    delay(1100);
    com_tx_string_with_delay(PORT, "ATE0X4V0AS0=1", 10, 10 );
    com_tx(PORT, 13); delay(10);
    printf ( "Waiting to answer modem...\n\n");
    delay(3500);
    a=b=d=0;
    while((!bioskey(1))&&(a==0)&&(!com_carrier(PORT)))
        if(!com_rx_empty(PORT))
        {
       a = com_rx(PORT);
       if ( a == 50 )
       {
        b = com_rx(PORT);
        if (b==13)
```

```
              {
               a = com_rx(PORT);
               b = 0;
              }
     }
  }
 delay(2000);
 if (!bioskey(1))
 {
    if(b==0) b = com_rx(PORT);
    if(b!=13) d = com_rx(PORT);
 }
 if ( b == 13 ) result = a - 48;
 else if ( d == 13 ) result = (a-48)*10 + (b-48);
 if (bioskey(1))
 {
    getkey();
    if (!com_carrier(PORT))
  com_tx(PORT,13);
    else
  hangup();
    return;
 }
 if ((com_carrier(PORT))&&(result!=ERROR)&&(result!=
NODIALTONE)&&(result!=NOCARRIER))
 {
    printf ("Waiting to connect...\n\n");
    com_flush_rx(PORT);
    connected = 1;
    delay(5000);
    do_link();
 }
 else if ( result == NODIALTONE )
 {
    busy = 1;
    printf ( "No Dial Tone...\n");
    delay(5000);
 }
 else if ( result == NOCARRIER )
 {
    busy = 1;
    printf ( "No Carrier...\n\n");
    delay(5000);
```

```
    }
    else
    {
       hangup();
       printf ( "Unable to connect. Please Try Again...\n");
       delay(5000);
       busy = 1;
     }
   }
 }
}
```

Dial Function

```
void dial()
{
 char a, b, d, result, inbuff[15];
 clrscr();
 if (!connected)
 {
    if ( busy && num_stored )
    {
       printf ("Redial previous number? (y/n)");
       a = getkey();
       while ( (a!='y') && (a!='n'))
       a = getkey();
       if ( a == 'y' )
       {
      com_raise_dtr(PORT);
      com_flush_rx(PORT);
      delay(1100);
      com_tx_string_with_delay(PORT, "A/", 10, 10);
      com_tx(PORT,13);
    }
 }
 if ( (!busy) || (a == 'n') )
 {
       printf ("Number: ");
       scanf ("%s", inbuff);
       com_flush_rx(PORT);
       com_raise_dtr(PORT);
       printf ("Dialing...\n\n");
       num_stored = 1;
       delay(1100);
```

```
        com_tx_string_with_delay(PORT, "ATE0X4V0DT", 10, 10 );
        com_tx_string_with_delay(PORT, inbuff, 10, 10);
        com_tx(PORT, 13);
}
delay(3500);
a=0;
while ((!bioskey(1))&&(!com_carrier(PORT)&&(a==0)))
        if(!com_rx_empty(PORT)) a = com_rx(PORT);
delay(2000);
if (!bioskey(1))
{
        b = com_rx(PORT);
        if(b!=13) d = com_rx(PORT);
}
if ( b == 13 ) result = a - 48;
else if ( d == 13 ) result = (a-48)*10 + (b-48);
if (bioskey(1))
{
        getkey();
        if (!com_carrier(PORT))
    com_tx(PORT,13);
        else
    hangup();
        return;
}
if ((com_carrier(PORT))&&(result!=ERROR)&&(result!=NODIALTONE)&&(re
sult!=NOCARRIER)&&(result!=BUSY))
{
        busy = num_stored = 0;
        printf ("Waiting to connect...\n\n");
        com_flush_rx(PORT);
        connected = busy = 1;
        delay(5000);
        do_link();
}
else if ( result == NODIALTONE )
{
        busy = 1;
        printf ( "No Dialtone...\n\n");
        delay(5000);
}
else if ( result == BUSY )
{
```

```c
        busy = 1;
        printf ( "Busy...\n\n");
        delay(5000);
    }
    else if ( result == NOCARRIER )
    {
        busy = 1;
        printf ( "No carrier...\n\n");
        delay(5000);
    }
    else
    {
        hangup();
        printf ("Unable to connect..Please try again...\n\n");
        delay(5000);
        busy = 1;
    }
  }
}
```

Check_Port Function

```c
int check_port()
{
 char a;
 long test;
 com_raise_dtr(PORT);
 com_flush_rx(PORT);
 delay(1100);
 com_tx_string_with_delay(PORT, "ATE0V0", 10, 10 );
 com_tx(PORT, 13); delay(10);
 delay(3500);
 a=test=0;
 while((com_rx_empty(PORT))&&(test<1500000))
 test++;
 if (!com_rx_empty(PORT)) a = com_rx(PORT);
 if (!com_rx_empty(PORT)) com_rx(PORT);
 com_lower_dtr(PORT);
 if (a == 48 ) return 1;
 else return 0;
}
```

Setup_Com Function

```c
int setup_com()
```

```c
{
 int com, ok = 0;
 char ch;
 // get COM port of serial device
 clrscr();
 printf ( "\n");
 printf ( "Select the COM port to which your modem or NULL modem
connection"); printf ( "\n");
 printf ( "is attached.");printf ( "\n\n");
 printf ( "Enter COM port number ( 1,2,3, or 4):");
 ch = getkey();
 while ( (ch<49) || (ch>52))
 {
    printf ( "\n");
    printf ( "Enter COM port number ( 1,2,3, or 4):");
    ch = getkey();
 }
 PORT = ch-48;
 if (com == com_install(PORT))
 {
 return(1);
 }
 SPEED=0;
 while (!SPEED)
 {
    clrscr();
    printf ( "\n");
    printf ("Please select the appropriate baud rate\n\n");
    printf ("(A) 2400\n");
    printf ("(B) 4800\n");
    printf ("(C) 9600\n");
    printf ("(D) 14400\n");
    printf ("(E) 28800\n");
    ch = toupper(getkey());
    switch(ch)
    {
  case 'A': SPEED = 2400; break;
  case 'B': SPEED = 4800; break;
  case 'C': SPEED = 9600; break;
  case 'D': SPEED = 14400; break;
  case 'E': SPEED = 28800; break;
    }
 }
 com_set_speed(PORT, SPEED );
```

```c
com_set_parity(PORT, COM_NONE, 1);
com_lower_dtr(PORT);
com_raise_dtr(PORT);
com_lower_dtr(PORT);
if (com_device=='m')
{
   printf ( "\n");
   printf ( "\nChecking Modem at COM Port %d...\n", PORT );
   if (check_port())
   {
com_raise_dtr(PORT);
com_tx_string ( PORT, "ATV0E0S0=0");
com_tx(PORT,13);
com_lower_dtr(PORT);
ok = 1;
   }
   if ((!ok)&&check_port())
   {
com_raise_dtr(PORT);
com_tx_string ( PORT, "ATV0E0S0=0");
com_tx(PORT,13);
com_lower_dtr(PORT);
ok = 1;
   }
   if ((!ok)&&check_port())
   {
com_raise_dtr(PORT);
com_tx_string ( PORT, "ATV0E0S0=0");
com_tx(PORT,13);
com_lower_dtr(PORT);
ok = 1;
   }
   if (!ok)
   {
clrscr();
   printf ( "\n\n\nThe system was unable to locate a modem at
the COM port specified" );
   printf ( "\n\nPlease check the connection and COM port.
It is imperative that" );
   printf ( "\nthe modem has a dedicated IRQ line. Check the
following chart to");
   printf ( "\ndetermine if you have a possible conflict");
   printf ( "\n\n\n");
   printf ( " Modem COM Port              COM Ports Not to Use");
```

150 CHAPTER 6

```
printf ( "\n\n");
printf ( " COM Port 1                         Ports - 3\n");
printf ( " COM Port 2                         Ports - 4\n");
printf ( " COM Port 3                         Ports - 1\n");
printf ( " COM Port 4                         Ports - 2\n");
printf ( "\n\n\n\n\n\n\n");
exit(1);
   }
  }
  else
  {
   printf ( "\n\nBypassing Modem setup...\n");
   delay(1000);
  }
  return(0);
}
```

Select_communication_device Function

```
int select_communication_device()
{
 char ch;
 int result;
 while (!com_device)
 {
    clrscr();
    printf ("\n\n\n");
    printf ("Please select the communication medium that you would like to
use:\n\n");
    printf ("(E)thernet connection\n");
    printf ("(I)nternet connection\n");
    printf ("(N)ull Modem connection\n");
    printf ("(M)odem connection\n");
    printf ("(S)ingle User\n");
    printf (":");
    ch = getkey();
    printf ("%c\n", ch);
    switch (toupper(ch))
    {
       case 'E': break;
       case 'I': com_device = 'i';
         break;
       case 'N': com_device = 'n';
         result = setup_com();
         break;
```

```
        case 'M': com_device = 'm';
        result = setup_com();
          break;
        case 'S': com_device = 's';
          result = 0;
          break;
   }
 }
 return(result);
 }
```

Create_link Function

```
int create_link()
{
 int got_one = 0, i, packet_length;
 char ch;
 switch(com_device)
 {
 case 'e': break;
 case 'i': break;
 case 'n': while (!got_one)
    {
     clrscr();
     printf ("Is this machine the originating or answering machine?\n");
     printf (":");
     ch = toupper(getkey());
     printf ("%c\n", ch);
     if (ch == 'O')
     {
      null_dial();
      got_one = 0;
     }
     if (ch == 'A')
     {
      null_answer();
      got_one = 0;
     }
     }
     return(1);
     break;
 case 'm': while (!got_one)
     {
     clrscr();
```

```
            printf ("Is this machine the originating or answering machine?\n");
            printf (":");
            ch = toupper(getkey());
            printf ("%c\n", ch);
            if (ch == 'O')
            {
             dial();
             got_one = 0;
            }
            if (ch == 'A')
            {
             answer();
             got_one = 0;
            }
             }
            return(1);
            break;
     }
     }
```

PROGRAMMING THE ETHERNET

Now that we have a complete graphical toolkit to use for our network game, we need to take a detailed look at the hardware and software the game will use to allow us to communicate with others. For this chapter, we are assuming that the game will be played on a local area network like those found in most offices. In a later chapter we will extend our communication to the Internet.

Interface to the Network

The network we will be working with is based on an ethernet protocol. This protocol allows for data to be transmitted over a coaxial cable at the rate of ten million bits per second or 10 MBits/sec. This is very fast when compared to say, a modem, which typically has a rate of fourteen thousand bits per second. Since we are communicating at such a high speed, the computer requires special hardware to access the network.

Figure 7.1 shows a typical network card. As you can see, it looks like just about any other card in your computer. However, one thing sets it apart: the BNC connector on the back of the card. A close-up view is shown in Figure 7.2. The cables that make up the network are attached to this connector using a T-connector.

Computer Interface

The network card is attached to the bus of the computer through the connectors in the back of the computer system. To communicate with the net-

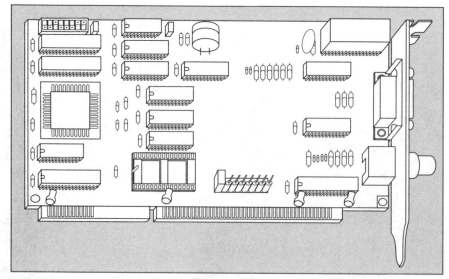

Figure 7.1   A typical network interface card.

Figure 7.2 The network card's BNC connector.

work card, the computer must assign I/O memory to the interface card as well as an interrupt line. The history of the PC has shown that it was designed with far too few interrupt lines. To help alleviate the problem, most network cards can use any number of different interrupt numbers.

The job of the interrupt is to notify the computer when the network card has received information. Since the job of the network card is to be an interface between the computer and the network cable, it really doesn't have time to do anything with the information it is sending and receiving. All it wants to do is take information from the computer and put it on the network cable, and receive information from the network cable and give it to the computer.

If you recall the speeds at which the ethernet line is capable of transferring information, you will see that we need to be able to service the network card and its interrupt line very quickly. There are two pieces of software that will do the job: a packet driver and the interface code to the packet driver.

Packet Drivers

When reasonably priced ethernet network cards began to hit the market several years ago, software application companies began to create software that would access the network cards. This is essentially how Novell Netware works. Along with Netware, other software applications were developed that would use the services of the network cards.

During all of the software development, a problem was created. When a piece of software was written to access the network card, the software generally took complete and total control of the card at its most basic level. This meant that if you were using, say, Novell Netware, you couldn't use any other piece of network software. The first application that gained control of the network card had sole access, and any other software system would be denied access to the card.

To get around the problem, a second or third ethernet card was installed in computer systems that needed to execute more than one type of network application. If you have ever installed PC-based interface cards, you already know the trouble that can be had. The multiple cards caused numerous problems both for the software and for the network administrators who had to install and configure the cards.

Toward the end of the 1980s, the network software house FTP Software, Inc. released a specification for a piece of software called a packet driver. A packet driver is a very small TSR (terminate-and-stay-resident) software program. The purpose of the packet driver is to control access to the network card.

How the Packet Driver Works

The basic format of a network packet provides a space for a packet type. This packet type is used to distinguish different packets from one another. For instance, the software package Novell Netware communicates on an ethernet network using the packet type 8137. However, the packet type 0xFFFF is used as a broadcast packet, while still another packet type 0x1234 might be used by some other piece of software.

Before the packet driver, we would have needed a minimum of two network cards to handle the different types of packets and the different software packages. The packet driver is able to use a single network card for the different packet types.

The whole packet driver system works by installing the packet driver upon booting up the computer system. The driver is installed at some particular software interrupt as opposed to a hardware interrupt. The IBM PC has a complete set of software interrupts that can be used to "talk" with TSRs or some other software application. Once the driver has been installed, it will look for an ethernet card at the PC location specified when the driver was loaded.

At this point, we don't have any software packages loaded into the computer, just the packet driver. Now we can load a software package that specifically uses a packet driver. The only thing that we have to tell the software package is that the packet driver is in the system at some specific software interrupt. The software we are loading will activate the packet driver and verify that a network card is installed in the system and that it is available to be used. After the packet driver informs the software application that a network card is available, the software application will tell the packet driver which packet types it is interested in receiving.

At the same time, we could load a second software application and have it register with the packet driver, telling it which packet types it wishes to receive. Figure 7.3 shows the setup we have in the computer.

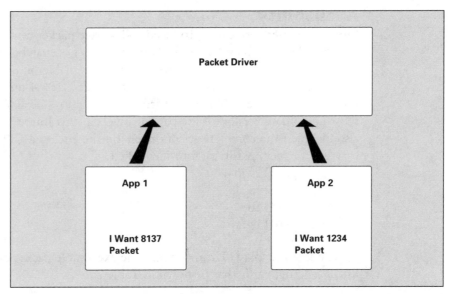

Figure 7.3 A packet driver and two applications registered with it.

As the network card receives packets, the packet driver will look at the packet type. If the packet type matches any of the types requested by registered applications, the packet driver will copy the packet from the network and send it to the requesting application. If the packet type of the new packet does not match any of the registered packet types, the packet is ignored by the packet driver. The entire sequence can be seen in Figure 7.4.

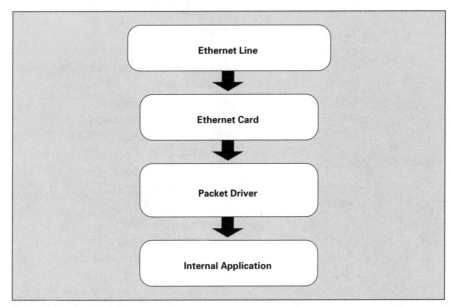

Figure 7.4 A packet driver sequence.

Availability

Most of the network cards produced today have packet drivers supplied with them by the manufacturers. Those that do not may be able to use several different public domain packet drivers available on the Internet. A good source for these packet drivers is at 128.252.135.4 under the directory /systems/msdos/simtel/pktdrv. You will always be able to find the most up-to-date version of the packet drivers at this Internet site. We have also included the complete set of drivers on the enclosed CD. In the directory /game_dev/pktdr are four files called

> pktd11.zip
> pktd11a.zip
> pktd11b.zip
> pktd11c.zip

The first file, pktd11.zip, contains the executable packet drivers for the list of ethernet cards that is shown in Table 7.1.

Table 7.1 Packet drivers included in pktd11.zip.

Packet driver	for
3C501.COM	3COM 3C501
3C503.COM	3COM 3C503
3C505.COM	3COM 3C505
3C507.COM	3COM 3C507
3C509.COM	3COM 3C509
3C523.COM	3COM 3C523
AQUILA.COM	ADI's Aquila cards
AR450.COM	Telesystems SLW ARLAN 450
ARCETHER.COM	ARCNET that simulates an Ethernet driver
ARCNET.COM	ARCNET
AT&T.COM	AT&T Ethernet and Starlan
AT&T_LP.COM	AT&T LanPACER/StarStation
AT1500.COM	Allied-Telesis 1500T and 1500BT
AT1700.COM	Allied-Telesis 1700T and 1700BT
CTRONDNI.COM	Cabletron DNI Exxxx
DAVIDSYS.COM	David Systems Inc Ether-T
DE600.COM	D-Link Pocket LAN Adapter
DEPCA.COM	Digital Equipment DEPCA
DK86960.COM	Fujitsu's NICE demo card
DK86965.COM	Fujitsu's EtherCoupler demo card
EN301.COM	Multitech EN-301
ES3210.COM	Racal/Interlan's ES3210 EISA adapter
ETHERSL.COM	SLIP that emulates an Ethernet driver

ETHIIE.COM	ICL EtherTeam16 (formerly Nokia Data Ethernet IIe)
EXOS205.COM	Microdyne (formerly EXOS/Excelan) EXOS205T
EXP16.COM	Intel EtherExpress
EXPRESS.COM	Mitel Express ISDN adapter
HPPCLAN.COM	HP EtherTwist
HPPCLANP.COM	HP EtherTwist, HP27242B, and HP27250A
IBMTOKEN.COM	IBM Token Ring Adapter
IPXPKT.COM	Novell IPX code (IP over IPX)
ISOLAN.COM	BICC Isolan 4110-0
ISOLINK.COM	BICC Isolan 4110-2/3
KODIAK.COM	Include file for Kodiak's drivers based on SEEQ 8005
KODIAK16.COM	Kodiak Technology's Kodiak~16 10BT
KODIAK8.COM	Kodiak Technology's Kodiak~8 10BT
KODIAKK.COM	Kodiak Technology's Kombo
MYLEX.COM	Mylex's LNE-890B
NB.COM	NetBIOS
NCRET105.COM	NCR ET-105
NE1000.COM	Novell NE1000
NE2.COM	Novell NE/2
NE2000.COM	Novell NE2000
NE2100.COM	Novell NE2100 and other PC-Net/ISA adapters
NI5010.COM	Interlan NI5010
NI5210.COM	MICOM-Interlan NI5210
NI6510.COM	Racal/Interlan NI6510
NI9210.COM	MICOM-Interlan NI9210
NTI16.COM	NTI 1002/DP-16
PI.COM	the Ottawa PI Amateur Radio board
SLIP8250.COM	SLIP driver using IBM-PC 8250
SMC_WD.COM	Western Digital WD-80?3*, SMC Elite series1
TCENET.COM	Thomas-Conrad's TC5045 adapter
TIARA.COM	Tiara LANcard/E
UBNICPC.COM	Ungermann-Bass PC/NIC
UBNICPS2.COM	Ungermann-Bass NIC-PS/2
VAXMATE.COM	DEC's Vaxmate

Packet Driver Installation

Installing a packet driver on your system is a process that will differ only slightly depending on the brand of network card that you have installed. We will go through the process using a packet driver for the SMC line of ethernet cards. Additional information for other packet drivers can be found on the PKTD11.ZIP file in the file Install.doc.

In my computer system is a Western Digital (now SMC) ethernet card called the EtherCard Elite 16. This network card is based on the WD/8003EP ethernet controller chipset. I can thus use the packet driver called SMC_WD.COM. The Install.doc file gives the following information for this packet driver:

> _SMC (formerly Western Digital) (also IBM) SMCWD
>   usage: smc_wd [options] packet_int_no [-o] [int_level [io_addr [mem_base]]]
>
> The SMC_WD driver runs the SMC (formerly Western Digital) E, EBT, EB, ET/A, and E/A Ethernet cards (but not the Ultra), and also on the IBM Microchannel Ethernet cards with POS ID's 0xEFE5, 0xEFD4 and 0xEFD5. The ISA SMC_WD requires three additional parameters — the hardware interrupt number, the I/O address, and the memory base address. The ISA defaults are 3 and 0x280 and 0xd000. The MCA SMC_WD picks up its default parameters from the POS registers, so you only need specify them it you have multiple adapters. The smc_wd cards do not enable their memory until configuration time. Some 386 memory mappers will map memory into the area that the card intends to use. You should be able to configure your software to leave this area of memory alone. Also the driver will refuse to map memory into occupied memory. The occupied memory test fails on some machines, so the optional switch -o allows you to disable the check for occupied memory.
> If you get the error "PROM ADDRESS Invalid", use EZSETUP to set all the parameters again (to the same values). Occasionally wayward programs will write to locations that don't belong to them. This can corrupt the EEPROM checksum on the card. EZSETUP will restore the correct checksum.

We usually need some additional information about our network card before we can properly execute the packet driver: the hardware interrupt, I/O address, and memory base address associated with the card. In my case, the hardware interrupt is 5, the I/O address is 0x300, and the memory base address is 0xCA00. Most all ethernet cards allow you to change all three of these values. You will want to select values that do not interfere with any other hardware cards installed in your computer.

In addition to the information from the network card, I need to specify a software interrupt value. The most common value to use is 0x60. You can execute the packet driver without any parameters at the command line, and the packet driver will give you a range of acceptable values to use.

Thus, to install the packet driver, I would execute the command

```
smc_wd 0x60 5 0x300 0xCA00
```

at a C: prompt under DOS. If I want the packet driver to be installed every time I boot my machine, I need to put the command in my autoexec.bat file.

The following script shows the outcome of the command:

> **C:\ccm\c>smc_wd 0x60 5 0x300 0xCA00**
> **Packet driver for SMC/WD/IBM Ethernet adapters, version 11.7.3**
> **Portions Copyright 1988, Robert C. Clements, K1BC**
> **Portions Copyright 1992, 1993, Crynwr Software**
> **Packet driver skeleton copyright 1988-93, Crynwr Software.**
> **This program is freely copyable; source must be available; NO WARRANTY.**
> **See the file COPYING.DOC for details; send FAX to +1-315-268-9201 for a copy.**
>
> **System: [345]86 processor, ISA bus, Two 8259s**
> **Packet driver software interrupt is 0x60 (96)**
> **Interrupt number 0x5 (5)**
> **I/O port 0x300 (768)**
> **Memory address 0xCA00 (51712)**
> **NIC 8390**
> **My Ethernet address is 00:00:C0:12:E4:25**
>
> **C:\ccm\c>**

As you can see from the script, the packet driver was able to install correctly because it returned to me the ethernet address of my ethernet card. We are now ready to interface with the packet driver software.

The Software Packet Driver

So far we have concentrated on the actions of the packet driver. Remember that the packet driver is simply in charge of determining which software applications receive specific packets based on their types. Once the packet driver determines that an application should receive a specific packet, the application must be prepared to receive it.

Recall that we gave the packet driver a software interrupt value that can be used to communicate with it. As it turns out, the packet driver can use the software interrupt to communicate with software applications.

Actually, this is how the packet driver tells a software application that it has a packet of its type available. It is then the responsibility of the software to copy the packet from the packet driver.

In order for the packet driver to access the application, it will use the software interrupt. This means that we have to write some piece of code in our application to acknowledge the software interrupt. To help us out, we need to take a look at the packet driver specification that FTP Software, Inc. released. When describing the code that should respond to the packet driver's software interrupt, the specification states:

> **When a packet is received, the receiver is called twice by the packet driver. The first time it is called to request a buffer from the application to copy the packet into. AX == 0 on this call. The application should return a pointer to the buffer in ES:DI. If the application has no buffers, it may return 0:0 in ES:DI, and the driver should throw away the packet and not perform the second call.**

> **It is important that the packet length (CX) be valid on the AX == 0 call, so that the receiver can allocate a buffer of the proper size. This length (as well as the copy performed prior to the AX == 1 call) must include the MAC header and all received data, but not the trailing Frame Check Sequence (if any).**

> **On the second call, AX == 1. This call indicates that the copy has been completed, and the application may do as it wishes with the buffer. The buffer that the packet was copied into is pointed to by DS:SI.**

As you can see, the code that responds to the software interrupt must be capable of handling two different calls. The first call tells the application that the packet driver has a packet available. It is during this call that the application must provide a buffer for the packet to be copied into. On the second call, the application can do whatever it wants with the packet.

A First Design

Now, considering that during its execution the application program will be receiving perhaps thousands of packets, the code that handles the communication with the packet driver must be as fast as possible. We will eventually want to do everything possible to make the code for the interface as fast and tight as possible.

Working directly from the specification description given above, a first design for our receiver interface code could look like:

```
If register AX = 0 then

    allocate a buffer the size of register CX

    assign the buffer to register ES:DI

    return control to the packet driver

endif

else if register AX = 1 then

    process the packet

endif
```

It would appear that this design might take a good deal of time to accomplish its task. When the code is first called, the application will allocate memory from a global heap of memory. This is an extensive process in itself. Upon the second call to the code, the packet must be processed. Processing a packet can be a simple or a complex task depending on the purpose of the packet.

With this design, processing takes a great deal of time. This means that during the time that one packet is being processed, there is a very good chance that a second packet will arrive and interrupt the processing of the first packet.

This may not be such a bad thing for all applications, but since the packets for our game are going to carry information about an opponent's movement or even death, they must be processed in the order that they are sent from other machines.

A Second Design

We can design a piece of code that is very quick and does minimal processing of the packets. The idea here is that the code that interacts with the packet driver should simply take packets and keep them in a queue. When the application needs a new packet, it will call another routine at its leisure to process a packet. Our new design looks like:

```
establish a static queue with head and tail indices

IF register AX = 0 THEN

    increment tail index

    give address of array position

    increment count

ENDIF
```

Creating the Queue

From reading the packet driver specification, we know that the size of a packet received by the network can vary. When the packet driver receives the packet from the network card, the size of the packet is given to the software application in the register CX. The software receiver code must provide the packet driver with a buffer of the appropriate size. Since we want to create a static queue to put packets in, we must make the individual slots of the queue large enough to handle any packet size. Since we are creating this code to handle packets coming from our own software application, we can determine the maximum size of the packets. In this case, we will say that no packets will be larger than 150 bytes.

We also need to determine how many slots we should have in the queue. This is always a tough decision, because we need enough slots to be sure that we will not lose any packets, but we don't want to waste memory on more slots than are needed. From experience, I have found that 30 slots are enough to handle packets arriving at the network very quickly.

Now, we can create the queue:

```
#define MAXSIZE 30
unsigned char packet_queue[MAXSIZE][150];
int queue_head = -1, queue_tail = -1;
```

With the queue, we can create the code that will handle the software interrupt from the packet driver.

Receiver Code

The receiver code must be written so that it is called automatically from the packet driver. The interface code will be called from the packet driver using a software interrupt. The interrupt will cause the application to stop working on its current instruction and move directly to the interface code. Because we are moving from one part of the application to another, we have to keep track of where we were and the state the computer was in. Fortunately, the compiler manufacturers take care of most of the details of this by using a special reserved word called **interrupt**. We can refer to the Borland C++ manuals to get the correct format of a C interrupt routine. The format is

```
void interrupt packet_receiver();
{
}
```

When a routine is designated as an interrupt routine, you have access to all of the variables of the CPU. From the specification, we know that the first thing we need to do is look at the AX register to determine if this is the first or second call to the receiver code. We can look at the register with the code:

```
void interrupt packet_receiver(bp, di, si, ds, es, dx, cx, bx, ax, ip, cs,
flags);
unsigned short bp, di, si, ds, es, dx, cx, bx, ax, ip, cs, flags;
```

```
{
    switch (ax)
    {
        case 0:
            break;
    }
}
```

Once we enter the routine, we look at the AX register, and if the register has the value 0 in it, then we are ready to do some work with the packet that the packet driver has available. Since we are using a queue, we must first increment the head index in the queue. After this we have to pass the segment and offset values for the slot in the receiver queue to the packet driver.

```
void interrupt packet_receiver(bp, di, si, ds, es, dx, cx, bx, ax, ip, cs,
flags);
unsigned short bp, di, si, ds, es, dx, cx, bx, ax, ip, cs, flags;
{
    switch (ax)
    {
        case 0: if (++receiver_head = maxsize) receiver_head = 0;
                es = FP_SEG(receiver_queue[receiver_head]);
                di = FP_OFF(receiver_queue[receiver_head]);
                if (++receiver_count==30)receiver_count = 30;
                if (receiver_tail == -1) receiver_tail = 0;
                break;
    }
}
```

Notice that the last thing we do is set the receiver tail index to 0. This tells our application that we have a packet in the queue available to be used, and at what position in the queue the packet is located.

The Length

As you can see from the preceding code, once the packet is copied into the receiver queue, we have no idea about its size. The size is an important piece of information that we may need once we start processing the packet. We can add a variable to each of the packets to hold this information. In order to add a variable to each of the packets, we will need an additional data structure. We could use an array, but that would add a second variable that we would have to keep track of. What we should do is create a data structure that will hold information about each of the packets. Our data structure will be:

```
typedef struct _packet_data {
            unsigned char packet_data[150];
            int packet_size;
            } PACKET_DATA;
```

With our new data structure, we need to make a few changes to the receiver code:

```
void interrupt packet_receiver(bp, di, si, ds, es, dx, cx, bx, ax, ip, cs,
flags);
unsigned short bp, di, si, ds, es, dx, cx, bx, ax, ip, cs, flags;
{
   switch (ax)
   {
     case 0: if (++receiver_head == MAXSIZE) receiver_head = 0;
             es = FP_SEG(receiver_queue[receiver_head].packet_data);
             di = FP_OFF(receiver_queue[receiver_head].packet_data);
             receiver_queue[receiver_head].packet_size = cx;
             if (receiver_tail == -1) receiver_tail = 0;
             break;
   }
}
```

Better Speed

The code above will do the job just as it should. However, in the spirit of speed, we want it to be as fast as possible; therefore, we will make one more change. Every time the packet driver is called, we have two calls, one to FP_SEG and one to FP_OFF. These function calls give the packet driver the address of the buffer that it should put the packet into. Since we are using a static queue, these addresses will never change. This means that we can add two additional parameters to the packet data structure: buffer_segment and buffer_offset.

```
typedef struct _packet_data {
     unsigned char packet_data[150];
     int packet_size;
     long buffer_offset;
     long buffer_segment;
     } PACKET_DATA;
```

When we execute our application program, we will run the following loop to initialize all of the buffer_offset and buffer_segment values:

```
for (i=0;i<30;i++)
```

```
{
    receiver_queue[i].buffer_segment=FP_SEG(receiver_queue[i].packet_data);
    receiver_queue[i].buffer_offset=FP_OFF(receiver_queue[i].packet_data);
}
```

Lastly, we need to make a small change to our receiver code:

```
void interrupt packet_receiver(bp, di, si, ds, es, dx, cx, bx, ax, ip, cs,
flags);
unsigned short bp, di, si, ds, es, dx, cx, bx, ax, ip, cs, flags;
{
    switch (ax)
    {
        case 0: if (++receiver_head == MAXSIZE) receiver_head = 0;
                es = receiver_queue[receiver_head].buffer_offset);
                di = receiver_queue[receiver_head].buffer_segment);
                receiver_queue[receiver_head].packet_size = cx;
                if (receiver_tail == -1) receiver_tail = 0;
                break;
    }
}
```

We now have very fast packet receiver code for our application. Every time the packet driver has a packet, it will automatically make a call to the function packet_receiver(). Packet_receiver() will put the packet into a queue of size 30. It is now the responsibility of the application to pull the packet off of the queue for its own use.

The Packet Driver Interface

Now that we are able to receive packets, we need to look at and create several support functions. These functions will allow us to initialize the packet driver (register the packet type we want to receive), send packets, and receive packets from the receiver queue.

Initializing the Packet Driver

Initializing the communication between our application and the packet driver is done in a series of nine or so calls to various functions. The initialization sequence is:

```
set_type (packet_type);
find_driver(interrupt_number);
driver_info(interrupt_number, handle, version, class, card_type, number,
```

```
basic);
access_type(interrupt_number, handle, class, ttype, number,
packet_type, 2);
get_address(interrupt_number, handle, our_address);
get_rcv_mode(interrupt_number, handle, mode);
if(mode<>3) set_rcv_mode(interrupt_number, handle, ADDRESS_ONLY);
```

Set_type();

The first function call is to the routine set_type();. This routine is defined as:

```
void set_type (unsigned int type)
{
    main_packet_type = type;
}
```

The purpose of this function is to simply set a global variable main_packet_type equal to the packet type value we wish to use in our application. This will be the packet type used throughout the application.

Find_driver();

The next function call, find_driver();, is the first function that accesses the packet driver. According to the packet driver specification, this function should scan the software interrupt areas of the PC and try to find a packet driver. Once a packet driver has been installed in your computer, it will have a signature called "PKT DRVR" located exactly four bytes from the start of the packet driver code. We can use the code shown in Listing 7.1 to find exactly where the packet driver is installed in the computer.

Listing 7.1

```
void find_driver(unsigned char * interrupt_number)
{
char the_word[] = "PKT DRVR",
    signature[8];
  int ok = 1;
  unsigned char i = 0x60;
  long old_handler;
  while ((ok) && (i<=0x80))
  {
  old_handler = (long)getvect(i);
  movedata(FP_SEG(old_handler), FP_OFF(old_handler)+3, FP_SEG(signature),
FP_OFF(signature), 8);
  if (strncmp ( the_word, signature, 8) == 0)
    ok = 0;
  else
```

```
    i ++;
  }
  if (ok) printf ("No Packet Driver Found\n");
  else
{
    printf ( "Packet Driver Found at interrupt %d\n", i);
  *interrupt_number = i;
  }
}
```

In order to find the packet driver, we start accessing all of the software interrupts from 0x60 to 0x80. Using the function getvect() we can find the address of any software installed at a particular interrupt. Using the address, we copy eight bytes starting at the fourth location from the start of the packet driver. The bytes copied from the software interrupt are compared with the string "PKT DRVR." If the compare is successful, we know that a packet driver has been found. We return the software interrupt number in the single parameter sent into the find_driver() function.

Driver_info();

Now that we have the interrupt number for the packet driver, we can use it to obtain additional information about the network card that we will need further down in the initialization sequence. The function is:

```
void driver_info(unsigned char interrupt_number,
        unsigned int *handle,
        unsigned int *version,
        unsigned char *driver_class,
        unsigned int *ttype,
        unsigned char *number,
        unsigned char *basic )
{
  union REGS regs;
  regs.x.bx = *handle;
  regs.h.ah = 1;
  regs.h.al = 0xff;
  int86 (interrupt_number, &regs, &regs);
  *version = regs.x.bx;
  *driver_class = regs.h.ch;
  *ttype = regs.x.dx;
  *number = regs.h.cl;
  *basic = regs.h.al;
}
```

The information gathered by this function includes:

- version: This is an internal hardware driver identifier. It would probably relate to the current version of your hardware chipset or ROM code.
- driver_class: The driver class relates to the types of packets that the ethernet card is able to handle, such as IEEE 802.3 Ethernet, IEEE 802.5 Token Ring, Appletalk, and so on.
- ttype: The type field is the specific interface for the class of the card. A typical response might be Interlan NI5210 or IBM Token Ring Adapter.
- number: The number field is a value assigned when there is more than one interface card installed in the computer with the same class and type fields.
- basic: This is the functionality of features supported by this card. The possible responses are:
  - 1 = basic functions present
  - 2 = basic and extended functions present
  - 5 = basic and high-performance functions present
  - 6 = basic, high-performance, and extended functions present
  - 255 = not installed

Access_type();

Now that we have the necessary interface card information, we can register our intentions with the packet driver. The access_type routine allows us to do this and is defined as:

```
void access_type (unsigned char interrupt_number,
        unsigned int *handle,
        unsigned char driver_class,
        unsigned int ttype,
        unsigned char number,
        unsigned int p_type,
        int type_length)
{
union REGS regs;
char iptype[2];
iptype[0] = (0xFF00 & p_type)>>8;
iptype[1] = (0x00FF & p_type);
*handle = regs.x.ax;
}
```

Once a call to the function access_type() is made, the application has officially informed the packet driver which packet types it wishes to receive and the address of the interrupt routine that should be called once a packet of this type arrives.

The next three routines are used to obtain additional information from the network card as well as determine that the card is in the correct reception mode.

Get_address();

When we begin sending packets through the packet driver, we will need to know our ethernet address. This address is hardwired into the ethernet card. We can access the address with the routine:

```c
void get_address(unsigned char interrupt_number, unsigned int handle)
{
 union REGS regs;
 struct SREGS sregs;
 regs.h.ah = 6;
 regs.x.bx = handle;
 sregs.es = FP_SEG(our_address);
 regs.x.di = FP_OFF(our_address);
 regs.x.cx = 0x0a;
 int86x (interrupt_number, &regs, &regs, &sregs);
}
```

Get_rcv_mode();

It's crucial that the network card is in the correct receiving mode. We can be sure of this by asking the network card which mode it is currently in with the code:

```c
void get_rcv_mode(unsigned char interrupt_number, unsigned int handle,
unsigned char *mode)
{
    union REGS regs;
    regs.h.ah = 21;
    regs.x.bx = handle;
    int86 (interrupt_number, &regs, &regs);
    *mode = regs.x.ax;
}
```

Set_rcv_mode();

Once we have the receive mode of the network card, we may need to change it using the following function:

```c
void set_rcv_mode (unsigned char interrupt_number, unsigned int handle, int
mode)
{
    union REGS regs;
    regs.h.ah = 20;
```

```
    regs.x.bx = handle;
    regs.x.cx = mode;
    int86(interrupt_number, &regs, &regs);
}
```

We want to make sure that the card is in mode 3. The possible modes are:

> 1 = turn off receiver
> 2 = receive only packets sent to this interface
> 3 = mode 2 plus broadcast packets
> 4 = mode 3 plus limited multicast packets
> 5 = mode 3 plus all multicast packets
> 6 = all packets

How to Prepare and Send Information

After all of the initialization, we are finally ready to look at sending packets down the ethernet line. We should first look at how to build a packet. The packets that we are going to be using in our application will consist of nine separate data areas:

1. TO address: a six-byte field ranging from bytes 0 to 5. The value put into this field is the ethernet address of the receiver of the packet.
2. FROM address: a six-byte field ranging from byte 6 to 11. The value put into this field is the ethernet address of the sender of the packet. Since we are the sender of the packet, we would put our ethernet address here.
3. Packet Type: the packet type we are using for our application. It is a two-byte field from bytes 12 to 13.
4. Misc Byte 1: a single-byte field, 14, that will be used for future purposes.
5. Misc Byte 2: a single-byte field, 15, that will be used for future purposes.
6. Misc Byte 3: a single-byte field, 16, that will be used for future purposes.
7. Misc Byte 4: a single-byte field, 17, that will be used for future purposes.
8. Packet Number: a two-byte field that will hold the sequence number for this packet. We will discuss this more in a later section. The range is bytes 18 to 19.
9. Data: The remaining bytes are used to hold data.

When building and sending packets, we must maintain a minimum packet size of 64 bytes. This means that if we are only sending a small amount of data to another machine, we will need to pad the packet with spaces or zeros. We must also keep to a maximum size of 150 bytes, since we have set up our packet queue to accommodate this size.

Every packet that we send to the packet driver must fall within these bounds and have all of the information discussed above. The easiest way to be sure that this occurs is to create a function, build_pkt(), that builds our packets. We will simply pass the necessary data to the function and the function will build the packet and then send it:

```
void build_pkt (unsigned char *packet, int *packet_length, unsigned char
*to_address, unsigned char *from_address, unsigned char *data, int
data_length)
{
  int i;
  for (i=0;i<6;i++)
   packet[i] = to_address[i];
  for (i=0;i<6;i++)
   packet[i+6] = from_address[i];
  packet[12] = (0xFF00 & main_packet_type) >> 8;
  packet[13] = (unsigned char)(0x00FF & main_packet_type);
  for (i=0;i<data_length;i++)
   packet[20+i] = data[i];
*packet_length = data_length + 20;
}
```

In order to build a packet, we give our new function several different parameters. The first is an array of type unsigned char. This is where the function will store all of the information that makes up the packet we are building. The second parameter is the final length of the packet being built. The third and fourth parameters are the ethernet addresses of the machine that will receive the packet being built and the address of the machine that is sending the packet. It is very important that the packet contain both the TO address and the FROM address. The fifth parameter is a pointer to the data that is to be put into the packet. The sixth parameter is the number of bytes that should be copied from the fourth parameter to the new packet.

Once we have our new packet, there may be times that we need to get a look at the parameters of the packet. We can do this using the function show_packet(). This function is:

```
void show_packet (unsigned char *packet)
{
   printf ( "To address -> %2X:%2X:%2X:%2X:%2X:%2X\n", packet[0], packet[1],
packet[2], packet[3], packet[4], packet[5] );
   printf ( "from address-> %2X:%2X:%2X:%2X:%2X:%2X\n", packet[6],
packet[7], packet[8], packet[9], packet[10], packet[11] );
   printf ( "Type field -> %2x%2x\n", packet[12], packet[13]);
```

```
   printf ( "temp stuff -> %2d %2d %2d %2d\n", packet[14], packet[15],
packet[16], packet[17]);
   printf( "Sequence # -> %2d%2d\n", packet[18], packet[19]);
}
```

We now have a new packet and are able to look at its contents. The
next step is to send the packet to the receiving machine. Fortunately, this
is not such a hard task because the ethernet card will perform most of the
work. What we have to do is let the packet driver know that we have a
packet to send and tell it where it is located in memory. This is performed
using the routine send_pkt():

```
void send_pkt(unsigned char interrupt_number, unsigned char *packet, int
packet_length)
{
 union REGS regs;
 struct SREGS sregs;
if (packet_length < 64) packet_length = 64;
 regs.h.ah = 4;
 regs.h.al = 0;
 regs.x.si = FP_OFF(packet);
 sregs.ds = FP_SEG(packet);
 regs.x.cx = packet_length;
 int86x(interrupt_number, &regs, &regs, &sregs);
}
```

Sending a Packet to the Packet Driver

Now that we have the sending functions created, we need to discuss the
actual steps involved in sending packets. Sending a packet to the packet
driver is a fairly simple process. One of the first things that we need is the
address of the ethernet card we are sending a packet to. This can be found
when a packet driver is installed on the computer. The ethernet address
must be put into a six-position array of type unsigned char. An example is:

```
    unsigned char their_address[6];

    their_address[0] = 0x00;
    their_address[1] = 0x00;
    their_address[2] = 0x23;
    their_address[3] = 0x34;
    their_address[4] = 0x45;
    their_address[5] = 0x02;
```

When sending a packet, we also need to know our address. We don't,
however, need to do anything special to get this information, since we

received it when we initialized our own ethernet card. This information is kept in the global variable our_address. The next thing we need is data.

No matter what we are sending in our packet to the other computer, we need to have the information in an array to be copied to the packet we are sending. This can be a problem, since we are only dealing with a string of bytes instead of characters, integers, or real numbers.

Obviously, copying characters to a byte string is a simple matter, since characters are bytes. Creating a byte string from an integer number can be accomplished using the C language functions itoa. If the data being sent to another computer is in the form of a structure or other complex variable, you will have to pick the data out of the structure or complex variable. This data will then have to be reconstructed on the receiving end of the communication link.

A Sending Example

We will create an example in which we will send the integer 45 to another machine located at the ethernet address 00:00:01:45:44:01.

```
unsigned char their_address[6], packet[1500], data[45];
int packet_length, data_length;

their_address[0] = 0x00;
their_address[1] = 0x00;
their_address[2] = 0x01;
their_address[3] = 0x45;
their_address[4] = 0x44;
their_address[5] = 0x01;
itoa(45, data, 10);
data_length = 2;
build_pkt(packet, packet_length, their_address, our_address, data,
data_length);
send_pkt(interrupt_number, packet, packet_length);
```

That's all there is to building and sending a packet to another machine. Now we have a packet on its way to another machine. The other machine will receive the packet through its ethernet card. The ethernet card will contact the packet driver, which will make a copy of the packet and store it in its internal buffer.

As we know, this internal buffer only has enough places to store 30 packets. The ethernet can transmit packets quickly enough to easily overrun this small buffer. Because we cannot guarantee that our application will process the packets fast enough, we will create a secondary buffer that will be large enough to hold the overflow of packets. This secondary buffer has another purpose that will be seen in the next section.

Receiving Information

To receive a packet from another machine, we will rely on a function called get_from_queue. The header for this function is

```
int get_from_queue (unsigned char *packet);
```

When this function is called, it will return an error code which indicates whether or not a packet was available. If the value returned is a 0, then a packet was not available from the queue. If the value returned is a 1, then a packet was available. A pointer to the packet is returned as the sole parameter to the function.

The code for the function is shown in Listing 7.2.

Listing 7.2

```
int get_from_queue(unsigned char *packet, int *packet_length, int type)
{
  SEC_PACKET *temp_record, *temp, *prev;
  int i;
  union REGS regs;
  struct SREGS sregs;
  while (receiver_count>0)
  {
// printf ( "Count > %d\n", receiver_count);
    temp_record = (SEC_PACKET *)malloc(sizeof(SEC_PACKET));
    if (temp_record == NULL)
    {
      release_type (interrupt_number, handle);
      terminate(interrupt_number, handle);
      exit(1);
    }
    temp_record->next = NULL;
    secondary_queue_count++;
    if (secondary_queue_head == NULL)
    {
      secondary_queue_head = temp_record;
      secondary_queue_tail = temp_record;
    }
    else
    {
      secondary_queue_tail->next = temp_record;
      secondary_queue_tail = temp_record;
    }
    temp_record->packet_length = receiver_queue[receiver_head].packet_size;
    for (i=0;i<receiver_queue[receiver_head].packet_size;i++)
```

```
          temp_record->data[i] = receiver_queue[receiver_head].packet_data[i];
     if(temp_record->data[14]!='a')
     {
        for(i=0;i<6;i++)
         ack_packet[i] = temp_record->data[6+i];
        ack_packet[18] = temp_record->data[18];
        ack_packet[19] = temp_record->data[19];
        regs.h.ah = 4;
        regs.h.al = 0;
        regs.x.si = FP_OFF(ack_packet);
        sregs.ds = FP_SEG(ack_packet);
        regs.x.cx = 64;
        int86x(interrupt_number, &regs, &regs, &sregs);
   }
  receiver_head++;
  if (receiver_head == MAXSIZE) receiver_head = 0;
  receiver_count--;
  if (receiver_count == 0)
   { receiver_head = receiver_tail = -1;}
 }
 if (secondary_queue_count > 0)
 {
// printf ( "In Here\n");
  temp = prev = secondary_queue_head;
  while (temp!=NULL)
  {
   i = (temp->data[18] << 8)+temp->data[19];
   if ((i==receiver_packet_number+1)&&(type==0)&&(temp->data[14] != 'a'))
   {
//  printf ( "Found Data %d\n", i);
//  printf ( "Sent = %d, Received = %d\n", send_packet_number,
receiver_packet_number);
        *packet_length = temp->packet_length;
        for(i=0;i<*packet_length;i++)
         packet[i] = temp->data[i];
        if (--secondary_queue_count == 0)
        {
         secondary_queue_head = NULL;
         secondary_queue_tail = NULL;
         free(temp);
        }
        else
        {
```

```
                   if (temp==prev)
                   {
                    secondary_queue_head = temp->next;
                    free(temp);
                   }
                   else
                   {
                    prev->next=temp->next;
                    free(temp);
                   }
                 }
                 receiver_packet_number++;
                 if (i==32766) receiver_packet_number = 0;
                 return 1;
             }
             else if ((i==send_packet_number-1)&&(type==1)&&(temp->data[14] == 'a'))
             {
//  printf ( "Found Ack %d\n", i);
                 if (—secondary_queue_count == 0)
                 {
                  secondary_queue_head = NULL;
                  secondary_queue_tail = NULL;
                  free(temp);
                 }
                 else
                 {
                  if (temp==prev)
                  {
                   secondary_queue_head = temp->next;
                   free(temp);
                  }
                  else
                  {
                   prev->next=temp->next;
                   free(temp);
                  }
                 }
                 return 2;
             }
             else
             {
                 prev = temp;
                 temp = temp->next;
```

```
            }
        }
    }
  else
    return 0;
}
```

In order to understand how this function works, we will run through several examples. When your application program is ready to process a packet from another machine, all it has to do is call the function get_from_queue(). The first thing that this function does is look at the main packet queue that we developed for the packet driver. Recall that this packet queue is used by the packet driver to directly hold the incoming packets from the ethernet card. Because this queue could fill up quickly, we need to take the packets from this queue and put them into a secondary application queue. Using a simple WHILE loop, the get_from_queue() function pulls all of the packets out of the main packet queue and puts them into a single linked list. Again, it may seem redundant to take the packets from the main queue and put them on a secondary queue, but there are several reasons for doing this that we will see in the next section.

There are three main variables and one data structure for the secondary packet queue. The data structure is:

```
typedef struct _secondary_packet {
                    unsigned char data[1500];
                    int packet_length;
                    struct_secondary_packet *next;
                    } SEC_PACKET;
```

The data structure contains a field to hold the data of the packet, **data**, a field for the length of the total packet, packet_length, and a pointer to another variable of type secondary_packet. This field is the main link for the linked list of packets.

To use the data structure, we have three variables:

```
SEC_PACKET *secondary_queue_head = NULL,
           *secondary_queue_tail = NULL;
int         secondary_queue_count = 0;
```

Obviously, the variable secondary_queue_count will hold a value indicating the total number of packets in the secondary queue. The variables secondary_queue_head and secondary_queue_tail are used to keep track of the beginning and the end of our linked list of packets. When a new packet is placed on the linked list, it is placed at the tail of the list.

Programming the Ethernet **181**

After the function get_from_queue() has pulled all of the packets from the main packet queue, it makes a check to see if there are packets in the secondary queue. If there are packets in the secondary queue, the function takes the packet at the beginning of the list and copies the packet to the first parameter sent to the function. The packet length is placed in the second parameter passed to the function.

Packet Dissection

Once the get_from_queue() function returns a packet to us, we need to access the different parts of it. We can do this using the function dissect_packet(), as we see from the following code:

```
void dissect_packet(unsigned char *packet, int packet_length, unsigned char
*their_address, unsigned char *data)
{
 int i;
 for(i=0;i<6;i++)
  their_address[i] = packet[i+6];
 for(i=0;i<packet_length-20;i++)
  data[i] = packet[20+i];
}
```

The dissect_packet function takes the packet and packet length returned by the get_from_queue function and returns the ethernet address of the sender and the data contained in the packet.

Of course, the data returned from the packet will have to be used according to your application and the manner in which the data was placed in the packet.

A Simple Test Program

We are now able to install a packet driver for our network card, initialize the packet driver, send and receive packets. Let's build a simple test program to make sure that we are able to transmit information back and forth between two different machines and ethernet cards.

The program we are going to use is shown in Listing 7.3.

Listing 7.3

```
#include <stdio.h>
#include <dos.h>
#include <alloc.h>
#include <conio.h>
```

```
#define MAXSIZE 30
/////Main Packet Queue/////
typedef struct _packet_data {
            unsigned char packet_data[1500];
            int packet_size;
            } PACKET_DATA;
PACKET_DATA receiver_queue[MAXSIZE];
int receiver_head=-1,
  receiver_tail=-1,
  receiver_count=0;


/////Secondary Packet Queue/////
typedef struct _secondary_packet {
              unsigned char            data[1500];
              int                      packet_length;
              struct _secondary_packet *next;
              } SEC_PACKET;
SEC_PACKET *secondary_queue_head = NULL,
      *secondary_queue_tail = NULL;
int      secondary_queue_count = 0;
unsigned char our_address[6];
unsigned char interrupt_number;
unsigned int  handle;
unsigned int  version;
unsigned char driver_class;
unsigned int  ttype;
unsigned char number;
unsigned char basic;
unsigned int  p_type;
unsigned int  main_packet_type;
/////temp variables/////
unsigned char pkt[1500],
      temp_pkt[1500],
      data[65];
unsigned char their_address[6];
int packet_length;
void _interrupt packet_receiver(bp, di, si, ds, es, dx, cx, bx, ax, ip, cs,
flags)
unsigned short bp, di, si, ds, es, dx, cx, bx, ax, ip, cs, flags;
{
  switch (ax)
  {
    case 0: if (++receiver_tail == MAXSIZE) receiver_tail = 0;
```

```c
        es = FP_SEG(receiver_queue[receiver_tail].packet_data);
        di = FP_OFF(receiver_queue[receiver_tail].packet_data);
        receiver_queue[receiver_tail].packet_size = cx;
        if (receiver_head == -1) receiver_head = 0;
        if (++receiver_count > 30) receiver_count = 30;
        break;
    }
}
void find_driver(unsigned char * interrupt_number)
{
 char the_word[] = "PKT DRVR",
      signature[8];
 int ok = 1;
 unsigned char i = 0x60;
 long old_handler;
 while ((ok) && (i<=0x80))
 {
  old_handler = (long)getvect(i);
  movedata(FP_SEG(old_handler), FP_OFF(old_handler)+3, FP_SEG(signature),
FP_OFF(signature), 8);
   if (strncmp ( the_word, signature, 8) == 0)
    ok = 0;
   else
    i++;
 }
 if (ok) printf ("No Packet Driver Found\n");
 else
 {
  printf ( "Packet Driver Found at interrupt %d\n", i);
  *interrupt_number = i;
 }
}
void driver_info(unsigned char interrupt_number,
      unsigned int *handle,
      unsigned int *version,
      unsigned char *driver_class,
      unsigned int *ttype,
      unsigned char *number,
      unsigned char *basic )
{
 union REGS regs;
 regs.x.bx = *handle;
 regs.h.ah = 1;
```

```c
 regs.h.al = 0xff;
 int86 (interrupt_number, &regs, &regs);
 *version = regs.x.bx;
 *driver_class = regs.h.ch;
 *ttype = regs.x.dx;
 *number = regs.h.cl;
 *basic = regs.h.al;
}
void access_type (unsigned char interrupt_number,
      unsigned int *handle,
      unsigned char driver_class,
      unsigned int ttype,
      unsigned char number,
      unsigned int p_type,
      int type_length)
{
 union REGS regs;
 struct SREGS sregs;
 char iptype[2];
 iptype[0] = (0xFF00 & p_type)>>8;
 iptype[1] = 0x00FF & p_type;
 regs.h.al = driver_class;
 regs.h.ah = 2;
 regs.x.bx = ttype;
 regs.h.dl = number;
 sregs.ds = FP_SEG(iptype);
 regs.x.si = FP_OFF(iptype);
 regs.x.cx = type_length;
 sregs.es = FP_SEG(packet_receiver);
 regs.x.di = FP_OFF(packet_receiver);
 int86x (interrupt_number, &regs, &regs, &sregs);
   *handle = regs.x.ax;
}
void get_address (unsigned char interrupt_number, unsigned int handle)
{
 union REGS regs;
 struct SREGS sregs;
 regs.h.ah = 6;
 regs.x.bx = handle;
 sregs.es = FP_SEG(our_address);
 regs.x.di = FP_OFF(our_address);
 regs.x.cx = 0x0a;
 int86x (interrupt_number, &regs, &regs, &sregs);
```

```c
}
void set_rcv_mode(unsigned int packet_type)
{
 main_packet_type = packet_type;
}
void build_pkt (unsigned char *packet, int *packet_length, unsigned char
*to_address, unsigned char *from_address,
        unsigned char *data, int data_length)
{
 int i;
 for (i=0;i<6;i++)
  packet[i] = to_address[i];
 for (i=0;i<6;i++)
  packet[i+6] = from_address[i];
 packet[12] = (0xFF00 & main_packet_type) >> 8;
 packet[13] = (unsigned char)(0x00FF & main_packet_type);
 for (i=0;i<data_length;i++)
  packet[20+i] = data[i];
 *packet_length = data_length+20;
}
void show_packet (unsigned char *packet, int packet_length)
{
 printf ( "To address -> %2X:%2X:%2X:%2X:%2X:%2X\n", packet[0], packet[1],
packet[2],
                  packet[3], packet[4], packet[5] );
 printf ( "from address-> %2X:%2X:%2X:%2X:%2X:%2X\n", packet[6], packet[7],
packet[8],
                  packet[9], packet[10], packet[11] );
 printf ( "Type field -> %2x%2x\n", packet[12], packet[13]);
 printf ( "temp stuff -> %2d %2d %2d %2d\n", packet[14], packet[15],
packet[16], packet[17]);
 printf ( "Sequence # -> %2d%2d\n", packet[18], packet[19]);
 printf ( "Packet Len -> %d\n", packet_length);
}
void set_type (unsigned int ptype)
{
 main_packet_type = ptype;
}
void send_pkt(unsigned char interrupt_number, unsigned char *packet, int
packet_length)
{
 union REGS regs;
 struct SREGS sregs;
```

```c
 regs.h.ah = 4;
 regs.h.al = 0;
 regs.x.si = FP_OFF(packet);
 sregs.ds = FP_SEG(packet);
 regs.x.cx = packet_length;
 int86x(interrupt_number, &regs, &regs, &sregs);
}
int get_from_queue(unsigned char *packet, int *packet_length)
{
 SEC_PACKET *temp_record;
 int i;
 while (receiver_count>0)
 {
  temp_record = (SEC_PACKET *)malloc(sizeof(SEC_PACKET));
  temp_record->next = NULL;
  secondary_queue_count++;
  if (secondary_queue_head == NULL)
  {
   secondary_queue_head = temp_record;
   secondary_queue_tail = temp_record;
  }
  else
  {
   secondary_queue_tail->next = temp_record;
   secondary_queue_tail = temp_record;
  }
  temp_record->packet_length = receiver_queue[receiver_head].packet_size;
  for (i=0;i<receiver_queue[receiver_head].packet_size;i++)
   temp_record->data[i] = receiver_queue[receiver_head].packet_data[i];
  receiver_head++;
  if (receiver_head == MAXSIZE) receiver_head = 0;
  receiver_count--;
  if (receiver_count == 0)
  {
   receiver_head = receiver_tail = -1;
  }
 }
 if (secondary_queue_count > 0)
 {
  *packet_length = secondary_queue_head->packet_length;
  for(i=0;i<*packet_length;i++)
   packet[i] = secondary_queue_head->data[i];
  temp_record = secondary_queue_head;
```

```c
     secondary_queue_head = secondary_queue_head->next;
     free (temp_record);
     secondary_queue_count--;
     if (secondary_queue_count == 0)
     {
       secondary_queue_head = secondary_queue_tail = NULL;
     }
     return 1;
   }
   else
     return 0;
}
void release_type (unsigned char interrupt_number, unsigned int handle)
{
  union REGS regs;
  regs.h.ah = 3;
  regs.x.bx = handle;
  int86(interrupt_number, &regs, &regs);
}
void terminate (unsigned char interrupt_number, unsigned int handle)
{
  union REGS regs;
  regs.h.ah = 5;
  regs.x.bx = handle;
  int86(interrupt_number, &regs, &regs);
}
void dissect_packet(unsigned char *packet, int packet_length, unsigned char
*their_address,
         unsigned char *data)
{
  int i;
  for(i=0;i<6;i++)
    their_address[i] = packet[i+6];
  for(i=0;i<packet_length-20;i++)
    data[i] = packet[20+i];
}
void get_their_address(unsigned char *address)
{
  clrscr();
  printf ( "Enter the six hexadecimal value of the receiver's ethernet
address\n");
  printf ( "Separate the values using spaces\n");
  printf ( "Address->");
```

```
     scanf ("%x %x %x %x %x %x", their_address[0], their_address[1],
their_address[2],
           their_address[3], their_address[4], their_address[5] );
 printf ( "\n\n");
}
void main()
{
 char ch;
 int received=0, sent=0, i;
 p_type = 0x1234;
 their_address[0] = 0;
 their_address[1] = 1;
 their_address[2] = 2;
 their_address[3] = 3;
 their_address[4] = 4;
 their_address[5] = 5;
 set_type (p_type);
 find_driver(&interrupt_number);
 driver_info(interrupt_number, &handle, &version, &driver_class, &ttype,
&number, &basic );
 access_type (interrupt_number, &handle, driver_class, ttype, number,
p_type, 2);
 get_address (interrupt_number, handle);
 their_address[0] = 0x00;
 their_address[1] = 0x00;
 their_address[2] = 0xC0;
 their_address[3] = 0x12;
 their_address[4] = 0xE4;
 their_address[5] = 0x25;
 data[0] = 'A';
 build_pkt (pkt, &packet_length, their_address, our_address, data, 5);
 printf ( "\n\nPress [R]eceiver or [S]ender\n");
 ch=getche();
 clrscr();
 while (!kbhit())
 {
  clrscr();
  if (ch=='r')
  {
   if (get_from_queue(pkt, &packet_length))
   {
   gotoxy(10,10);
   printf ( "%d", ++received);
```

```
        }
      }
    else
    {
      send_pkt(interrupt_number, pkt, packet_length);
      gotoxy(10,10);
      printf ("%d", ++sent);
    }
  }
  release_type(interrupt_number, handle);
  terminate(interrupt_number, handle);
}
```

The program works by asking each of the machines the ethernet address of the computer it should communicate with. It uses this ethernet address to construct a very simple packet with very little in its data field.

Next the program asks whether or not the machine it is currently executing on should be the sender or the receiver of packets. Once each of the machines has been assigned its respective task, the two machines will pass and receive packets between themselves. A running indicator shows the progress of the test program.

This is by far the simplest type of communication program possible using the ethernet. When tested on a dedicated network, with only two machines tied together, the program is able to transmit and receive hundreds of packets every second. This is a great deal of information. However, we all know that not everything is as ideal as a dedicated network with only two machines on it.

In many cases, your access to a network may be at your place of business or at school. There could be hundreds or thousands of computers placed on the network system. Personal computers will be communicating with other personal computers as well as with large mainframes. Your packets will not be the only ones travelling on the electronic highway.

All of this is leading to the conclusion that there may be problems with the system we have created. We know that when we send a packet to another computer, we just accept that the packet will arrive. Can we make this assumption?

The answer is no. During a real-world test of the basic communication system developed above, it became apparent that there wasn't just one type of error that could occur, but several. The errors that can occur are:
- lost packets
- duplicate packets
- delayed packets

All of the errors basically have something to do with the transmission of the packet. Notice that this list does not include corrupted data. The reason is that the ethernet card takes care of this for us. When a packet is transmitted by the ethernet card, a checksum value is attached to it. When the packet is received by another ethernet card, if the packet does not match the checksum value, the packet is discarded. Once the packet is discarded, it is lost.

Creating Guaranteed Communication

We are trying to achieve a guaranteed communication scheme. With this scheme, we will be able to create a system that keeps track of packets that have been sent and received and detect whether any packets have been lost.

We will begin our scheme by looking at the lost packet situation. How do we determine that a packet has been lost? The easiest way is to ask the receiver to tell the sender when the packet has arrived. We can do this using an acknowledgment packet. But how does this solve our lost packet problem? The answer is that once we send a packet to a receiver, we will be expecting an acknowledgment packet to be sent back to us. If the acknowledgment packet does not arrive, we know that our original packet was not received.

The scheme works like this:

SENDER: send packet to receiver
RECEIVER: wait for packet
SENDER: wait for acknowledgment
RECEIVER: packet received, send acknowledgment
SENDER: acknowledgment received, packet sent okay!

This scheme is illustrated in Figure 7.5.

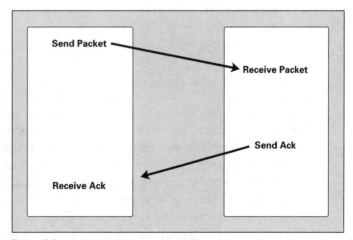

Figure 7.5 Acknowledgment scheme diagram.

As you examine the scheme, you may be thinking to yourself, "What if the acknowledgment packet is lost?" This is a very good question. The sender will be waiting for that acknowledgment packet to arrive before it does any further processing. We can anticipate this lost acknowledgment packet by setting up a time frame for the reception of the acknowledgment packet.

Instead of the sender machine simply waiting for an acknowledgment packet to arrive anytime, we set up a simple timer that gives the acknowledgment packet only so much time to arrive. If the timer expires without an acknowledgment packet being received, then we send another data packet to the receiver and reset the timer.

In order to implement this scheme, we have to make three changes to our code. The first change is to add variable for the acknowledgment packet. Since we will have to acknowledge every packet that arrives at our computer, we had better have an acknowledgment packet already made up and ready to send. The variable we are going to use for our acknowledgment packet is:

```
unsigned char ack_packet[64];
```

Notice that we are defining the packet as the smallest possible packet size.

Next we need to create the packet. We will do this using the function create_ack_packet:

```
void create_ack_packet()
{
   int i;
   for(i=0;i<6;i++)
     ack_packet[6+i] = our_address[i];
   ack_packet[12] = (0xFF00 & main_packet_type)>>8;
   ack_packet[13] = (unsigned char)(0x00FF & main_packet_type);
   ack_packet[14] = 'a';
   ack_packet[15] = 'c';
   ack_packet[16] = 'k';
}
```

As you can see, our acknowledgment packet makes use of three of the four reserved bytes starting at location 14. We put the three letters "ack" in the reserved area to make sure that this packet is not taken as a data packet.

Now that we have our acknowledgment packet, we need to make a change to the get_from_queue() function. We know that every time a packet is received by our machine, we want to send an acknowledgment packet back to the other computer. What do we do when we receive an acknowledgment packet? Do we acknowledge it as well? The answer is no. Once an acknowledgment packet is received, it is simply discarded. The code we added begins by looking at the characters placed in the reserved section of the packet just copied from the main packet queue. If the packet has the letter "a" in position 14 and the letter "k" in position 16, we know that this packet is an acknowledgment packet and we don't need to do any further processing. However, if the packet is not an acknowledgment packet, we need to send an acknowledgment packet to the sender. We first extract the sender's address from the packet and place it in the acknowledgment packet. This lets the packet know which machine it is acknowledging. This is followed by a direct sending of the packet.

After the acknowledgment packet is sent to the sender machine, we are ready to return a packet to the caller of the get_from_queue function. As you will see, we have made a slight change to this function. At the end of the header line, we have added a third parameter called **type**. This parameter is used to tell the get_from_queue function whether we are looking for an acknowledgment packet or a data packet in the secondary queue of packets.

To help explain the need for the **type** parameter, we should look at the changes that we made to the send_pkt routine. We know that when we send a packet to another machine, we need to wait and find out if the packet was received. We can accomplish this task using a new send_pkt routine as shown:

```
void send_pkt(unsigned char interrupt_number, unsigned char *packet, int
packet_length)
{
    union REGS regs;
    struct SREGS sregs;
    do
    {
    regs.h.ah = 4;
    regs.h.al = 0;
    regs.x.si = FP_OFF(packet);
    sregs.ds = FP_SEG(packet);
    regs.x.cx = packet_length;
    int86x(interrupt_number, &regs, &regs, &sregs);
 }
 while (get_ack());
}
```

The new routine begins with a DO statement followed by the standard code for sending packets. After the sending code, we have a WHILE statement with a condition of get_ack(), which is a function that looks for an acknowledgment packet. The DO..WHILE loop ensures that we send a minimum of one packet. The get_ack() function is where we really do the processing. The function is:

```
int get_ack()
{
```

```
SEC_PACKET *temp, *prev;
struct time start, finish;
int start_time, no_ack = 1, length;
unsigned char *pkt;
gettime (&start);
start_time = start.ti_min*60+start.ti_sec;
while (no_ack)
{
 if (get_from_queue(pkt, &length, 1)==2) return 0;
 gettime(&finish);
 if((finish.ti_min*60+finish.ti_sec)-start_time > 3) return 1;
}
 return 1;
}
```

The get_ack function begins by assigning the current system time to the variable **start**. The current minute and second values are combined and assigned to the variable start_time. This value gives us the current time in seconds past the hour. We will use this value to time the acknowledgment packet.

Once we enter a WHILE loop, we make a call to the function get_from_queue. Notice that the last parameter in the call is the value 1. This value corresponds to the type variable in the get_from_queue function. The value of 1 tells the function that we are not looking for a data packet but only an acknowledgment packet.

If you flip back a few pages and look at the code that makes up the get_from_queue() routine, you will see that the function tests to see if the type variable is a 1 and if the reserved bytes in the first packet on the secondary queue have the letters "a" and "k." If this statement evaluates to TRUE, then we know that we have an acknowledgment packet. We remove the packet from the queue and return a value of 2 to the calling function.

The calling function, get_ack(), recognizes the 2 and returns a value of 0 to the send_pkt routine, which exits its DO..WHILE loop. This sequence of events happens for a successful packet transmission.

If the get_from_queue() routine does not find an acknowledgment packet within three seconds, the get_ack() function will return of value of 1 to the send_pkt() routine and a copy of the original packet will be sent to the other machine.

Duplicate Packets

As you may have guessed from the last paragraph, we may have a problem with just sending another packet to the other machine when an acknowledgment packet is not received right away. On a typical network, packets can be delayed or lost. If our original packet was lost, then sending a copy is the appropriate thing to do; but if the original packet—or the acknowledgment packet, for that matter—is just delayed, the receiving machine may get both the original packet and a duplicate of the original. The receiving machine will not know that it should disregard one of these packets, and it will process the duplicate just as it does all its other packets. If the packet contains movement data for our game, then it will seriously throw off the play of the game. We need a way to be sure that no packets are duplicated on either end of our transmissions.

Just a List

When a packet arrives at our machine, the only way that we know it differs from some other packet is the data in the packet. One packet may contain movement data and another may contain shooting data. In order to tell whether or not a packet just received is a duplicate of another packet, we would need to keep a list of all the packets that have arrived at our machine and search through the data area of each of the packets to see if any of the data matches the data in our new packet.

Obviously, this type of scheme will not work for two reasons: first, because storing all of the packets that arrive at our machine would consume a large amount of memory, and second, because it would be impossible to recognize duplicate acknowledgment packets, since the data areas of these packets are empty.

If you recall the format of our packets, you will remember that we have two bytes reserved for a packet number. Every time we send a new packet to the receiver machine, we will assign a unique number to the packet. When the receiver machine receives the packet it can look at the number embedded in the packet to see if it has received the packet before.

This can be accomplished in the following way. We create two variables, send_packet_number and receiver_packet_number, and set these variables equal to 1 and 0 respectively. When our machine sends its first packet, it will put the value of the send_packet_number variable into the packet. Since each packet must have a unique packet number, the sending machine will increment the value in the send_packet_number variable in preparation for the next packet.

When the packet is received, the receiver machine will extract the packet number and compare it to the value in the variable receiver_packet_number. If the packet number is greater than the value in the variable, then the packet is not a duplicate. Since we are going to accept this packet, we need to increment that value of the receiver_packet_number variable to indicate that we have received all of the packets up to the value located in this variable.

Now if the sender machine sends a second packet, it will embed the packet number value 2 into the packet. When the packet is received, the value 2 will be greater than the value of 1 located in the receiver_packet_number.

To see that the system does work, consider the situation if our first packet does not arrive at the receiver machine. The sender machine will time out because it has not received an acknowledgment packet and will send a copy of the original packet with an embedded packet number value of 1 in it. Since the receiver machine did not receive the first packet, the variable receiver_packet_number is still holding the value of 0. The packet value of 1 is greater than the value of 0, so the packet will be accepted as a new packet.

To implement the packet number scheme, we need to make a change to the send_pkt() and get_from_queue() routines.

The new send_pkt routine is:

```
void send_pkt(unsigned char interrupt_number, unsigned char
*packet, int packet_length)
{
 union REGS regs;
 struct SREGS sregs;
 packet[18] = (0xFF00 & send_packet_number) >> 8;
 packet[19] = (unsigned char)(0x00FF & send_packet_number);
 if(++send_packet_number > 32766) send_packet_number = 1;
 do
 {
  regs.h.ah = 4;
  regs.h.al = 0;
  regs.x.si = FP_OFF(packet);
  sregs.ds = FP_SEG(packet);
  regs.x.cx = packet_length;
  int86x(interrupt_number, &regs, &regs, &sregs);
 }
 while (get_ack());
}
```

Notice that in the new send_pkt() routine, we have to place the code for adding the packet number to the packet outside of the DO..WHILE loop. If we put the code inside the loop, we would assign a new packet number to every new packet as well as any copy packets that need to be sent. This would throw off our scheme.

Conclusion

You can now be sure that you can reliably send packets between any two machines using packet drivers and an ethernet card. The packets will be received reliably and without any losses.

Adding Ethernet Support to ACK3D

Being able to communicate and share our game with another user using the NULL modem cable or modem is exciting, but just think about doing the same thing over the company or school network. The following discussion gives you all the information you need to take the network code from the previous chapter and add the necessary interface code. Fortunately, most of the foundation code for adding network support to our game has already been added when we provided serial port support.

Initialization

Just as was the case for the serial port, we must initialize the ethernet code. Remember that we must already have a packet driver installed in our system in order for us to be able to interface with the network card. Our initialization process is just like that used in the previous chapter for our test communication program. The most obvious place to put the initialization code is in the select_communication_device() function. In this function, we present the player with a list of possible communication devices to be used to link to the opponent. One of the options is the ethernet. By pressing the E key, the player indicates a wish to use the ethernet as the communication device. The code is able to determine that the player pressed the E key using a SWITCH statement and a CASE statement. In the select_communication_device() function you will find the code:

```
case 'E': com_device = 'e';
          break;
```

Between com_device='e'; and the break; command you should place the following code:

```
p_type = 0x1234;
set_type (p_type);
find_driver(&interrupt_number);
driver_info(interrupt_number, &handle, &version, &driver_class, &ttype,
&number, &basic );
access_type (interrupt_number, &handle, driver_class, ttype, number,
p_type, 2);
get_address (interrupt_number, handle);
```

This initialization code begins by setting the global variable p_type equal to the packet type 0x1234; This is our one personal packet type to be used throughout our entire game. After setting the global variable, we find the packet driver that we installed in our computer and let the packet driver know that we want to use 0x1234 packets only. Once the packet driver is initialized, we get the address of our ethernet card.

Creating the Ethernet Link

Once the ethernet link and interface are initialized, we are ready to create a link to the opponent. When programming for the serial port, we need to know which of the players would be the answerer and which the originator. This is also the case for the ethernet link. In the function create_link(), we must place linking information in the CASE statement for the ethernet. The new code is:

```
case 'e': clrscr();
   printf ("Are we the (O)riginator or (A)nswerer?\n");
   printf (":");
   ch = toupper(getkey());
   printf ("%c\n", ch);
   if (ch == 'O')
   {
   for (i=0;i<6;i++)
      data_packet[6+i] = 0xff;
   data_packet[20] = 'x';
   send_pkt(interrupt_number, data_packet, 64);
   while (!get_from_queue(data_packet, &packet_length, 0))
      NULL;
   if (data_packet[20] == 'y')
   {
      for(i=0;i<6;i++)
         their_address[i] = data_packet[6+i];
      build_packets();
   }
   }
   else
   {
   while (!get_from_queue(data_packet, &packet_length, 0))
      NULL;
   if (data_packet[20] == 'x')
   {
      data_packet[20] = 'y';
      for (i=0;i<6;i++)
         data_packet[i] = data_packet[6+i];
      for (i=0;i<6;i++)
         data_packet[i+6] = our_address[i];
```

```
        }
    }
    break;
```

The code begins by asking the originator question. Once the program determines which player's machine will be the originator, it must begin looking for the answering machine. In the program running on the originator's computer, we start by creating a data packet to send out on the network. This data packet will be called a broadcast packet. To create a broadcast packet, we fill in the TO address of an ethernet packet with the value 0xFF. We have defined a global variable called data_packet which has a length of 64 bytes. This will be a universal packet used throughout the game. The code for filling in the TO address is:

```
for (i=0;i<6;i++)
  data_packet[6+i] = 0xff;
```

After the TO address is filled in, the FROM ethernet address as well as the packet type of the packet must be filled in. The code is:

```
for (i=0;i<6;i++)
  data_packet[i] = our_address[i];
ack_packet[12] = (0xFF00 & main_packet_type) >> 8;
ack_packet[13] = (unsigned char)(0x00FF & main_packet_type);
```

We are going to include one more piece of information in our data packet. This information is a single character that will be used to let the receiving machine know that this particular broadcast packet is part of the initialization code.

```
data_packet[20] = 'x';
```

Now that all of the information is placed in the packet, we can send out the packet on the network using the send_pkt() function. The code is:

```
send_pkt(interrupt_number, data_packet, 64);
```

Notice that we are indicating that the total length of the packet is 64 bytes, even though we only have one character in the packet. This is because all packets must be at least 64 bytes.

After the packet is sent out on the network, the sender must wait for a reply from the opponent's machine. The code that does the wait is:

```
while (!get_from_queue(data_packet, &packet_length, 0))
  NULL;
```

This simple loop makes repeated calls to the function get_from_queue(). Recall that this function goes to the packet queue where all of the data packets are stored and tries to return a packet to the calling function. If no packet is available, the function returns a value of 0. We are assuming that a value of 0 will be returned, so we negate the value using the ! operator. This makes the code stay in the WHILE loop. The only statement in the WHILE loop is a NULL, so we immediately return to the top of the loop, where we make another call to the get_from_queue() function. When a packet arrives at the originator machine that matches our 0x1234 packet type, the get_from_queue() function will return a value of 1. This exits the loop.

We makes a quick check of the contents of the twentieth position in the data packet. If the position contains the character "y," we know that the broadcast packet found the opponent. The reason for this will be seen shortly, when we look at the answerer code. For now, remember that we sent our packet with the character "x" in position 20. The answerer code will change the "x"' to "y."

```
if (data_packet[20] == 'y')
{
 for(i=0;i<6;i++)
    their_address[i] = data_packet[6+i];
 build_packets();
}
```

Now that the originator has a data packet from the opponent, the ethernet packet is recorded so that the originator will be able to send other packets without using the broadcast method. This is very important, since if we were to use the broadcast mode in our network game we would create problems for the network administrator. When a broadcast packet is put on the network, it will be received by every computer on the network. Only those machines that have asked for packet type 0x1234 will do anything with the packet, but it will be received by all machines. When a machine receives a packet it has to do some work. The amount of work is small, but there is work to do. If the machines on the network were to be bombarded with broadcast packets from our game, the applications running on the other computers would be slowed, and sometimes the slowdown can be dramatic. For this reason we will record our opponent's ethernet address so the machines can communicate directly. After we record the address, we make a call to the function build_packets(). This function builds packets used later in the play of the game. It will be discussed shortly. After building the necessary packets, we end with a call to do_link(), which exchanges person information (information about which player is which) with the opponent.

Now that we know what the originator machine is doing, let's look at the answerer. The code for the answerer is very much like the code for the originator. It begins with a loop. The loop works just like the WHILE

loop for the originator. It constantly makes a call to the function
get_from_queue(), looking for a packet. The answerer is waiting for the
originator machine to send a packet identifying itself.

```
while (!get_from_queue(data_packet, &packet_length, 0))
  NULL;
```

Once a packet arrives at the answering machine, we make a quick
check to see if it is the appropriate data packet. This is really just a safety
step, since we are the only ones on the network using the 0x1234 packet
type. If the twentieth position of the packet is an "x," we enter a short IF
block. The block begins by replacing the "x" character in the data packet
with a "y" character, after which we copy the ethernet address of the
sender of the packet into the global variable their_packet and transfer the
address to the TO part of the ethernet packet that we are sending back to
the originator machine. The sender must also copy its ethernet address
into the packet so that the originator machine knows who it is.

```
if (data_packet[20] == 'x')
{
 data_packet[20] = 'y';
 for (i=0;i<6;i++)
   {
                 their_address[i] = data_packet[6+i];
      data_packet[i] = data_packet[6+i];
   }
 for (i=0;i<6;i++)
    data_packet[i+6] = our_address[i];
}
send_pkt(interrupt_number, data_packet, 64);
build_packets();
}
```

After the data packet is complete, we send it using the send_pkt() function, make a call to the packet-building function build_packets(), and call
do_link() to exchange person information. At this point in the game, each of
the machines knows who the opponent is, or at least what the opponent's
ethernet address is. This is all the information that we need to start the game.

Build_packets()

During our game, we will be sending information to our opponent to indicate
our movements in the game as well as other information. Our movements in

the game are coded to a single character. When the receiving machine gets the character, our graphical figure object on the opponent's machine is moved the appropriate distance. Because we will be moving very quickly, we have to make sure that the movement information is sent to our opponent as fast as possible. For this reason we create a function build_packets(). The purpose of this function is to create several packets for our use throughout the game. These packets contain information about the data they are to contain as well as about the machine that is to receive the information. The code for build_packets() is:

```c
void build_packets()
{
 int i;
 for (i=6;i<12;i++)
 {
    ack_packet[i] = our_address[i-6];
    data_packet[i] = our_address[i-6];
    get_packet[i] = our_address[i-6];
 }
 for (i=0;i<6;i++)
 {
    ack_packet[i] = their_address[i];
    data_packet[i] = their_address[i];
    get_packet[i] = their_address[i];
 }
 ack_packet[12] = (0xFF00 & main_packet_type) >> 8;
 ack_packet[13] = (unsigned char)(0x00FF & main_packet_type);
 get_packet[12] = data_packet[12] = ack_packet[12];
 get_packet[13] = data_packet[13] = ack_packet[13];
 ack_packet[14] = 'a';
 ack_packet[15] = 'c';
 ack_packet[16] = 'k';
}
```

The build_packets() function builds a total of three packets. The first packet is called data_packet and is a simple temporary packet that we can use to send any information to our opponent. The second packet is our acknowledgment packet that is used internally by the network interface code. The third packet is a packet that we will use to get information from the opponent.

Transmitting Information

With all of our information packets created, it's time to send them. Recall from Chapter 6 on the serial interface to our game that we placed code to send our movement characters directly in the keyboard handling code. The code that we are going to add to each of our keyboard controls is

```
if (com_device=='e') send_pkt(interrupt_number, packet, length);
```

It is imperative that we include the IF statement so that the send_pkt() function is used only when we are connected by the ethernet. The code added to each of the keyboard routines appears as:

```
switch(ch)
{
 case LEFT : if ((com_device == 'n') || (com_device == 'm'))com_tx(PORT, 'd');
    if (com_device=='e')
    {
    data_packet[20] = 'd';
    send_pkt (interrupt_number,data_packet, 64);
    }
    ae->PlayerAngle += (-INT_ANGLE_2 * 5);
    pan = 1;
    break;
 case RIGHT: if ((com_device == 'n') || (com_device == 'm'))com_tx(PORT, 'c');
    if (com_device=='e')
    {
      data_packet[20] = 'c';
      send_pkt (interrupt_number,data_packet, 64);
    }
    ae->PlayerAngle += INT_ANGLE_2 * 5;
    pan = 1;
    break;
 case UP: if ((com_device == 'n') || (com_device == 'm'))com_tx(PORT, 'a');
    if (com_device=='e')
    {
      data_packet[20] = 'a'
      send_pkt (interrupt_number,data_packet, 64);
    }
    AckMovePOV(ae,ae->PlayerAngle,16);
    break;
 case DOWN: if ((com_device == 'n') || (com_device == 'm'))com_tx(PORT, 'b');
    if (com_device=='e')
    {
      data_packet[20] = 'b';
      send_pkt (interrupt_number,data_packet, 64);
    }
    temp= ae->PlayerAngle + INT_ANGLE_180;
```

```
if (temp >= INT_ANGLE_360)
  temp -= INT_ANGLE_360;
AckMovePOV(ae,temp,16);
break;
```

Notice that we are using our prepared movement character packets.

Receiving via Ethernet

Transmitting movement information is just half of the story. We also need to be able to receive movement information. We will do this using the code:

```
if (com_device == 'e')
  if (get_from_queue(get_packet, &packet_length, 0))
    process_communications(get_packet[20]);
```

This code is placed in the main() function directly under the reception code for the serial ports. The code first checks to make sure that we are using an ethernet connection link. If we are, the code makes one check of the get_from_queue() function to determine if a packet is available for us. If a packet is available, we know that the movement character is located in position 20, so we immediately make a call to process_communications() to process the movement character.

New do_link

During the course of adding ethernet support, we find that several of our routines are specific to the serial port. The do_link() function is one of them. Notice that in this function the connection is assumed to be through the serial port:

```
void do_link()
{
 char ours, theirs, do_again = 1;
 randomize();
 while ( do_again )
 {
    do_again = 0;
    randomize();
```

```
      ours = random(50);
      com_tx(PORT, ours);
      theirs = com_rx(PORT);
      if (ours<theirs) person = 0;
      else person = 1;
      if (ours==theirs) do_again = 1;
   }
}
```

We need to change the code so that the appropriate medium is used for transferring our message. The new code looks like:

```
void do_link()
{
 char ours, theirs, do_again = 1;
 int packet_length;
 randomize();
 while ( do_again )
 {
    do_again = 0;
    randomize();
    ours = random(50);
    if ((com_device == 'n') || (com_device == 'm')) com_tx(PORT, ours);
    if (com_device=='e')
    {
       data_packet[20] = ours;
       send_pkt (interrupt_number,d_packet, 64);
    }
    if ((com_device == 'n') || (com_device == 'm'))theirs=com_rx(PORT);
    if (com_device=='e') {
       while (!get_from_queue(data_packet, &packet_length, 0))
       NULL;
       theirs = data_packet[20];
    }
    if (ours<theirs) person = 0;
    else person = 1;
    if (ours==theirs) do_again = 1;
 }
}
```

In the network code, we pass all of the information using position 20 of the data packet. This is a convenient way of sending small pieces of data between the computers.

New Hangup

In addition to the do_link() function, our hangup() function needs to be changed. Notice that all of the code assumes that the communication is via the serial port link. To change things so that we don't bother the serial port when we use the ethernet, we need to add a single IF statement. The new code is:

```
void hangup()
{
 if ((com_device=='n') || (com_device=='m'))
 {
 com_lower_dtr(PORT);
 delay(1100);
 if (com_carrier(PORT))
 {
   com_tx_string_with_delay(PORT, "+++", 10, 10);
   delay(1100);
   com_tx(PORT, 13); delay(10);
   com_tx_string_with_delay(PORT, "ATH", 10, 10);
   com_tx(PORT, 13); delay(10);
 }
   com_flush_rx(PORT);
   com_flush_tx(PORT);
   busy = num_stored = null_modem = connected = 0;
 }
 }
```

Conclusion

As you can tell, adding ethernet support to our game is really a very simple matter once the network code is written. We have been able to use all of the support functions that we developed when adding serial port support. In the next chapter, we will extend our support of communication links by going worldwide.

The code changes we have made are listed in the following.

Global Variables

```
//Ethernet variables
extern unsigned char    our_address[6];
extern unsigned char    their_address[6];
```

```
extern unsigned char     interrupt_number;
extern unsigned int      handle;
extern unsigned int      version;
extern unsigned char     driver_class;
extern unsigned int      ttype;
extern unsigned char     number;
extern unsigned char     basic;
extern unsigned int      p_type;
extern unsigned int      main_packet_type;
extern unsigned char     ack_packet[64];
unsigned char data_packet[64], get_packet[64];
```

Main Function

```
int main(void)
{
 int      result,
    done = 0,
    pan = 0,
    i;
 int      temp,
    packet_length;
 unsigned ch_val;
 char buf[35] = "Line 1", ch;
 int x, y, buttons, joy_centx, joy_centy, moves = 0;
 if (select_communication_device())
   {
     printf ( "Error setting up communication device\n");
     return(1);
   }
 if (com_device != 's')
    if (create_link())
    {
    printf ("Error creating communication link\n");
    return(1);
 }
 if (result==AppInitialize())
 {
    printf("Error initializing: ErrorCode = %d\n",result);
    return(1);
 }
 if (result==AppSetupEngine())
 {
```

```c
      printf("Error setting up ACK engine: ErrorCode = %d\n",result);
      AckWrapUp(ae);
      return(1);
   }
   if (result==AppLoadBitmaps())
   {
      printf("Error loading bitmaps: ErrorCode = %d\n",result);
      AckWrapUp(ae);
      return(1);
   }
   if (result==AppSetGraphics())
   {
      AckSetTextmode();
      printf("Error loading palette: ErrorCode = %d\n",result);
      AckWrapUp(ae);
      return(1);
   }
   if (result == AppSetupOverlay())
   {
      printf("Error loading overlay: ErrorCode = %d\n",result);
      AckWrapUp(ae);
      return(1);
   }
   if (LoadSmallFont())
   {
      AckSetTextmode();
      printf("Error loading font: ErrorCode = %d\n",result);
      AckWrapUp(ae);
      return(1);
   }
   if (result==AppSetObject())
   {
      AckSetTextmode();
      printf("Error loading palette: ErrorCode = %d\n",result);
      AckWrapUp(ae);
      return(1);
   }
   AppSetupPalRanges();
   //if person == 1 then we need to switch locations of us and opponent
   if (person)
   {
      temp = ae->ObjList[other_guy].x;
      ae->ObjList[other_guy].x = ae->xPlayer;
```

```
        ae->xPlayer = temp;
        temp = ae->ObjList[other_guy].y;
        ae->ObjList[other_guy].y = ae->yPlayer;
        ae->yPlayer = temp;
        ae->ObjList[other_guy].mPos = (ae->ObjList[other_guy].y & 0xFFC0)
+ (ae->ObjList[other_guy].x >> 6);
        temp = ae->ObjList[other_guy].Dir;
        ae->ObjList[other_guy].Dir = ae->PlayerAngle;
        ae->PlayerAngle = temp;
    }
    if (use_joystick)
        joystick_read(&joy_centx, &joy_centy, &buttons);
    while (!done)
    {
        if (pan)
        {
        pan = 0;
        if (ae->PlayerAngle >= INT_ANGLE_360)
            ae->PlayerAngle -= INT_ANGLE_360;
        if (ae->PlayerAngle < 0)
            ae->PlayerAngle += INT_ANGLE_360;
        }
        AckBuildView(ae);
        AckDisplayScreen(ae);
        if ((com_device == 'n') || (com_device == 'm'))
        {
        if ((!com_carrier(PORT)) && (!null_modem))
        {
            hangup();
            AckSetTextmode();
            printf("Lost communication link");
            AckWrapUp(ae);
            delay(5000);
            exit(1);
        }
        if (!com_rx_empty(PORT))
        {
            process_communications(com_rx(PORT));
        }
        }
        if (com_device == 'e')
        {
        if (get_from_queue(get_packet, &packet_length, 0))
```

```
                    {
                        process_communications(get_packet[20]);
                    }
                }
                if (bioskey(1))
                {
                ch_val = getkey();
                if (ch_val==ESC) break;
                switch(ch_val)
                {
                    case LEFT : if ((com_device == 'n') || (com_device == 'm'))com_tx(PORT, 'd');
                            if (com_device=='e')
                            {
                            data_packet[20] = 'd';
                            send_pkt (interrupt_number,data_packet,64);
                            }
                            ae->PlayerAngle += (-INT_ANGLE_2 * 5);
                            pan = 1;
                            break;
                    case RIGHT: if ((com_device == 'n') || (com_device == 'm'))com_tx(PORT, 'c');
                            if (com_device=='e')
                            {
                            data_packet[20] = 'c';
                            send_pkt (interrupt_number,data_packet, 64);
                            }
                            ae->PlayerAngle += INT_ANGLE_2 * 5;
                            pan = 1;
                            break;
                    case UP: if ((com_device == 'n') || (com_device == 'm'))com_tx(PORT, 'a');
                            if (com_device=='e')
                            {
                            data_packet[20] = 'a';
                            send_pkt (interrupt_number,data_packet, 64);
                            }
                            result = AckMovePOV(ae,ae->PlayerAngle,16);
                            break;
                    case DOWN: if ((com_device == 'n') || (com_device == 'm'))com_tx(PORT, 'b');
                            if (com_device=='e')
                            {
                            data_packet[20] = 'b';
                            send_pkt (interrupt_number,data_packet, 64);
                            }
                            temp= ae->PlayerAngle + INT_ANGLE_180;
```

```
                if (temp >= INT_ANGLE_360) temp -= INT_ANGLE_360;
                if (temp < 0) temp += INT_ANGLE_360;
                result = AckMovePOV(ae,temp,16);
                break;
        }
    }
}
```

Process_communication Function

```
int select_communication_device()
{
 char ch;
 int result;
 while (!com_device)
 {
  clrscr();
  printf ("\n\n\n");
  printf ("Please select the communication medium that you would like to
  use:\n\n");
  printf ("(E)thernet connection\n");
  printf ("(I)nternet connection\n");
  printf ("(N)ull Modem connection\n");
  printf ("(M)odem connection\n");
  printf ("(S)ingle User\n");
  printf (":");
  ch = getkey();
  printf ("%c\n", ch);
  switch (toupper(ch))
  {
    case 'E': com_device = 'e';
         p_type = 0x1234;
         set_type (p_type);
         find_driver(&interrupt_number);
         driver_info(interrupt_number, &handle, &version, &driver_class,
&ttype, &number, &basic );
         access_type (interrupt_number, &handle, driver_class, ttype,
number, p_type, 2);
         get_address (interrupt_number, handle);
         result = 0;
         break;
    case 'I': break;
    case 'N': com_device = 'n';
         result = setup_com();
```

```
        break;
    case 'M': com_device = 'm';
        result = setup_com();
        break;
    case 'S': com_device = 's';
        result = 0;
        break;
    }
 }
 return(result);
}
```

Create_link Function

```
int create_link()
{
 int got_one = 0, i, packet_length;
 char ch, buffer[40];
 switch(com_device)
 {
  case 'e': clrscr();
    printf ("Are we the (O)riginator or (A)nswerer?\n");
    printf (":");
    ch = toupper(getkey());
    printf ("%c\n", ch);
    if (ch == 'O')
    {
    for (i=0;i<6;i++)
       their_address[i] = 0xff; //0;
    build_packets();
    data_packet[20] = 'x';
    send_pkt(interrupt_number, data_packet, 64);
    while (!get_from_queue(get_packet, &packet_length, 0))
       { if (kbhit()) exit(1); }
    if (get_packet[20] == 'y')
    {
       for(i=0;i<6;i++)
          their_address[i] = get_packet[6+i];
       build_packets();
       do_link();
    }
    }
    else
    {
```

```
        build_packets();
        while (!get_from_queue(get_packet, &packet_length, 0))
        { if (kbhit()) exit(1); }
        if (get_packet[20] == 'x')
        {
            data_packet[20] = 'y';
            for (i=0;i<6;i++)
        {
            data_packet[i] = get_packet[6+i];
            their_address[i] = get_packet[i];
        }
            for (i=0;i<6;i++)
                data_packet[i+6] = our_address[i];
            send_pkt(interrupt_number, data_packet, 64);
            build_packets();
            do_link();
        }
        }
        break;
    case 'i':
        break;
    case 'n': while (!got_one)
        {
        clrscr();
        printf ("Is this machine the originating or answering machine?\n");
        printf (":");
        ch = toupper(getkey());
        printf ("%c\n", ch);
        if (ch == 'O')
        {
            null_dial();
            return(0);
        }
        if (ch == 'A')
        {
            null_answer();
            return(0);
        }
        }
        return(1);
    case 'm': while (!got_one)
        {
        clrscr();
```

```c
    printf ("Is this machine the originating or answering machine?\n");
    printf (":");
    ch = toupper(getkey());
    printf ("%c\n", ch);
    if (ch == 'O')
    {
       dial();
       return(0);
    }
    if (ch == 'A')
    {
       answer();
       return(0);
    }
    }
    return(1);
 }
 return(0);
 }
```

CHAPTER 9

ADDING INTERNET SUPPORT

It's the time we have all been waiting for—playing games over the Internet! Internet programming is such an important concept because the Internet connects millions of people from all over the world. Players will love a game with Internet capability because it gives them an almost unlimited number of opponents, and for most people, Internet access is much cheaper than long-distance phone bills! In this chapter, we will not only give you the changes necessary to use the Internet with our game but we will also introduce you to a freeware TCP/IP package that can be used in any of your programs. This TCP/IP package, developed at the University of Waterloo, takes care of the details involved in Internet communication.

WATTCP

As the instructions for the package WATTCP state, the author of the package, Erick Engelke, was frustrated with the lack of TCP/IP interface packages for the PC. In his frustration, he developed WATTCP. On the enclosed CD ROM, you will find the complete source code to WATTCP as well as compiled libraries. The libraries are designed to be used specifically with the Borland line of C/C++ compilers. This is good news for us, since we are using the Borland compilers for our ACK3D game.

While the documentation for the WATTCP libraries is sparse, it does give the necessary information to begin using the libraries. A programmer's manual is available for the WATTCP package. Check the readme files in the \WATTCP directory for more details.

What Is TCP/IP?

TCP/IP is a protocol for allowing different computers to share information on a network. The protocol was developed for the ARPAnet, which connected a community of researchers. Now TCP/IP isn't just one single protocol, but is part of a suite of protocols for the Internet called the "Internet Protocol Suite."

Machines connected to the net have an IP address assigned to them. The IP address is usually a four- or five-segment number such as 128.252.135.4. Using IP addresses, a machine can communicate with any other machine on the Internet. Since the machines will typically not be in the same geographical area, a series of gateway machines and other devices are used to translate the IP address in such a way that the information packet is routed to the correct machine. The IP address is by far the most important thing you need to know about a machine on the net.

To understand how the TCP/IP system works, let's look at the very simple example of sending mail. When you use a mail service to send mail, you are using an application that includes all of the functions necessary for entering your message and indicating who the message is for. Once you tell the main system to send your message, the mail code will call upon the TCP protocol. The TCP protocol is part of a layering system that will be responsible for getting your mail to its recipient.

Once the TCP layer receives your message, it is responsible for breaking your message up into datagrams, transmitting the datagrams, keeping track of any lost datagrams, and reassembling the datagrams into your original message at the recipient's machine. This should sound kind of familiar, as these are some of the tasks that we had to handle when we developed our ethernet code.

As the TCP layer is transmitting the datagrams, it will call upon the IP layer to actually handle the routing of the datagrams to the receiving machine. This is a very important part of the transmission of your message to the other machine, because your message will more than likely pass through many different networks. Each of these networks will have to pass your message to another network. By using a common protocol such as IP, all of the networks will know exactly how to handle the routing.

There are many other operations that the TCP/IP protocols must handle and work with, but for our purposes this is enough description of what is going on. Thankfully we don't have to handle any of these details because the WATTCP package does it for us.

(reating a Simple (ommunication Test Program Using WATT(P

To begin using the TCP/IP libraries, we need to have a foundation program. The program we will use starts as:

```
#include <stdio.h>
#include "tcp.h"
void main()
{
}
```

The only statement that differs from other programs is the #include "tcp.h" line. We must include the TCP.H file in order for the system to have access to the different functions of the TCP library.

There are four global variables that we are going to declare in our test program. These variables are:

```
tcp_Socket s, s2;
word status = 0;
int person = 0;
```

The first three variables are needed by all programs that use the
WATTCP package. The first two variables s and s2 are declared as type
tcp_Socket. (Note that the S is capitalized in Socket.) These variables
are used internally by the WATTCP functions, although you can call
them anything you want. The third variable, status, will be set by a
WATTCP function if an internal error occurs. The error will typically be
a lost connection. The lost connection is handled by the function
sock_err, which must be included in any WATTCP function. The code
for the function is:

```
void sock_err()
{
 switch ( status ) {
    case 1 : cputs("Connection closed");
       exit(1);
       break;
    case -1: cputs("REMOTE HOST CLOSED CONNECTION");
       sock_close ( &s );
       sock_wait_closed ( &s, sock_delay, NULL, &status ); exit(1);
       break;
 }
}
```

The specific functions in this function will be discussed as they occur in
the main() function of our test program. Next we will turn our attention
to the main() function of our test program.

Test Program main( ) Function

The main() function of our test program will be where we do all of the
initialization of the program. When we use the test program, one of the
users will execute the test program with the command **test** and the other
user will execute the test program with the command **test** *other computer's IP address*. We will use this fact later in our program.

We will begin our main() function with the following code:

```
void main(int argc, char *argv[])
{
 word status;
 longword remoteip;
```

```
char *host;
sock_init();
clrscr();
printf ( "Waiting for connect\n\n" );
```

Probably the most important statement in this code is the call to the function sock_init(). This function performs all of the internal housekeeping for communicating using the TCP/IP protocol. Once the program and TCP/IP code has been initialized, we clear the screen of the computer and display a waiting message.

We now turn to the code that determines which of the computers executed the program with the **test** command alone and which one used the test command followed by an IP address. The code is:

```
if (argc < 2)
{
    tcp_listen( &s, TCP_PORT, 0, 0, NULL, 0 );
    sock_mode( &s, TCP_MODE_BINARY );
    sock_wait_established( &s, 0, NULL, &status);

    printf ( "Press any key to begin" );
    getch();

    sock_write ( &s, &temp, sizeof ( temp ) );
    person = 1;
}
else
{
  host = argv[1];
  if (!( remoteip = resolve( host )))
  {
    cprintf("\n\rUnable to resolve '%s'\n\r", host );
    exit( 3 );
  }
  if ( !tcp_open( &s, 0, remoteip, TCP_PORT, NULL ))
  {
    cputs("Unable to open connection.");
    exit( 1 );
  }
    sock_mode( &s, TCP_MODE_BINARY );
    sock_wait_established( &s, sock_delay,NULL, &status);
    sock_read ( &s, &temp, sizeof ( temp ));
    person = 0;
}
```

As you can see, there is quite a bit of processing occurring in the code. The first IF statement looks at the variable argc to determine if the IP address follows the test command. If argc is less than 2, then the IP address does not follow the test command. In this case, the machine the program is running on will be the answering machine, if you use the paradigm that we have been following for the other communication schemes.

The first three lines of code

```
tcp_listen( &s, TCP_PORT, 0, 0, NULL, 0 );
sock_mode( &s, TCP_MODE_BINARY );
sock_wait_established( &s, 0, NULL, &status);
```

are used to open half of the communication line to the other computer. The code continues by waiting for a connection to be made with our computer. The function sock_wait_established() does not return until a connection is made. After the connection is created, we ask the user to press a key. Upon a key press, we send a simple piece of data to the other machine. The last line of code sets a global variable equal to the value 1.

Now we need to look at the other side of the connection. The user that enters the command test followed by the IP address will enter the ELSE part of the IF statement. The IP address will be located in the second position of the argv variable. The code sends the received IP address to the function resolve() to verify that this is a true IP address. The code looks like:

```
host = argv[1];

if (!( remoteip = resolve( host )))
{
    cprintf("\n\rUnable to resolve '%s'\n\r", host );
    exit( 3 );
}
```

If the IP address is good, the code will try to open the connection to the other computer. Once the connection is established, this computer tries to read information from the other computer.

```
if ( !tcp_open( &s, 0, remoteip, TCP_PORT, NULL ))
{
    cputs("Unable to open connection.");
    exit( 1 );
}
sock_mode( &s, TCP_MODE_BINARY );
sock_wait_established( &s, sock_delay,NULL, &status);
sock_read ( &s, &temp, sizeof ( temp ));
```

```
person = 0;
```

The last thing the code does is set the global variable equal to 0.

After a connection is established, the code calls the function main_loop() to begin a communication session between the computers.

The main_loop() function is a loop that terminates when a user presses a key or a connection error occurs. One of the machines will constantly send the character "a" to the other computer. The other computer will receive the "a" character and display it on the screen. When enough activity has been done to verify that the connection is good, we press a key to stop the main loop. The program ends by releasing the connection. The code is:

```
sock_close(&s);
sock_wait_closed ( &s, sock_delay, NULL, &status );
exit(0);
```

Here is the complete test program:

```
#include <stdio.h>
#include "tcp.h"
#define TCP_PORT 23
tcp_Socket s, s2;
int person = 0;
word status = 0;
int main_loop()
{
 char ch;
 int who_closed = 0;
 ch = 'a';
 while ((!kbhit()) && ( tcp_tick ( &s )))
 {
    if (person == 0)
       sock_write ( &s, &ch, 1);
    if (person == 1)
    {
       if ( sock_dataready ( &s ) )
       {
          sock_read ( &s, &ch, 1);
          printf ( "%c\n", ch);
       }
    }
 }
 getch();
```

```
    }
void sock_err()
{
    switch ( status ) {
       case 1 : cputs("Connection closed");
       exit(1);
        break;
       case -1: cputs("REMOTE HOST CLOSED CONNECTION");
        sock_close ( &s );
        sock_wait_closed ( &s, sock_delay, NULL, &status );
        exit(1);
        break;
    }
}
void main(int argc, char *argv[])
{
 word status;
 longword remoteip;
 char *host;
 sock_init();
 clrscr();
 printf ( "Waiting for connect\n\n" );
 if (argc < 2)
 {
    tcp_listen( &s, TCP_PORT, 0, 0, NULL, 0 );
       sock_mode( &s, TCP_MODE_BINARY );
       sock_wait_established( &s, 0, NULL, &status);
    printf ( "Press any key to begin" );
    getch();
    sock_write ( &s, &temp, sizeof ( temp ) );
    person = 1;
 }
 else
 {
    host = argv[1];
    if (!( remoteip = resolve( host )))
    {
       cprintf("\n\rUnable to resolve '%s'\n\r", host );
       exit( 3 );
 }
 if ( !tcp_open( &s, 0, remoteip, TCP_PORT, NULL ))
 {
       cputs("Unable to open connection.");
```

```
        exit( 1 );
    }
    sock_mode( &s, TCP_MODE_BINARY );
    sock_wait_established( &s, sock_delay,NULL, &status);
    sock_read ( &s, &temp, sizeof ( temp ));
    person = 0;
}
main_loop();
sock_close(&s);
sock_wait_closed ( &s, sock_delay, NULL, &status );
exit(0);
}
```

Adding WATTCP to ACK3D

With the capabilities of the WATTCP package, we can add Internet support
to our game. What we are adding is *support* to use the game over the
Internet. This support will only be available to those who have a direct connection to the Internet. This means that players must have a network card
installed in their computers and a connection to a gateway machine. They
will also have to have a valid IP address. The IP address is used to contact
players from anywhere on the Net. Those who are using a dial-up service
such as PPP will not be able to use the Internet support at this time.

   We will now look at taking the functions used to create our test program earlier in the chapter and putting them inside our simple program.

Global Variables

As in the test program, we will need a few global variables for our
Internet link. The first variable is a variable for the connection to our
opponent's machine. This variable

```
    tcp_Socket our_socket;
```

will be used throughout the Internet code.

   The remaining global variables are

```
word status;
longword remoteip;
char host[25];
```

   The variable remoteip will be used to hold an internal translation of
our opponent's IP. The variable host will be used to accept keyboard
input from the user. These variables should be placed at the top of the
MINOTAUR.c source code.

Error Function

We must include a function called sock_err() in any program that uses the WATTCP package. This function can be called by just about any of the functions within the WATTCP package. The main purpose of the function is to shut down the Internet link if the link has been cut by the other player or somewhere along the connection route. The code is:

```
void sock_err()
{
 //sock_err:
 switch ( status ) {
    case 1 : cputs("Connection closed");
        AckWrapUp();
        exit(1);
    break;
     case -1: cputs("REMOTE HOST CLOSED CONNECTION");
    sock_close ( &our_socket );
    sock_wait_closed ( &our_socket, sock_delay, NULL, &status );
    AckWrapUp();
    exit(1);
    break;
 }
}
```

Select_communication Function

The select_communication_device() function is where players select the connection link that they wish to use for this session. When we developed the code, we had already put in a case statement for the Internet connection. This case statement recognizes the I key. When the user selects the I key on the keyboard, we need to make sure that an Internet link is possible. This is where we will place the sock_init() function. This is the only function that needs to be set up before the program actually tries to create the link. The added code is:

```
 case 'I': com_device = 'i';
    sock_init();
    break;
```

Create_link Function

After the ability to create a link is set up, we can move to the next step and try the link. This code is basically the same as that used in our test program:

```
 case 'i': while (!got_one)
    {
```

```
clrscr();
printf ("Is this machine the originating or answering machine?\n");
printf (":");
ch = toupper(getkey());
printf ( "%c\n", ch);
if (ch=='A')
{
    tcp_listen( &our_socket, PORT, 0, 0, NULL, 0 );
    sock_mode( &our_socket, TCP_MODE_BINARY );
    sock_wait_established( &our_socket, 0, NULL, &status);
    got_one = 1;
}
else if (ch=='O')
{
    clrscr();
    printf ( "Enter IP Address of answering machine as
xxx:xxx:xxx:xxx\n");
    printf ( ":" );
    scanf ("%s", host);
    if (!( remoteip = resolve(host)))
    {
        cprintf("\n\rUnable to resolve '%s'\n\r", host );
        exit( 3 );
    }
    if ( !tcp_open( &our_socket, 0, remoteip, PORT, NULL ))
    {
        cputs("Unable to open connection.");
        exit( 1 );
    }
    sock_mode( &our_socket, TCP_MODE_BINARY );
    sock_wait_established( &our_socket, sock_delay, NULL, &status);
    got_one = 1;
}
}
break;
```

The code is added to the "i" case of the create_link() function. The
first detail that makes the code different from the code in our test program is that we have to determine which of the machines will be the originator and which will be the answerer. The originator will need to have the
IP address of the answerer in order to make the link between machines.

The second difference is the code

```
clrscr();
```

```
        printf ( "Enter IP Address of answering machine as
xxx:xxx:xxx:xxx\n");
        printf ( ":" );
        scanf ("%s", host);
```

This code asks for an IP address to be entered by the player. The IP address must be entered as a single string of characters such as 129.72.6.43. The string of characters is stored in the HOST variable.

Do_link Function

Once the link has been established between the two machines, the do_link() function must be executed. Recall that this function exchanges several values between machines in order to determine which of the machines will be Player 0 and which will be Player 1. We must add the following lines of code to the function:

```
if (com_device == 'i') sock_write (&our_socket, &ours, 1);


if (com_device =='i')
  if (sock_dataready (&our_socket))
  sock_read (&our_socket, &theirs, 1);
```

The first IF statement is placed with the IF statements for the "m," "n," and "e" cases in which a random number is sent to the other machine. The second IF statement is placed with the IF statements for receiving the random number from the other machine.

Keyboard Handling Function

We have initialized our Internet link, created the link, and exchanged information about which machine is which player. We are now ready to begin sending and receiving movement data between machines. The first thing we will consider is sending our movement data to the opponent. The code for sending a forward movement value to the other machine is:

```
        ch = 'a';
        if (com_device=='i')sock_write ( &our_socket, &ch, 1);
```

These two lines of code should be placed in the CASE UP part of the keyboard handling code. You will notice that we have to do a little bit more work to get the "a" character sent to the other machine. The reason for this is that the sock_write() function requires a memory address and the number of bytes to send from the memory address. We cannot simply use the function call

```
        sock_write(&our_socket, 'a', 1);
```

because the system will not be able to create a correct address for the "a" constant. So we must first put the character "a" in a character variable and send the function the address of the variable.

Processing Data

We must also be able to receive data from our opponent. Once we receive data from our opponent, we have to pass it to the process_communications() function in order for it to be processed. The code for receiving data from our opponent is

```
if (com_device == 'i')
   if ( sock_dataready ( &our_socket ) )
   {
   sock_read ( &our_socket, &ch, 1);
   process_communications(ch);
   }
```

This code should be placed in the main() function where we receive data from our opponent during a serial or ethernet link. The most important thing about this code is the sock_dataready() function. This function looks at the incoming data buffer for the TCP/IP link and determines whether or not data is available for us to access. If data is not available, then we don't want to call the sock_read() function.

Hangup Function

The last function that we have to consider changing is hangup(). In this function we need to add the code:

```
else if (com_device == 'i')
{
   sock_close (&our_socket);
   sock_wait_closed(&our_socket, sock_delay, NULL, &status);
}
```

to the end of the function code.

Conclusion

Adding Internet support to a game opens up a world of opportunities to players. Your players can now play the game with anyone in the world who has a direct Internet connection. In addition, you now have access to a TCP/IP Internet package that you can add to any of your own programs.

The following functions have been changed in our game code.

Main Code

```c
int main(void)
{
  int    result,
         done = 0,
         pan = 0;
  int    temp,
         packet_length;
  unsigned ch;
  if (select_communication_device())
  {
    printf ( "Error setting up communication device\n");
    return(1);
  }
  if (com_device != 's')
    if (create_link())
    {
        printf ("Error creating communication link\n");
        return(1);
    }
    if (result==AppInitialize())
    {
    printf("Error initializing: ErrorCode = %d\n",result);
    return(1);
    }
    if (result==AppSetupEngine())
    {
     printf("Error setting up ACK engine: ErrorCode = %d\n",result);
     AckWrapUp(ae);
     return(1);
  }
  if (result==AppLoadBitmaps())
  {
     printf("Error loading bitmaps: ErrorCode = %d\n",result);
     AckWrapUp(ae);
     return(1);
  }
  if (result==AppSetGraphics())
  {
     AckSetTextmode();
     printf("Error loading palette: ErrorCode = %d\n",result);
     AckWrapUp(ae);
```

```
          return(1);
      }
      if (result==AppSetObject())
      {
          AckSetTextmode();
          printf("Error loading palette: ErrorCode = %d\n",result);
          AckWrapUp(ae);
          return(1);
      }
      AppSetupPalRanges();
      //if person == 1 then we need to switch locations of us and opponent
      if (person)
      {
          temp = ae->ObjList[other_guy].x;
          ae->ObjList[other_guy].x = ae->xPlayer;
          ae->xPlayer = temp;
          temp = ae->ObjList[other_guy].y;
          ae->ObjList[other_guy].y = ae->yPlayer;
          ae->yPlayer = temp;
      }
      while (!done)
      {
          AckCheckObjectMovement(ae);
          if (pan)
          {
          pan = 0;
          if (ae->PlayerAngle >= INT_ANGLE_360)
              ae->PlayerAngle -= INT_ANGLE_360;
          if (ae->PlayerAngle < 0)
              ae->PlayerAngle += INT_ANGLE_360;
      }
      AppShow3D();
      if ((com_device == 'n') || (com_device == 'm'))
      {
        if ((!com_carrier(PORT)) && (!null_modem))
        {
        hangup();
        AckSetTextmode();
        printf("Lost communication link");
        AckWrapUp(ae);
        delay(5000);
        exit(1);
        }
```

```
            if (!com_rx_empty(PORT)) process_communications(com_rx(PORT));
    }
    if (com_device == 'i')
    if ( sock_dataready ( &our_socket ) )
    {
       sock_read ( &our_socket, &ch, 1);
       process_communications(ch);
    }
    if (bioskey(1))
    {
      ch = getkey();
      if (ch==ESC) break;
      switch(ch)
      {
       case LEFT : if ((com_device == 'n') || (com_device == 'm'))com_tx(PORT, 'd');
          if (com_device=='e')send_pkt (interrupt_number,d_packet, 64);
          ch = 'd';
          if (com_device=='i')sock_write ( &our_socket, &ch, 1);
          ae->PlayerAngle += (-INT_ANGLE_2 * 5);
          pan = 1;
          break;
       case RIGHT: if ((com_device == 'n') || (com_device == 'm'))com_tx(PORT, 'c');
          if (com_device=='e')send_pkt (interrupt_number,c_packet, 64);
          ch = 'c';
          if (com_device=='i')sock_write ( &our_socket, &ch, 1);
          ae->PlayerAngle += INT_ANGLE_2 * 5;
          pan = 1;
          break;
       case UP: if ((com_device == 'n') || (com_device == 'm'))com_tx(PORT, 'a');
          if (com_device=='e')send_pkt (interrupt_number,a_packet, 64);
           ch = 'a';
          if (com_device=='i')sock_write ( &our_socket, &ch, 1);
          AckMovePOV(ae,ae->PlayerAngle,16);
          break;
       case DOWN: if ((com_device == 'n') || (com_device == 'm'))com_tx(PORT, 'b');
          if (com_device=='e')send_pkt (interrupt_number,b_packet, 64);
           ch = 'b';
          if (com_device=='i')sock_write ( &our_socket, &ch, 1);
          temp= ae->PlayerAngle + INT_ANGLE_180;
          if (temp >= INT_ANGLE_360)
            temp -= INT_ANGLE_360;

          AckMovePOV(ae,temp,16);
```

```
        break;
    }
  }
 }
 AckWrapUp(ae);
 AckSetTextmode();
 return(0);
}
```

Select_communication_device

```
int select_communication_device()
{
 char ch;
 int result;
 while (!com_device)
 {
    clrscr();
    printf ("\n\n\n");
    printf ("Please select the communication medium that you would like to
use:\n\n");
    printf ("(E)thernet connection\n");
    printf ("(I)nternet connection\n");
    printf ("(N)ull Modem connection\n");
    printf ("(M)odem connection\n");
    printf ("(S)ingle User\n");
    printf (":");
    ch = getkey();
    printf ("%c\n", ch);
    switch (toupper(ch))
    {
     case 'E': com_device = 'e';
                p_type = 0x1234;
                set_type (p_type);
                find_driver(&interrupt_number);
                driver_info(interrupt_number, &handle, &version,
&driver_class, &ttype, &number, &basic );
                access_type (interrupt_number, &handle, driver_class,
ttype, number, p_type, 2);
                get_address (interrupt_number, handle);
                break;
     case 'I': com_device = 'i';
      sock_init();
      break;
```

```
        case 'N': com_device = 'n';
         result = setup_com();
         break;
        case 'M': com_device = 'm';
         result = setup_com();
         break;
        case 'S': com_device = 's';
         result = 0;
         break;
     }
   }
  return(result);
}
```

Create_link

```
int create_link()
{
 int got_one = 0, i, packet_length;
 char ch;
 switch(com_device)
 {
 case 'e': clrscr();
    printf ("Are we the (O)riginator or (A)nswerer?\n");
    printf (":");
    ch = toupper(getkey());
    printf ("%c\n", ch);
    if (ch == 'O')
    {
      for (i=0;i<6;i++)
       data_packet[6+i] = 0xff;
      data_packet[20] = 'x';
      send_pkt(interrupt_number, data_packet, 64);
      while (!get_from_queue(data_packet, &packet_length, 0))
       NULL;
      if (data_packet[20] == 'y')
      {
       for(i=0;i<6;i++)
         their_address[i] = data_packet[6+i];
       build_packets();
       do_link();
      }
    }
    else
```

```c
     {
       while (!get_from_queue(data_packet, &packet_length, 0))
        NULL;
       if (data_packet[20] == 'x')
       {
        data_packet[20] = 'y';
        for (i=0;i<6;i++)
         data_packet[i] = data_packet[6+i];
        for (i=0;i<6;i++)
         data_packet[i+6] = our_address[i];
        send_pkt(interrupt_number, data_packet, 64);
        build_packets();
        do_link();
       }
     }
     break;
case 'i': while (!got_one)
     {
       clrscr();
       printf ("Is this machine the originating or answering machine?\n");
       printf (":");
       ch = toupper(getkey());
       printf ( "%c\n", ch);
       if (ch=='A')
       {
        tcp_listen( &our_socket, TCP_PORT, 0, 0, NULL, 0 );
        sock_mode( &our_socket, TCP_MODE_BINARY );
        sock_wait_established( &our_socket, 0, NULL, &status);
        got_one = 1;
       }
       else if (ch=='O')
       {
        clrscr();
        printf ( "Enter IP Address of answering machine as xxx:xxx:xxx:xxx\n");
        printf ( ":" );
        scanf ("%s", host);
        if (!( remoteip = resolve(host)))
        {
         cprintf("\n\rUnable to resolve '%s'\n\r", host );
         exit( 3 );
        }
        if ( !tcp_open( &our_socket, 0, remoteip, TCP_PORT, NULL ))
        {
```

```c
            cputs("Unable to open connection.");
            exit( 1 );
         }
         sock_mode( &our_socket, TCP_MODE_BINARY );
         sock_wait_established( &our_socket, sock_delay, NULL, &status);
         got_one = 1;
         }
      }
   break;
case 'n': while (!got_one)
   {
      clrscr();
      printf ("Is this machine the originating or answering machine?\n");
      printf (":");
      ch = toupper(getkey());
      printf ("%c\n", ch);
      if (ch == 'O')
      {
       null_dial();
       got_one = 0;
      }
      if (ch == 'A')
      {
       null_answer();
       got_one = 0;
      }
   }
   return(1);
   break;
case 'm': while (!got_one)
   {
      clrscr();
      printf ("Is this machine the originating or answering machine?\n");
      printf (":");
      ch = toupper(getkey());
      printf ("%c\n", ch);
      if (ch == 'O')
      {
       dial();
       got_one = 0;
      }
      if (ch == 'A')
      {
```

```
        answer();
        got_one = 0;
      }
    }
    return(1);
    break;
  }
}
```

Do_link

```
void do_link()
{
 char ours, theirs, do_again = 1;
 int packet_length;
 randomize();
 while ( do_again )
 {
   do_again = 0;
   randomize();
   ours = random(50);
   if ((com_device == 'n') || (com_device == 'm')) com_tx(PORT, ours);
   if (com_device=='e')
   {
    data_packet[20] = ours;
    send_pkt (interrupt_number,d_packet, 64);
   }
   if (com_device == 'i') sock_write (&our_socket, &ours, 1);
   if ((com_device == 'n') || (com_device == 'm'))theirs=com_rx(PORT);
   if (com_device=='e')
   {
    while (!get_from_queue(data_packet, &packet_length, 0))
       NULL;
    theirs = data_packet[20];
  }
  if (com_device =='i')
    if (sock_dataready (&our_socket))
      sock_read (&our_socket, &theirs, 1);
    if (ours<theirs) person = 0;
    else person = 1;
    if (ours==theirs) do_again = 1;
 }
}
```

Hangup

```
void hangup()
{
 if (com_device == 'm')
 {
    com_lower_dtr(PORT);
    delay(1100);
    if (com_carrier(PORT))
    {
       com_tx_string_with_delay(PORT, "+++", 10, 10);
       delay(1100);
       com_tx(PORT, 13); delay(10);
       com_tx_string_with_delay(PORT, "ATH", 10, 10);
       com_tx(PORT, 13); delay(10);
    }
    com_flush_rx(PORT);
    com_flush_tx(PORT);
    busy = num_stored = null_modem = connected = 0;
 }
 else if (com_device == 'i')
 {
    sock_close (&our_socket);
    sock_wait_closed(&our_socket, sock_delay, NULL, &status);
 }
}
```

Sock_err

The sock_err function was added to our program.

```
void sock_err()
{
 //sock_err:
 switch ( status ) {
    case 1 : cputs("Connection closed");
      break;
    case -1: cputs("REMOTE HOST CLOSED CONNECTION");
      sock_close ( &our_socket );
      sock_wait_closed ( &our_socket, sock_delay, NULL, &status );
      break;
 }
}
```

CHAPTER 10

ADDING SUPPORT FOR THREE OR MORE PLAYERS

Enabling two people to play a single game over several different connection schemes is an achievement in itself. We can play our game with anyone around the entire world. We have our choice of several different connection links including serial, ethernet, and Internet. As we look toward the future, we see that using just two people in our game may be limiting. We should have the ability to connect more than two people. However, moving from a single connection with two people is far simpler than adding just one more opponent for a three-player game. In this chapter, we will look at some of the necessary code for adding more opponents.

Adding More Opponents

When we first developed our game, we only intended to support two players. In this scenario, we only have two machines that have to be kept aware of positions. When Player A moves, Player A's machine sends the necessary movement values to Player B's machine, and when Player B moves, Player A's machine receives its movement values and changes the position of the graphical figure object used to represent the opponent. This two-player scheme is shown in Figure 10.1.

Let's look at adding one more player. Figure 10.2 illustrates this situation. Here are just a few of the things that we have to concern ourselves with:

figure objects—For each of the opponents in our game, we need to have a graphical figure.

figure movements—As a player moves in the game, the movement

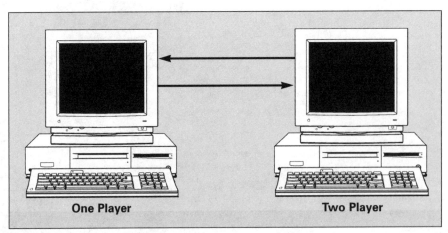

One Player   **Two Player**

Figure 10.1 Two-player scheme.

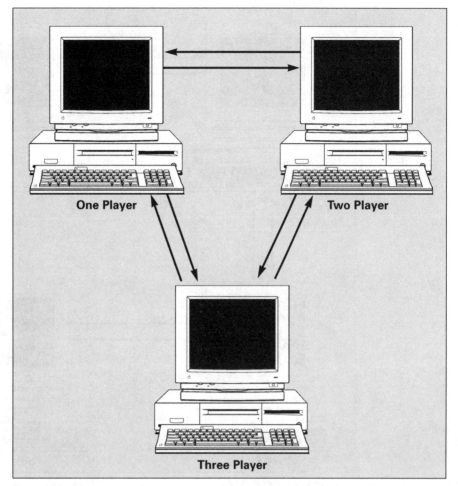

Figure 10.2 Three-player scheme.

information will have to be sent to *each* of the opponents' computers. In addition, we have to expect movement information *from* each of the opponents. When the information is received, the graphical figures have to be moved appropriately.

What happens with four players? As Figure 10.3 shows, for our four-player scheme, we need a total of six communication links. Each of the players will have to communicate with eight opponents, both receiving and transmitting. As you can see, the more players we add to our game, the more housekeeping has to be performed. In the remainder of the chapter, we will look at the specific components that we have to add to our game to allow for more players, and the necessary code that makes it happen.

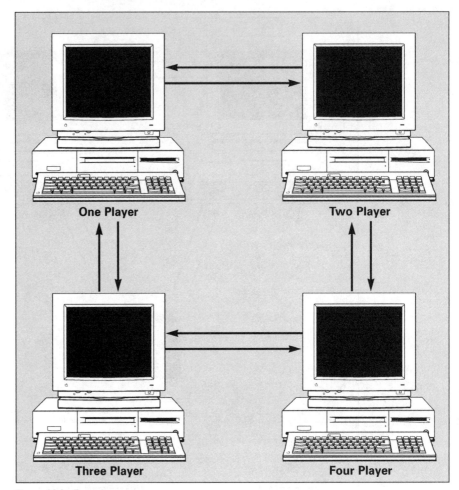

Figure 10.3 Four-player scheme.

Selecting the Link

To even think about adding additional opponents to our game, we have to look at how we are going to connect them. In the simplest situation, all of the computers will be in the same room and we can just connect them via their serial ports. But wait a minute—how are we going to connect three, four, or more computers via serial ports? We could use multiple serial ports in each of the computers, but this gets complicated—besides which, it requires that everyone playing is in one room. So we will not consider using serial ports for more than two players.

Now if we rule out the serial ports, what about the modem? We could use several modems in our machine for connecting more than two opponents. This really isn't a problem nowadays—many BBSs have many incoming lines using multiple modems. But, even if we have numerous modems in our computer, what about the phone lines? If we have two opponents, we will need two phone lines. Three opponents, three phone lines and three modems. This is getting a bit much. It's true that two phone lines aren't out of the ordinary, but three lines or four lines—! Well, I think we should drop the thought of using the modem for more than two players. This leaves us with the ethernet and the Internet. Both of these communication schemes are suited for accessing many connections to different locations at the same time. We will use these connections to build ourselves a multi-player game. As you will see in the next few sections, we are going to start with the cosmetics and then get into the interface coding.

Creating Representations of the Opponents

When we developed the two-player game, we had to include a graphical figure object for the opponent. The purpose of the figure object was to enable a player to know precisely where the opponent was at all times during game play. The same has to be true for a multiple-player game. Each and every opponent in the game must have a graphical figure object so that each player can keep track of them. We used a #define statement to create a constant value that we could use to access our single graphical figure in the two-player version:

```
#define other_guy 0
```

We will need to define several different constants for our many additional opponents. The constants could be something like

```
#define opponent_one 0
#define opponent_two 1
#define opponent_three 2
```

When writing a game for more than one opponent, we must be consistent with how we keep track of the graphical figure objects as well as any other variables we might use.

But wait a minute, how do we define all of these #define statements when we don't even know how many opponents there will be? Well, the answer is that we need to put a limit on the total number of people that are allowed in the game. We need the limit not only for memory concerns but also for some of the programming like the #define statements. Also, we have already seen that the more opponents we add, the more links we need between opponents. So, for the sake of argument, we will assume that we have a maximum of three opponents.

For each of the opponents, there absolutely must be a graphical figure object. Thus, we will need to have on hand three opponent objects, each of which will have four separate views. We could just use one graphical figure object for all of the opponents, so that all of the opponents would look the same. However, to make things look a bit more realistic, each of the opponents should look different—maybe a big muscular blond half-man, half-horse, a wizard, and a redheaded woman fighter. Each of these would be available to the other opponents.

We could enhance our game even more by developing eight or so graphical objects and giving each of the players the ability to pick which of the graphical objects they want to be represented as on the opponents' machines.

To read in all of our graphical figure objects, we need to add to the code in the function AppSetObject(). In addition, we need to add the specific bitmaps to the array at the beginning of our code. The code is shown as:

```
BMTABLE bmTable[] = {
  1  ,TYPE_WALL    ,"wall.lbm",
  1 ,TYPE_OBJECT ,"man1.lbm",
  2 ,TYPE_OBJECT ,"man2.lbm",
  3 ,TYPE_OBJECT ,"man3.lbm",
  4 ,TYPE_OBJECT ,"man4.lbm",
  -1 ,-1              ,""          /* End of table */
  };
```

To show how to expand our array, we will add bitmaps for three additional opponents. Our new bitmaps appear as:

```
BMTABLE bmTable[] = {
  1  ,TYPE_WALL    ,"wall.lbm",
  1 ,TYPE_OBJECT ,"opp11.lbm",
  2 ,TYPE_OBJECT ,"opp12.lbm",
  3 ,TYPE_OBJECT ,"opp13.lbm",
  4 ,TYPE_OBJECT ,"opp14.lbm",
  5 ,TYPE_OBJECT ,"opp21.lbm",
  6 ,TYPE_OBJECT ,"opp22.lbm",
  7 ,TYPE_OBJECT ,"opp23.lbm",
  8 ,TYPE_OBJECT ,"opp24.lbm",
  9 ,TYPE_OBJECT ,"opp31.lbm",
  10 ,TYPE_OBJECT ,"opp32.lbm",
  11 ,TYPE_OBJECT ,"opp33.lbm",
  12 ,TYPE_OBJECT ,"opp34.lbm",
  13 ,TYPE_OBJECT ,"opp41.lbm",
  14 ,TYPE_OBJECT ,"opp42.lbm",
```

```
15 ,TYPE_OBJECT ,"opp43.lbm",
16 ,TYPE_OBJECT ,"opp44.lbm",
-1 ,-1                ,""       /* End of table */
};
```

We now have all of the bitmaps for our opponents ready to be loaded.
Now we just change the AppSetObject to load the bitmaps and set up the
objects (see the following code). In the next section we will begin to look
at the code that will move them.

```
int AppSetObject(void)
{
 UCHAR bitmaps[3];
 int result;

//Load Opponent One
 bitmaps[0] = 1; bitmaps[1] = 3; bitmaps[2] = 2; bitmaps[3] = 4;
 ae->ObjList[other_guy].Flags |= OF_PASSABLE;
 ae->ObjList[other_guy].Speed = 1;
 ae->ObjList[other_guy].Dir = 0;
 AckCreateObject (ae, opponent_one, 4, bitmaps);

//Load Opponent Two
 bitmaps[0] = 5; bitmaps[1] = 7; bitmaps[2] = 6; bitmaps[3] = 8;
 ae->ObjList[other_guy].Flags |= OF_PASSABLE;
 ae->ObjList[other_guy].Speed = 1;
 ae->ObjList[other_guy].Dir = 0;
 AckCreateObject (ae, opponent_two, 4, bitmaps);

//Load Opponent Three
 bitmaps[0] = 9; bitmaps[1] = 11; bitmaps[2] = 10; bitmaps[3] = 12;
 ae->ObjList[other_guy].Flags |= OF_PASSABLE;
 ae->ObjList[other_guy].Speed = 1;
 ae->ObjList[other_guy].Dir = 0;
 AckCreateObject (ae, opponent_three, 4, bitmaps);

//Load Opponent Four
 bitmaps[0] = 13; bitmaps[1] = 15; bitmaps[2] = 14; bitmaps[3] = 16;
 ae->ObjList[other_guy].Flags |= OF_PASSABLE;
 ae->ObjList[other_guy].Speed = 1;
 ae->ObjList[other_guy].Dir = 0;
 AckCreateObject (ae, other_guy, 4, bitmaps);

 return(0);
}
```

Keeping Track of the Opponents Movements

The most important part of our two-player game is the communication between players. By adding more opponents, we just complicate things. We have to get information not only about our movements, but about the movements of all our opponents. To help things out, we will need to know up front how many people will be playing as opponents. This number will be held in a global variable defined as

```
int TOTAL_PLAYERS;
```

Now that we know how many people will be our opponents, we can begin getting connected to them. We must consider both ethernet connections and Internet connections. We will look at the Internet first, since it is easier.

In our two-player game, one of the players is the originator and one is the answerer. We are going to keep this type of setup for our multi-player game as well. This is how we want things to work:

- Select one machine as originator—all others are answerers
- Originator uses answerer IPs to create separate connections

The code for creating the links in our current program is located in the create_link() function. We are going to change this code and add three more global variables. The global variables that we are going to add will be used to keep our TCP/IP links separate. The code is:

```
tcp_Socket       *opponent_one_socket,
                 *opponent_two_socket,
                 *opponent_three_socket;
```

Once we have all of our global variables, we can look at the code in the create_link() function. The way the code works right now is that the machine that is the originator will take the IP address for the answerer machine and try to make a connection with it. Our new code should work the same way, except that we have up to three connections to make. We will present the originator's code in pseudo-code form:

```
For TOTAL_PLAYERS do
    Get player IP
    Establish connection
    Store connection information in appropriate
        opponent_one_socket (or two or three)
End Loop
```

The code for each of the connections looks just like the current code in the create_link() function. Once the originator has established all of the connections, it must inform all of the opponent machines of the other players in the game, since they will all have to communicate with each other. An algorithm for the originator is:

```
Send IP of opponent1 to all players
Send IP of opponent2 to all players
Send IP of opponent3 to all players
```

The algorithm for all of the opponents is:

```
Receive IP of opponent1
Receive IP of opponent2
Receive IP of opponent3

find which opponent IP is our own
create link with opponent
save as opponent_two_socket
create link with opponent
save as opponent_three_socket1
```

After all of the code has been formed, each of the players in the game will have three opponents, with their socket connections in the variables opponent_one_socket, opponent_two_socket, and opponent_three_socket.

Ethernet

The code for the ethernet is much like the Internet code. We used a broadcast packet to find the opponent in our two-player game. We will do the same thing in our multi-player game by sending out the number of broadcast packets equal to the number of opponents there will be in the game. The algorithm for the originator appears as:

```
for TOTAL_OPPONENTS
   send broadcast packet
   create link
end FOR
```

Once the originator code is finished, the originator is aware of all of the opponents and their ethernet addresses. Just as in the case of the Internet, once the originator has all of the addresses, it needs to send them to the opponents. The opponents will use the ethernet addresses to create a link with all of the other opponents, just as in the algorithm for the Internet.

Getting the Information

We now have all of the communication links with our opponents. The last step is to send and receive information between the players. When we send information to another computer, we need to make sure that our movement value is assigned to our graphical figure object. Thus, the receiving machines must be able to keep track of the movement values and who they came from. The Internet connection is easy, since each of the connections with the opponent computers has its own socket variable. We can just keep track of which socket variable we receive information from and make sure we update the appropriate graphical figure object.

For the ethernet connection, we don't have the luxury of different incoming variables. All of the information comes in from a single input buffer. To keep track of the incoming data, each of the opponents should be given a single value from the originator machine of the game. This number, such as 2, would be sent with each movement value. Each machine in the game would have a different value and therefore the appropriate object would be updated as different values came streaming in from the communication link.

 # Conclusion

As you can see, adding players to our two-player game entails a great deal of work. If you want to go beyond a two-player or four-player game, techniques other than those given here should be used, as we don't want to hold open eight, ten, or more connections to all the opponents. The most important thing to consider is keeping all of the information passing between all of the players up-to-date and accurate. In addition to the viewpoints and graphical figure objects, a multi-player game will have to consider all of the monsters in the game, as well as objects that are movable, like doors, and items to be picked up.

CHAPTER **11**

ADDING MONSTERS

How much fun would our game be without a couple of monsters in it? In this chapter, we'll look at the really fun stuff—adding two different types of monsters to our game. One of the monsters will fire acidballs, and the second monster will be moving around looking for someone to chop up with its axe. The two monsters give us very different ways of controlling them and determining their movements. In addition, we'll look at adding intelligence to our monsters to make them more worthy opponents.

 # The Medusa

The first monster that we are going to add will be a stationary medusa head that fires bullets at us. The head is a single bitmap that will be placed in one of the areas of the map. It will be firing bullets in a random fashion whenever a player approaches it.

As with the other objects that we have added to the game, the first step is to add the bitmap for the head to the global bitmap table. After the bitmap is added to the table, it will automatically be added to the game's bitmaps.

The next step is to create the medusa object using the bitmap. We create our objects in the AppCreateObject() function. For our medusa head, we have the following code:

```
bitmaps[0] = 8;
ae->ObjList[9].Flags = 0;
ae->ObjList[9].Speed = 0;
ae->ObjList[9].Dir = 0;
ae->ObjList[9].Active = 1;
AckCreateObject (ae, medusa, 1, bitmaps);
```

Notice that we are only using a single bitmap (shown in Figure 11.1) to represent the entire head.

Obviously, a "real" medusa head would be a three-dimensional object. Therefore, in our three-dimensional game, shouldn't we have different views of it? What happens when we go around to the back of the head?

Well, we could have three or more other views of the head so that you could go around the head and see the back, but would it really be necessary? The way the system works now is that when you move around the medusa head, you will always get to see the bitmap in Figure 11.1. It will appear that the head is always looking at you. No matter where you move, the medusa will be looking and firing spitballs at you.

Another reason for only using a single bitmap and having the same view all of the time is to save on memory. We will be pushing the limits of

Figure 11.1 Medusa head.

the conventional memory in our computer, and using only one bitmap reduces our memory requirements by 12 KB. We can use this 12 KB to create or animate another object.

Once we have the code for creating the object, we need to place the medusa head object in our map. We do this by first making an entry in our game's resource file and then using the map editor to place the object. The medusa object appears in our resource file as the bold text in the following code:

```
; Description file for ACK-3D demo program
Walls:
 Files:
 1 , wall.lbm
 60, roman3.lbm
 61, wall.lbm
 62, roman3.lbm
 EndFiles:
EndWalls:

Objects:
 Files:
 1, manf1.lbm
 2, manl1.lbm
 3, manb1.lbm
 4, manr1.lbm
 5, mon1.lbm
 6, ammocase.lbm
 7, bullet.lbm
 18, medusa.lbm
EndFiles:
```

```
;Other guy figure
Number: 1
Direction: 0
Speed: 1
Bitmaps: 1,2,3,4

Number: 2
Direction:180
Speed: 1
Bitmaps: 5

Number: 3
Direction: 0
Speed: 0
Bitmaps: 6

Number: 4
Direction: 0
Speed: 0
Bitmaps: 6

Number: 5
Direction: 0
Speed: 0
Bitmaps: 6

Number: 6
Direction: 0
Speed: 0
Bitmaps: 7

Number: 9
Direction: 0
Speed: 0
Bitmaps: 18
EndObjects:
MapFile: simple.MAP
PalFile: simple.PAL
; Palette ranges - starting color, number of colors
RANGE: 16,16
RANGE: 32,16
RANGE: 48,16
RANGE: 64,16
RANGE: 80,16
```

```
RANGE: 96,8
RANGE: 104,8
RANGE: 112,8
RANGE: 120,8
RANGE: 128,8
RANGE: 136,8
RANGE: 144,8
RANGE: 152,8
RANGE: 160,8
RANGE: 168,8
RANGE: 176,8
RANGE: 184,8
RANGE: 192,16
RANGE: 208,16
RANGE: 224,8
RANGE: 232,8
```

Using the resource file, execute the map editor. Remember to click on the large objects icon before placing the object in the map. Figure 11.2 shows what happens when we bring up the medusa head object in the map editor.

After we place the medusa head in the map, its object number will appear in one of the grid positions, as we see in Figure 11.3. If you

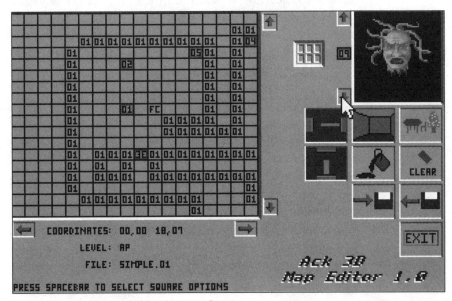

Figure 11.2 Medusa head object in map editor.

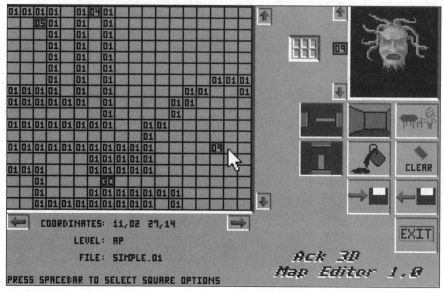

Figure 11.3 Medusa head placed in map.

thought of trying to place a couple of medusa heads in the map, and tried to click on a second grid position, you ran into a problem. The way that the ACK3D engine is set up only allows an object to be placed in one grid position. If you wanted to have another medusa head, you would need to create an entirely different object to handle the second head.

With the object placed in the map, we can move to the code that will allow the object to fire. We want the object to fire randomly and consistently. To start things off, we are going to create a global variable called is_shooting. This variable will be used in our main loop code to call the function monster_shooting(). The code will look like

```
if ((person==0)&&(is_shooting)) monster_shooting();
```

The statement can be placed anywhere in the main loop of the program, just so long as it is executed every loop. Now when the loop gets to our code, it will check to see whether the medusa head is currently firing a bullet—and whether we are currently person 0. This is something that we need to discuss. If we had both of the computers controlling the firing of the medusa head, then we would be doing double work. We can just have one computer doing the actual movement of the bullet, and it can inform the opponent's machine whenever the bullet moves. We will see this happen in the code to follow. If the head is firing, a call is made to the function monster_shooting(). The code for monster_shooting() is:

```
void monster_shoot()
{
```

```
   int result;
   result = AckMoveObjectPOV(ae, monster_bullet, ae-
:>ObjList[monster_bullet].Dir, ae->ObjList[monster_bullet].Speed);
   if ((com_device == 'n') || (com_device == 'm'))
   {
      com_tx(PORT, 'x');
      com_tx(PORT, ((ae->ObjList[monster_bullet].x & 0xFF00)>>8));
      com_tx(PORT, (ae->ObjList[monster_bullet].x & 0x00FF));
      com_tx(PORT, ((ae->ObjList[monster_bullet].y & 0xFF00)>>8));
      com_tx(PORT, (ae->ObjList[monster_bullet].y & 0x00FF));
   }
   if (com_device=='e')
   {
      data_packet[20] = 'x';
      data_packet[21] = (ae->ObjList[monster_bullet].x & 0xFF00)>>8;
      data_packet[22] = (ae->ObjList[monster_bullet].x & 0x00FF);
      data_packet[23] = (ae->ObjList[monster_bullet].y & 0xFF00)>>8;
      data_packet[24] = ae->ObjList[monster_bullet].y & 0x00FF;
      send_pkt (interrupt_number,data_packet, 64);
   }
   if (result != POV_NOTHING)
   {
      ae->ObjList[monster_bullet].Active = 0;
      monster_shooting = 0;
      result = AckGetObjectHit();
      if (result == POV_PLAYER)
      {
         ammo = 0;
         if ((com_device == 'n') || (com_device == 'm')) com_tx(PORT, 'o');
         AckFadeOut(0, 255);
         reset_game();
         AckFadeIn(0, 255, colordat);
         AckDeleteObject(ae, other_guy);
         AckDeleteObject(ae, other_guy_bullet);
   }
   if (com_device=='e')
   {
      data_packet[20] = 'o';
      send_pkt (interrupt_number,data_packet, 64);
   }
}
else if (result == POV_OBJECT)
{
```

```
    ae->ObjList[other_guy].Active = 0;
    if ((com_device == 'n') || (com_device == 'm')) com_tx(PORT, 'w');
    if (com_device=='e')
    {
     data_packet[20] = 'w';
     send_pkt (interrupt_number,data_packet, 64);
    }
    AckFadeOut(0, 255);
    reset_game();
    AckFadeIn(0, 255, colordat);
}
if (monster_shooting == 0)
{

    monster_shooting = 1;
    ae->ObjList[monster_bullet].x = ae->ObjList[medusa].x;
    ae->ObjList[monster_bullet].y = ae->ObjList[medusa].y;
    ae->ObjList[monster_bullet].Dir = random (INT_ANGLE_360);
    ae->ObjList[monster_bullet].mPos = (ae->ObjList[monster_bullet].y &
0xFFC0) + (ae->ObjList[monster_bullet].x >> 6);
    ae->ObjList[monster_bullet].VidRow = 100;
    ae->ObjList[monster_bullet].Active = 1;
 }
}
```

The code for this function starts out by moving the bullet forward in the
game. Notice that we get the results of the move and put it in the variable
result. This is very important, since we need to see if the bullet hits anything.

Next, we tell our opponent where the bullet currently is in the map. This
is the point where instead of sending a character, as we do when we move
our player using the keyboard or joystick, we are going to send the actual x
and y location of the bullet. Since we are using bytes to send information
back and forth between the computers, we have to translate, or pick apart,
each of the x and y locations because they are integers In other words, if we
have the decimal value 1, this is represented in hexidecimal as 0x0001. Since
we can only send 8-bit values over our communication lines, we have to send
the value 00 and then the value 01. These values will be received and translated back into the decimal value 1 by the reciving machine. The first part of
this translation code takes the top byte of the integer and shifts it down to
the lower byte. This lower byte is then sent to the opponent. The second
part of the translation code takes the lower part of the integer and sends it to
the opponent. As we will see in a moment, the opponent must put the integers back together. We also use a character "x" to indicate to the other computer exactly what the information it is receiving should be used for.

After moving the bullet and sending the necessary information to the other computer, we make a quick check to see if the bullet has hit anything. If the code

```
if (result != POV_NOTHING)
```

is evaluated as true, then we know that the bullet has hit something. At this point, we deactivate the bullet on both our machine and our opponent's machine.

Once the bullet is deactivated, we check the value of the result variable. If the result variable is equal to POV_PLAYER, then we change the value of our ammo to 0. If the result variable is equal to POV_OBJECT, then we know that the opponent was hit by the bullet. In this case, we deactivate the opponent's object on our machine and send a character code to the opponent letting the opponent know that he or she has been shot.

In both cases, we also reset the game. This indicates that one of the players was killed and the game should start over. To reset the game, we do a few things. First note the code we are using:

```
AckFadeOut(0, 255);
reset_game();
AckFadeIn(0, 255, colordat);
```

The first line of code is an ACK3D internal function. It takes the current palette used in the game and cycles all of the colors to black. This has the effect of slowly blanking out the screen. After the screen has gone to black, we have a call to the function reset_game(). This function is defined as

```
void reset_game()
{
// Reset player
ae->xPlayer = player_start_x;
ae->yPlayer = player_start_y;
ae->PlayerAngle = player_start_angle;
// Reset medusa monster1
ae->ObjList[monster1].x = monster_start_x;
ae->ObjList[monster1].y = monster_start_y;
ae->ObjList[monster1].Dir = monster_start_angle;
ae->ObjList[monster1].mPos = (ae->ObjList[monster1].y & 0xFFC0) + (ae-
>ObjList[monster1].x >> 6);
ae->ObjList[monster1].Active = 1;
// Reset opponent monster
ae->ObjList[other_guy].x = opponent_start_x;
ae->ObjList[other_guy].y = opponent_start_y;
ae->ObjList[other_guy].Dir = opponent_start_angle;
```

```
ae->ObjList[other_guy].mPos = (ae->ObjList[other_guy].y & 0xFFC0) + (ae-
>ObjList[other_guy].x >> 6);
ae->ObjList[other_guy].Active = 1;
// Put all of the ammo cans back on screen
ae->ObjList[3].Active = 1;
ae->ObjList[4].Active = 1;
ae->ObjList[5].Active = 1;
// Reset total ammo we are carrying
ammo = 5;
}
```

This function sets all of the objects and our player back to their original positions. The original positions were recorded into several variables at the start of the game. In the main() function, just before we enter our main_loop, we have the following code:

```
//Get starting positions
player_start_x = ae->xPlayer;
player_start_y = ae->yPlayer;
player_start_angle = ae->PlayerAngle;
opponent_start_x = ae->ObjList[other_guy].x;
opponent_start_y = ae->ObjList[other_guy].y;
opponent_start_angle = ae->ObjList[other_guy].Dir;
monster_start_x = ae->ObjList[monster1].x;
monster_start_y = ae->ObjList[monster1].y;
monster_start_angle = ae->ObjList[monster1].Dir;
```

This code records the exact positions of the player, the opponent, and the medusa monster. These are the only objects in the game that have movement. Once all of the objects are placed into their original positions, we fade the screen back to its original palette and start the game over again.

That's it for the medusa head. When you are designing a game yourself, you should make the result of the bullet greater than just decreasing the ammo and fading the screen. You should let the player (as well his or her opponent) know that he or she has been shot. The obvious way to indicate that someone has been shot is to have the body slump to the floor. This can be accomplished using several different objects and placing them at the point the object died.

The Minotaur

The medusa head wasn't a very difficult object because it doesn't move around. It is stationary and just keeps firing in random patterns. Our second monster is different. This monster, a Minotaur, is a walking nightmare. He holds an axe in his hand and his goal is to slice you up.

Since the Minotaur is a moving creature, we will have many more bitmaps than just one. The bitmaps that we are going to be using are:

      mino1.lbm — Initial position of legs—front view
      mino2.lbm — Standing positon—front view
      mino3.lbm — Ending position of legs—front view

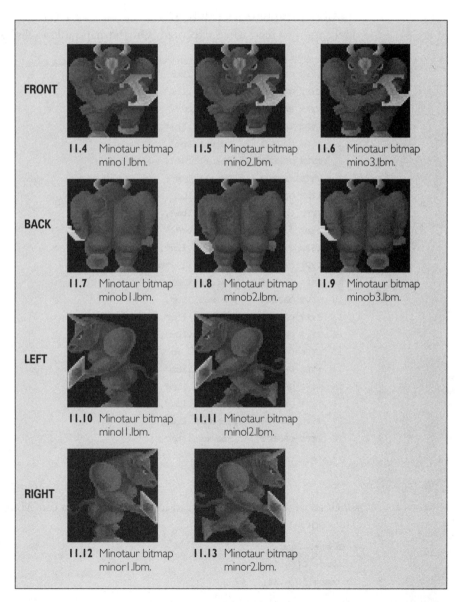

FRONT

11.4 Minotaur bitmap mino1.lbm.

11.5 Minotaur bitmap mino2.lbm.

11.6 Minotaur bitmap mino3.lbm.

BACK

11.7 Minotaur bitmap minob1.lbm.

11.8 Minotaur bitmap minob2.lbm.

11.9 Minotaur bitmap minob3.lbm.

LEFT

11.10 Minotaur bitmap minol1.lbm.

11.11 Minotaur bitmap minol2.lbm.

RIGHT

11.12 Minotaur bitmap minor1.lbm.

11.13 Minotaur bitmap minor2.lbm.

minob1.lbm— Initial position of legs—back view

minob2.lbm— Standing position—back view

minob3.lbm— Ending position of legs—back view

minol1.lbm — Left leg forward/right left back—left view

minol2.lbm — Left leg back/right leg forward—left view

minor1.lbm — Left leg forward/right leg back—right view

minor2.lbm — Left leg back/right leg forward—right view

The bitmaps are shown in Figures 11.4 through 11.13.2

All of these bitmaps will be placed in our global bitmap table for the application to read when executed. Our bitmap table looks like:

```
BMTABLE bmTable[] = {
   1 ,TYPE_WALL       ,"wall.lbm",
  60 ,TYPE_WALL       ,"roman3.lbm",
  61 ,TYPE_WALL       ,"wall.lbm",
  62 ,TYPE_WALL       ,"roman3.lbm",
   1 ,TYPE_OBJECT     ,"manb1.lbm",
   2 ,TYPE_OBJECT     ,"manf1.lbm",
   3 ,TYPE_OBJECT     ,"manl1.lbm",
   4 ,TYPE_OBJECT     ,"manr2.lbm",
   5 ,TYPE_OBJECT     ,"mino1.lbm",
   6 ,TYPE_OBJECT     ,"ammo.lbm",
   7 ,TYPE_OBJECT     ,"bullet.lbm",
   8 ,TYPE_OBJECT     ,"spitball.lbm",
   9 ,TYPE_OBJECT     ,"mino2.lbm",
  10 ,TYPE_OBJECT     ,"mino3.lbm",
  11 ,TYPE_OBJECT     ,"minob1.lbm",
  12 ,TYPE_OBJECT     ,"minob2.lbm",
  13 ,TYPE_OBJECT     ,"minob3.lbm",
  14 ,TYPE_OBJECT     ,"minol1.lbm",
  15 ,TYPE_OBJECT     ,"minol2.lbm",
  16 ,TYPE_OBJECT     ,"minor1.lbm",
  17 ,TYPE_OBJECT     ,"minor2.lbm",
  18 ,TYPE_OBJECT     ,"medusa.lbm",
  -1 ,-1              ,""          /* End of table */
  };
```

Once all of the bitmaps are read in, we must set up our Minotaur object. The code to do this is:

```
//Monster Load
 bitmaps[0] = 11;
 bitmaps[1] = 14;
```

```
bitmaps[2] = 5;
bitmaps[3] = 16;
ae->ObjList[monster1].Speed = 1;
ae->ObjList[monster1].Dir = INT_ANGLE_90;
AckCreateObject (ae, monster1, 4, bitmaps);
```

Using the positions of the bitmaps in our table, we can set up the object
and its initial views.

After the object is created, it's time to give the monster intelligence
and movement. The goal of the Minotaur is to hunt you down and chop
you up. We will need a routine that does the movement. This routine is
called move_monsters(). As in the case of the medusa object, only the
code for one player, Player 0, will actually be controlling the monster.

In our main loop we have the code

```
if (player==0) move_monsters();
```

The move_monsters() function is:

```
void move_monsters()
{
  int x1, y1, x, y, px, py, dx, dy, angle, result, dx1, dy1;
 monster_moves++;
 if (ae->ObjList[monster1].Active == 1)
 {
    x = ae->ObjList[monster1].x;
    y = ae->ObjList[monster1].y;
    x1 = ae->ObjList[other_guy].x;
    y1 = ae->ObjList[other_guy].y;
    px = ae->xPlayer;
    py = ae->yPlayer;
    dx = abs(px - x);
    dy = abs(py - y);
 if(com_device != 's')
 {
    dx1 = abs(px - x1);
    dy1 = abs(py - y1);
    if (dx1 < dx)
    {
       dx = dx1;
       dy = dy1;
       x = x1;
       y = y1;
    }
 }
```

```
        if (dx > dy)
           py = y;
        if (dx < dy)
           px = x;
        if (py == y)
        {
           if (px < x) angle = INT_ANGLE_180;
           if (px > x) angle = 0;
        }
        if (px == x)
        {
           if (py < y) angle = INT_ANGLE_270;
           if (py > y) angle = INT_ANGLE_90;
        }
        if (monster_moves == 7) monster_moves = 0;
        if (angle == 0)
        {
           if (monster_moves == 3)
           {
              ae->ObjList[monster1].bmNum[0] = 11;
              ae->ObjList[monster1].bmNum[1] = 14;
              ae->ObjList[monster1].bmNum[2] = 5;
              ae->ObjList[monster1].bmNum[3] = 16;
           }
           else if (monster_moves == 6)
           {
              ae->ObjList[monster1].bmNum[0] = 13;
              ae->ObjList[monster1].bmNum[1] = 15;
              ae->ObjList[monster1].bmNum[2] = 10;
              ae->ObjList[monster1].bmNum[3] = 17;
           }
        }
        else if (angle == INT_ANGLE_90)
        {
           if (monster_moves == 3)
           {
              ae->ObjList[monster1].bmNum[0] = 16;
              ae->ObjList[monster1].bmNum[1] = 11;
              ae->ObjList[monster1].bmNum[2] = 14;
              ae->ObjList[monster1].bmNum[3] = 5;
           }
           else if (monster_moves == 6)
           {
```

```
         ae->ObjList[monster1].bmNum[0] = 17;
         ae->ObjList[monster1].bmNum[1] = 13;
         ae->ObjList[monster1].bmNum[2] = 15;
         ae->ObjList[monster1].bmNum[3] = 10;
      }
   }
   else if (angle == INT_ANGLE_180)
   {
      if (monster_moves == 3)
      {
         ae->ObjList[monster1].bmNum[0] = 5;
         ae->ObjList[monster1].bmNum[1] = 16;
         ae->ObjList[monster1].bmNum[2] = 11;
         ae->ObjList[monster1].bmNum[3] = 14;
      }
      else if (monster_moves == 6)
      {
         ae->ObjList[monster1].bmNum[0] = 10;
         ae->ObjList[monster1].bmNum[1] = 17;
         ae->ObjList[monster1].bmNum[2] = 13;
         ae->ObjList[monster1].bmNum[3] = 15;
      }
   }
   else
   {
      if (monster_moves == 3)
      {
         ae->ObjList[monster1].bmNum[0] = 14;
         ae->ObjList[monster1].bmNum[1] = 5 ;
         ae->ObjList[monster1].bmNum[2] = 16;
         ae->ObjList[monster1].bmNum[3] = 11;
      }
      else if (monster_moves == 6)
      {
         ae->ObjList[monster1].bmNum[0] = 15;
         ae->ObjList[monster1].bmNum[1] = 10;
         ae->ObjList[monster1].bmNum[2] = 17;
         ae->ObjList[monster1].bmNum[3] = 13;
      }
   }
   ae->ObjList[monster1].Active = 1;
   ae->ObjList[monster1].Dir = angle;
   result = AckMoveObjectPOV(ae,monster1,ae-:>ObjList[monster1].Dir,ae-
```

```
      >ObjList[monster1].Speed);
    if ((com_device == 'n') || (com_device == 'm'))
    {
        com_tx(PORT,  'y');
        com_tx(PORT, ((ae->ObjList[monster1].x & 0xFF00)>>8));
        com_tx(PORT, (ae->ObjList[monster1].x & 0x00FF));
        com_tx(PORT, ((ae->ObjList[monster1].y & 0xFF00)>>8));
        com_tx(PORT, (ae->ObjList[monster1].y & 0x00FF));
        com_tx(PORT, ((ae->ObjList[monster1].Dir & 0xFF00)>>8));
        com_tx(PORT, (ae->ObjList[monster1].Dir & 0x00FF));
    }
    if (com_device=='e')
    {
        data_packet[20] = 'y';
        data_packet[21] = (ae->ObjList[monster1].x & 0xFF00)>>8;
        data_packet[22] = (ae->ObjList[monster1].x & 0x00FF);
        data_packet[23] = (ae->ObjList[monster1].y & 0xFF00)>>8;
        data_packet[24] = ae->ObjList[monster1].y & 0x00FF;
        data_packet[25] = (ae->ObjList[monster1].Dir & 0xFF00)>>8;
        data_packet[26] = ae->ObjList[monster1].Dir & 0x00FF;
        send_pkt (interrupt_number,data_packet, 64);
    }
    if (result == POV_PLAYER)
    {
        ammo = 0;
        if ((com_device == 'n') || (com_device == 'm')) com_tx(PORT, 'o');
        if (com_device=='e')
        {
            data_packet[20] = 'o';
            send_pkt (interrupt_number,data_packet, 64);
        }
        AckFadeOut(0, 255);
        reset_game();
        AckFadeIn(0, 255, colordat);
        AckDeleteObject(ae, other_guy);
        AckDeleteObject(ae, other_guy_bullet);
    }
    else if (result == POV_OBJECT)
    {
        AckDeleteObject(ae, other_guy);
        AckDeleteObject(ae, other_guy_bullet);
        AckFadeOut(0, 255);
        reset_game();
```

```
    AckFadeIn(0, 255, colordat);

    if ((com_device == 'n') || (com_device == 'm')) com_tx(PORT, 'w');

    if (com_device=='e')
    {
        data_packet[20] = 'w';
        send_pkt (interrupt_number,data_packet, 64);
    }
  }
 }
}
```

Most of the work for giving our monster some intelligence and movement is in the first part of this function. We begin by getting the current location of the player, the opponent, and the monster. We then measure the distance between the current location of the monster and the player as well as between the monster and the opponent.

If we are using the system in a multi-player mode, we allow the monster to chase either the player or the opponent, depending upon which is closer to the monster. The monster's direction will change depending on where the player or opponent is located.

The next part of the code does the actual animation of the monster. We have three different positions available to the monster. Each time the function move_monsters( ) is called, the global variable monster_move is incremented. When the variable is 3, 6, or 9, the monster is put into one of the three different positions. These positions give the illusion that the monster is running.

After the monster is put into one of the three positions, it is moved with the AckMoveObjectPOV routine, and the result of the function is put in the result variable. After the monster is moved, we send the coordinates of its new position to the opponent's machine.

Once both of the machines haved moved the monster, we have to check to see if the Minotaur has chopped us into pieces. We do this by looking at the result value that was returned when we moved the monster. If the result value is equal to POV_PLAYER, then the Minotaur has chopped us up. We put the ammo variable to 0 and send a character to the other machine, letting it know that it should remove our graphical figure from the playing screen.

Opponent Reception

Everything that we have done so far occurs in our machine and not the opponent's. As we noted earlier, only Player 0 handles the movement of the Minotaur. We will have to transmit a number of things to the opponent machine. Let's look at each of the monsters.

Medusa

The medusa has two actions: she fires a spitball, and then she determines if the spitball has hit an object. We have to first tell the opponent that she is getting ready to fire a new spitball. We do this by transmitting the letter "x" followed by the x,y position of the bullet's starting point.

```
if (com_device=='e')
  {
    data_packet[20] = 'x';
    data_packet[21] = (ae->ObjList[monster_bullet].x & 0xFF00)>>8;
    data_packet[22] = (ae->ObjList[monster_bullet].x & 0x00FF);
    data_packet[23] = (ae->ObjList[monster_bullet].y & 0xFF00)>>8;
    data_packet[24] = ae->ObjList[monster_bullet].y & 0x00FF;
    send_pkt (interrupt_number,data_packet, 64);
  }
```

The opponent receives the letter "x" and sends it to the process_communications() function. In this function, the following code receives and processes the position of the spitball:

```
case 'x': if ((com_device == 'm') || (com_device == 'n'))
    {
      ae->ObjList[monster_bullet].x = (com_rx(PORT)<<8)+(com_rx(PORT));
      ae->ObjList[monster_bullet].y = (com_rx(PORT)<<8)+(com_rx(PORT));
    }
    if(com_device == 'e')
    {
      ae->ObjList[monster_bullet].x = (get_packet[21] << 8)+get_packet[22];
      ae->ObjList[monster_bullet].y = (get_packet[23] << 8)+get_packet[24];
    }
    ae->ObjList[monster_bullet].mPos = ((ae->ObjList[monster_bullet].y &
0xFFC0) + (ae->ObjList[monster_bullet].x >> 6));
    ae->ObjList[monster_bullet].VidRow = 100;
    ae->ObjList[monster_bullet].Active = 1;
    break;
```

Notice that we have to do different things depending on whether the connection between the players is a modem/serial port or an ethernet. The Internet connection is shown in the code specific to the Internet connection—MINOINTR.c. Once the x and y positions are extracted from the information sent by Player 0, the spitball object is placed at the appropriate position on the opponent's screen.

Every time Player 0's machine executes the code for keeping track of the medusa's spitball, it will send the letter "x" to the opponent so that each machine has a spitball moving at the same time. In addition to moving the spitball, the medusa code will check to see if the spitball has hit either of the players. If a spitball has hit Player 0, the code will send the letter "o" to the opponent. The process_communications function will process the "o" with the code

```
case 'o': AckDeleteObject(ae, other_guy);
    AckDeleteObject(ae, other_guy_bullet);
    AckFadeOut(0, 255);
    reset_game();
    AckFadeIn(0, 255, colordat);
    break;
```

Since it is Player 0 that has been killed, the graphical object that is representing Player 0 is removed from the opponent's screen. We also reset the game at this point and start over.

The medusa head can also kill the opponent. If the opponent is killed, the code sends the letter "w" to the opponent's machine. Upon reception, the following code is executed:

```
case 'w': ammo = 0;
    AckFadeOut(0, 255);
    reset_game();
    AckFadeIn(0, 255, colordat);
    break;
```

As you can see, this looks like the code for the letter "o" except that it doesn't remove the graphical representation of Player 0.

Minotaur

Now it's time to take a look at the Minotaur. The code for determining and sending a character upon a kill by the Minotaur is the same as that for the medusa head. The real difference between the two monsters is that the Minotaur can move. Each time the Minotaur moves, the opponent must be informed. This is done by transmitting the character "y" to the opponent. The code that does the transmitting is

```
if ((com_device == 'n') || (com_device == 'm'))
{
    com_tx(PORT, 'y');
    com_tx(PORT, ((ae->ObjList[monster1].x & 0xFF00)>>8));
    com_tx(PORT, (ae->ObjList[monster1].x & 0x00FF));
```

```
   com_tx(PORT, ((ae->ObjList[monster1].y & 0xFF00)>>8));
   com_tx(PORT, (ae->ObjList[monster1].y & 0x00FF));
   com_tx(PORT, ((ae->ObjList[monster1].Dir & 0xFF00)>>8));
   com_tx(PORT, (ae->ObjList[monster1].Dir & 0x00FF));
}
```

In addition to the letter "y," we also send the x and y coordinates of the Minotaur. The opponent receives the letter "y" and processes it with the code

```
case 'y': if ((com_device == 'm') || (com_device == 'n'))
 {
    ae->ObjList[monster1].x = (com_rx(PORT)<<8)+(com_rx(PORT));
    ae->ObjList[monster1].y = (com_rx(PORT)<<8)+(com_rx(PORT));
    ae->ObjList[monster1].Dir = (com_rx(PORT)<<8)+(com_rx(PORT));
 }
 if (com_device=='e')
 {
    ae->ObjList[monster1].x = (get_packet[21] << 8)+get_packet[22];
    ae->ObjList[monster1].y = (get_packet[23] << 8)+get_packet[24];
    ae->ObjList[monster1].Dir = (get_packet[25] << 8)+get_packet[26];
}
      angle = ae->ObjList[monster1].Dir;
// Just as in the case of the opponent, the minotaur monster has animation
// in its movements. We have to change the bitmaps accordingly.
 if (++monster_moves == 7) monster_moves = 0;
 if (angle == 0)
 {
    if (monster_moves == 3)
    {
      ae->ObjList[monster1].bmNum[0] = 11;
      ae->ObjList[monster1].bmNum[1] = 14;
      ae->ObjList[monster1].bmNum[2] = 5;
      ae->ObjList[monster1].bmNum[3] = 16;
    }
    else if (monster_moves == 6)
    {
      ae->ObjList[monster1].bmNum[0] = 13;
      ae->ObjList[monster1].bmNum[1] = 15;
      ae->ObjList[monster1].bmNum[2] = 10;
      ae->ObjList[monster1].bmNum[3] = 17;
    }
 }
    else if (angle == INT_ANGLE_90)
```

```
{
   if (monster_moves == 3)
   {
      ae->ObjList[monster1].bmNum[0] = 16;
      ae->ObjList[monster1].bmNum[1] = 11;
      ae->ObjList[monster1].bmNum[2] = 14;
      ae->ObjList[monster1].bmNum[3] = 5;
   }
   else if (monster_moves == 6)
   {
      ae->ObjList[monster1].bmNum[0] = 17;
      ae->ObjList[monster1].bmNum[1] = 13;
      ae->ObjList[monster1].bmNum[2] = 15;
      ae->ObjList[monster1].bmNum[3] = 10;
   }
}
else if (angle == INT_ANGLE_180)
{
   if (monster_moves == 3)
   {
      ae->ObjList[monster1].bmNum[0] = 5;
      ae->ObjList[monster1].bmNum[1] = 16;
      ae->ObjList[monster1].bmNum[2] = 11;
      ae->ObjList[monster1].bmNum[3] = 14;
   }
   else if (monster_moves == 6)
   {
      ae->ObjList[monster1].bmNum[0] = 10;
      ae->ObjList[monster1].bmNum[1] = 17;
      ae->ObjList[monster1].bmNum[2] = 13;
      ae->ObjList[monster1].bmNum[3] = 15;
   }
}
else
{
   if (monster_moves == 3)
   {
      ae->ObjList[monster1].bmNum[0] = 14;
      ae->ObjList[monster1].bmNum[1] = 5 ;
      ae->ObjList[monster1].bmNum[2] = 16;
      ae->ObjList[monster1].bmNum[3] = 11;
   }
   else if (monster_moves == 6)
```

```
    {
        ae->ObjList[monster1].bmNum[0] = 15;
        ae->ObjList[monster1].bmNum[1] = 10;
        ae->ObjList[monster1].bmNum[2] = 17;
        ae->ObjList[monster1].bmNum[3] = 13;
    }
}
ae->ObjList[monster1].mPos = ((ae->ObjList[monster1].y & 0xFFC0) + (ae-
>ObjList[monster1].x >> 6));
ae->ObjList[monster1].Active = 1;
break;
```

As you can see, the opponent's machine has a great deal of work to do each time it receives the letter "y." This code does exactly the same thing that Player 0's machine does each time the Minotaur moves. It must determine which bitmaps should make up the Minotaur at this particular moment. The bitmaps are determined based on the direction that the Minotaur is facing and the step it is currently on. Each time the Minotaur moves, we have to change position of the feet so that it looks like the Minotaur is actually walking as it moves.

Intelligence

Now that you have seen the development of two rather simple monsters, let's discuss intelligence. The Minotaur monster we created has a limited amount of intelligence. You will notice that it can lock onto a person and

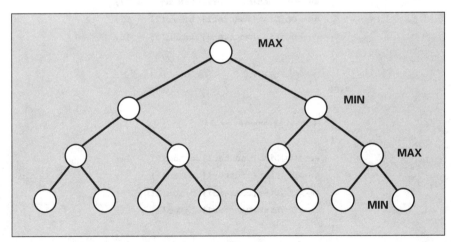

Figure 11.14 Basic minmax tree.

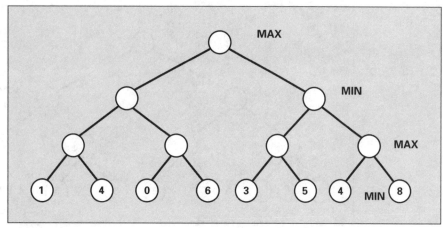

Figure 11.15 Minmax tree with assigned values.

move toward the person. In addition, the Minotaur is able to determine which of the players is closer to it. It will generally move toward the closer player.

This system works well enough, but what if you want to create a commercial game with objects that are very smart? This last part of our monster chapter will introduce to you the concept of *minmax*, which is used in many strategy games. Using a tree of possible moves, we are able to create a monster that can move anywhere with great confidence.

Tree

The first thing that we have to do is create a tree based on possible moves. The tree is shown in Figure 11.14. It consists of 15 nodes and four levels. Each of the levels is described as either MIN or MAX. The object of minmax is to either MINimize or MAXimize the point possible at each level. Let's add some values to our minmax tree. All of the leaf nodes (nodes at the bottom of the tree) will indicate possible point values assigned the movements of the monster in our game. With point values assigned to specific movements, we have the tree shown in Figure 11.15.

What the numbers will represent is not important here, but just for sake of clarity, we could say that specific numbers represent movement in a particular direction. Now, it should be obvious that when the monster moves, he wants to maximize his movement toward us, and when we are moving we will generally want to minimize our movement away from the monster. The minmax tree takes this into consideration. We first propagate the movement number up to the next (maximize) level. We do this by just picking the best number on the left part of the tree, as shown in Figure 11.16.

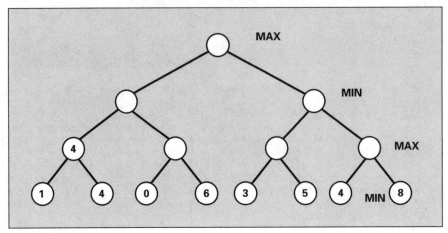

Figure 11.16 First move.

Now we move the max number (4) up to the min level. What we want to do is select the minimum number from both of the left and right child nodes of the current min node. Since we don't know what the right number is, we have to go down this path and find out what it is. Since the right node is a max, we choose the max of the two leaf nodes for Figure 11.17.

Now we can fully evaluate the minimize node for the value 4. This value is sent to the root maximize node. We now do the same operations on the right part of the tree to obtain the final tree, shown in Figure 11.18.

We see that the best move possible will be the value 5. This selection is based on the possible moves by the object we are tracking.

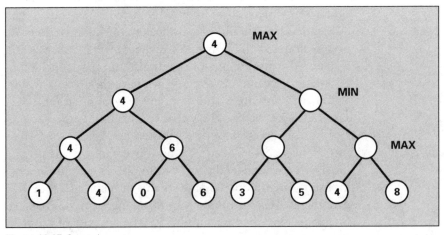

Figure 11.17 Second move.

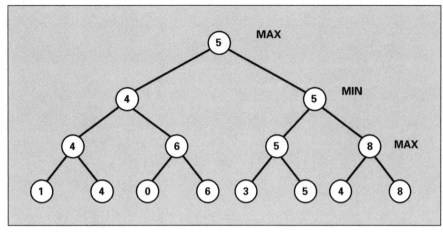

Figure 11.18 Final tree.

In a real application, the trees can get quite large. Most chess programs use a form of minmax called alpha-beta which performs additional operations to cut down on the amount of work necessary in the tree.

 # Conclusion

Adding monsters to our game is the fun part. We have the freedom to come up with very interesting creations. The ACK3D system lets you add just about any type of monster you can think up.

ADDING SOUND

One of the more enjoyable parts of any game is hearing the music. Whether it's background music or sound effects added to certain movements, sound adds something to the game. In this chapter, we are going to look at the addition of sound to our game. We will be demonstrating the use of a shareware package that allows us to use many different sound cards.

RUCKDAC

RUCKUS-DAC is a RUCKUS sound toolkit for DOS. It has the capability to play digital data in the formats VOC, WAV, and MOD. Using very simple code, you can play any sound files in these formats to any of the following devices:

- the PC speaker
- a DAC on the parallel port
- Disney Sound Source
- Adlib MSC
- SoundBlaster
- SoundBlaster Pro

In addition, the system will support just about any sound card that attempts to emulate one of these devices.

I chose to include information about this sound toolkit because of its ease of use. I was able to add sound support to the game in just under ten minutes. Simply by cutting and pasting source code from a sample program, I was instantly able to add a sound effect to the firing of the gun.

In the remainder of this chapter, we will investigate the code that I added to the game for sound. I will not go into the details of the code because the RUCKDAC toolkit includes a very good documentation file that follows the example code which comes with the toolkit.

We are adding code to the MINOSND.C file because of the memory requirements of the RUCKUS toolkit and the sound file that is loaded. Because of the number of bitmaps and communication link code that is in our game, we must use the MINOSND.C code instead of MINOSND.C. TheMINOSND.C program does not use as much memory so we will have the space necessary to add the sound toolkit. You will need to balance your use of sound to available memory. When you run the MINOSND.EXE file with the sound file code activated, you may find that the screen overlay does not show up. This is due to memory limitations. Try and release more memory and the overlay should appear.

Possible Places for Sound

There are many different places that sound could be added to our program. These places include:
- Door openings
- Player firing
- Opponent firing
- Medusa firing
- Minotaur chopping and walking
- Explosions

We are going to look at one of these places: when the player fires.

The player can fire using the keyboard, mouse, or joystick, so we will need to add code in all of these places.

Adding a Shooting Sound

Adding sound code using the RUCKUS toolkit has basically four parts: finding a sound source, initializing the sound source, loading the sound, and playing the sound.

Finding a Sound Source

To find any sound sources on the PC, we can use a function defined in the RUCKUS toolkit. The function SysInfoDac() analyzes the PC to see if any of the sound sources listed above are installed in the computer. We are going to use a function called pick_device() that was defined in one of the RUCKUS sample programs. The function is

```
int pick_device(int *devID, int *XMSflag)
{
 int td=0;
 char nums[9] = {7};
 SIP.Func = SysInfoDac;
 rez = RUCKDAC(&SIP);
 if (rez == 0) {
   printf("\n0. End program");
     printf("\n1. PC speaker at port 42h");
     if (SIP.SD[1].device)
       printf("\n2. LPT-DAC on LPT1, port %xh",SIP.SD[1].Port);
     if (SIP.SD[2].device)
```

```
        printf("\n3. Disney Sound Source port %xh",SIP.SD[2].Port);
    if (SIP.SD[3].device)
        printf("\n\n4. AdLib Music Synthesizer Card, port %xh",SIP.SD[3].Port);
    if (SIP.SD[4].device)
        printf("\n5. SoundBlaster, port %xh",SIP.SD[4].Port);
    if (SIP.SD[5].device)
        printf("\n6. SoundBlaster Pro, port %xh",SIP.SD[5].Port);
    if (SIP.SD[4].device)
        printf("\n\n7. SoundBlaster as 5 but use XMS (if applicable)");
    if (SIP.SD[5].device)
        printf("\n8. SoundBlaster Pro as 6 but use XMS (if applicable)\n");
    printf("\nSelection: ");
    td = atoi(cgets(nums));
    td--; /* since devices are numbered 0 to 5 */
    if (td > 6) {
      *XMSflag = 1; /* XMS memory selected with SB */
      td-=2;        /* map to appropriate device */
    }
    if ((td >=0) && (td <=5)) { /* validate device selected available */
        if (SIP.SD[td].device == 0)
            td = -1;
    }
    else
        td = -1;
    }
    *devID = td;
    return(rez);
}
```

The function calls the SysInfoDac() function to find any sources. Based on the information returned, the routine lists the devices that were found. The user can select any of the devices just by entering the appropriate key. After a little manipulation, the code returns an internal value for the selected sound device.

Initializing the Sound Source

After a sound source has been selected, it has to be initialized. The function init_device() will do the initialization for us. This function is

```
int init_device(int devID)

{
/*
Initialize RUCKDAC and device and register ExitDac with _atexit
The IP.port for devices 0 and 3 are set to 0 for low-rez mode,
```

```
             or their respective actual ports for hi-rez mode (0x42 and 0x388)
             */
             IP.Func = InitDac;
             IP.DeviceID = devID;
             IP.IOport = SIP.SD[devID].Port;
             IP.IRQline = SIP.SD[devID].IRQ;
             IP.DMAch = SIP.SD[devID].DMA;
             if ((devID == 0) || (devID == 3)) /* use low-rez mode for */
             IP.IOport = 0;                    /* PC speaker and Adlib */
             rez = RUCKDAC(&IP);               /* Initialize */
             if (rez == 0) {
                XP.Func = AtExitDac;
                rez2 = RUCKDAC(&XP);
                if (rez2 != 0) {
                   printf("AtExitDac failed, press Enter to continue");
                   getchar();
                }
                /*
                Increase SB Pro main and vol volumes to max
                */
                if (devID == 5) {
                   SPP.Func = SetVolMainSBP;
                   SPP.Volume = 0x0F0F;
                   rez2 = RUCKDAC(&SPP);
                   SPP.Func = SetVolVocSBP;
                   SPP.VolVoc = 0x0F0F;
                   rez2 = RUCKDAC(&SPP);
                }
             }
             return(rez);
             }
```

The code in the initialization function sets several internal fields, main-
ly for the SoundBlaster and its compatible sound cards. You will note that
the last part of this initialization function sets the SoundBlaster Pro volume to MAXIMUM. You may want to change this to a value smaller than
0xF0F like 0x0100. If you are using powered speakers, simply adjust their
volume instead of this variable.

Loading a Sound

The third part of our sound process sequence is to load a sound and get it
ready for use. We will do this with the function do_sound(). This function
is placed in the main() function of the program. It will make calls to both

the pick_device() and init_device() functions. Once these functions have been called and a sound source is ready to be used, the sound is loaded. The do_sound() function is as follows:

```
void do_sound()
{
  int devID=-1, XMSflag=0;
    rez = pick_device(&devID, &XMSflag);
    if (devID >= 0)
    {
        printf ("Initializing devID %u\n", devID);
        rez = init_device(devID);
        if (rez == 0)
        {
            play_sound = 1;
            /* load file and setup playback parameters */
            LP.Func = LoadDac;
            LP.FilenamePtr = "phaser3.voc";
            LP.StartPos = 0L; /* start at first byte */
            LP.LoadSize = 0L; /* autoload entire file */
            LP.XMMflag = XMSflag;
            rez = RUCKDAC(&LP);
            if (rez == 0)
            {
                PBP.Func = PlayDac;
                if (devID >= 4)
                    PBP.Mode = 2;
                else
                {
                    PBP.Mode = 1;
                    if (DACDATA.SampleRate < 11025)
                    SP.IntRate = DACDATA.SampleRate;
                else
            SP.IntRate = 8643;
                SP.Func = SetIntRateDac;
                rez = RUCKDAC(&SP); /* set the playback rate */
            }
            if (LP.XMMflag == 0)
            {
                PBP.XMMhandle = 0;
                PBP.LoadPtr = LP.LoadPtr;
            }
            else
            {
```

```
                PBP.XMMhandle = LP.XMMhandle;
                PBP.LoadPtr = NULL;
            }
        }
    }
  }
}
```

The filename of the sound that we want to load is placed in the global variable LP. The code is

```
LP.Func = LoadDac;
LP.FilenamePtr = "phaser3.voc";
LP.StartPos = 0L; /* start at first byte */
LP.LoadSize = 0L; /* autoload entire file */
LP.XMMflag = XMSflag;
rez = RUCKDAC(&LP);
```

As you read the RUCKUS documentation and the sample source code, you will notice that all of the function calls to the toolkit are through one function called RUCKDAC(). The author of the package does this to insure compatibility with all types of C compilers. In order for the RUCK-DAC function to tell what it is supposed to do, the individual function is placed in the Func field of the appropriate global variable. Once the file is loaded, we have to set up several more global variables that set the starting point of the sound file and the playback rate. After all of this, we are ready to use the sound.

Playing the Sound

Playing the sound that we have just loaded is very simple. We just place the function call

```
rez = RUCKDAC(&PBP);
```

where we want the sound to be played. The sound will be played in the background until the end of the sound file is encountered.

Loading and Playing More Than One Sound

In most games, you will want to have more than one sound. To do this, you will just need to have multiple copies of the sound global variables. The global variables used in our single sound example are

```
//SOUND variables
#pragma pack(1)
extern struct DacDataArea pascal DACDATA;
```

```
struct SysInfoPack SIP;
struct InitPack IP;
struct XitPack XP;
struct LoadPack LP;
struct SetPack SP;
struct SetProPack SPP;
struct PlaybackPack PBP;
struct GetDataPack GDP;
struct DeallocPack DP;
#pragma pack()
```

You will need to have separate variables for LP, SP, SPP, and PBP, which are all initialized in the do_sound() function. You can make all of the variables look the same except LP, which will have a different filename.

Conclusion

We have just scratched the surface of adding sound to our game. I would recommend that you register the RUCKUS sound package, as it provides very easy instructions for adding sound to your game. In fact, the RUCKUS package allows you to take total advantage of the sound cards installed in most computers. You could even allow the players to record their own voices during game play for added effect.

Completing the Game

By now you have made a determination as to your game and how you are going to allow the players to be connected. The game really isn't that exciting yet, since all the players can do is run around. We need to add a few things to the game in order to make it playable. This chapter will discuss:

- Static overlays
- Writing to the overlay
- Adding objects that can be picked up from the floor
- Firing weapons
- Using the joystick
- Using the mouse
- Doors
- Memory

Adding a Static Overlay with Changing Values

If you have played other 3D games, you will notice that most of them have some type of overlay that is visible on top of the playing field of the game. This overlay is typically used to give the players valuable information about their current state. The overlay that we are going to add to our game is shown in Figure 13.1.

You can see that the overlay will occupy the bottom part of the screen. On the left side is the name of our game—Minotaur. In the center of the

Figure 13.1 Game overlay.

screen is a face. In other 3D games, the programmers have used the face to indicate the health of the player. As the player is hit or attacked by opponents or monsters, the face on the overlay begins to get bloody. This is something that you can add to your game by simply creating smaller bitmaps that you can overlay on the overlay. On the right side of the overlay we have an indicator called AMMO. We will be putting a number in the blank part to the right of the word AMMO.

Building the Overlay

The overlay that we are adding to the game is built using the paint program MVP Paint and the current palette. The size of the palette should be 320 x 200 x 256 colors and converted to the LBM file format using the VPIC view program. You can use any color from the palette without regard for shading, because the overlay is not shaded by the game, so the overlay's colors never change.

Code for Adding the Overlay

With the overlay designed and converted to the LBM format, we need to add it to our program. The code necessary for overlay support is added in several locations. The first location is in the global variable part of the program. The code is:

```
char        *PictureFile = "dashboar.lbm";
UCHAR far   *OverlayPic;
```

The first variable, PictureFile, is used to hold the name of the file that contains the overlay. The second variable, OverlayPic, is a temporary variable that will hold our overlay when it is read into the game.

These variables are used in a function called AppSetupOverlay(). This function is in charge of reading in the overlay and letting the application know that we are going to be using it.

```
int AppSetupOverlay(void)
{
 int result = 0;
 UCHAR far *Video;
 OverlayPic = AckReadiff(PictureFile);
 if (OverlayPic == NULL)
   return(-1);
 Video = MK_FP(0xA000,0);
 memmove(Video,&OverlayPic[4],64000);
 result = AckCreateOverlay(ae,&OverlayPic[4]);
 free(OverlayPic);
```

```
    return(result);
}
```

The function starts by using the AckReadiff() function to read in the file in the variable PictureFile and storing it in the new file in the variable OverlayPic. After the call to the read function, we have to make a quick check of the OverlayPic to make sure that the file was actually read into the system.

If the file was read in correctly, we put the graphics file into the video buffer of the VGA card and then make a call to the function AckCreateOverlay(). The function AckCreateOverlay() is an internal ACK3D function that takes the current contents of the VGA buffer and puts it into an internal buffer so that the ACK system has easy access to the overlay. The last thing that we do is release the memory that we allocated when we first read the overlay into the game. Since the ACK3D system has a copy of the overlay in its internal data structures, we no longer need to keep a separate copy of it.

Now that we have a way of reading in the overlay, we need to make a call to the AppSetupOverlay() function. The code that makes the call is:

```
if (result == AppSetupOverlay())
  {
  printf("Error loading overlay: ErrorCode = %d\n",result);
  AckWrapUp(ae);
  return(1);
  }
```

This code is placed in the main program just after the call to the AppSetGraphics() function. After the call to the function, we can have the ACK3D display the overlay in our game. The code for displaying the overlay is:

```
AckBuildView(ae);
AckDrawOverlay(ae->ScreenBuffer,ae->OverlayBuffer);
AckDisplayScreen(ae);
```

You will recognize the first and third lines of code from our original skeleton code. The second line is a call to the function AckDrawOverlay(). This function draws the overlay *after* the ACK3D system has drawn the wall in our game using the AckBuildView() function.

Now we need to do one last thing in order to use the overlay. When we originally designed the game, we had to set the boundaries of the drawing screen. The variables are:

Figure 13.2 Our final overlay and the game.

```
VIEW_X
VIEW_X1
VIEW_Y
VIEW_Y1
```

These variables are located in the MINOTAUR.h file. The VIEW_X and VIEW_Y variables are the upper left corner coordinates of the drawing screen, and VIEW_X1 and VIEW_Y1 are the lower right corner. We need to change the VIEW_X1 and VIEW_Y1 variables upward so that the corner of the drawing screen is at the top of the visible part of the overlay.

Figure 13.2 shows the overlay when it is combined with the game.

Fonts for Writing Text

We also want to be able to write to the screen overlay. To do this, we are going to use some code that was included in an ACK3D demo released to the public domain. The code for writing to the screen is shown in four different routines. The first routine loads the fonts into the game:

```
int LoadSmallFont(void)
{
   int   ht,wt,len;
smFont = AckReadiff("spfont.bbm");
if (smFont == NULL)
   return(-1);
```

```
ht = (*(int *)smFont);
wt = (*(int *)&smFont[2]);
len = ht * wt;
memmove(smFont,&smFont[4],len);
return(0);
}
```

The LoadSmallFont() function reads the file Spfont.bbm into a global variable called smFont. This variable will be used by the routines smWriteChar() and smWriteString() for writing to the screen. The smWriteChar() function is:

```
void smWriteChar(int x,int y,unsigned char ch)
{
    int    FontOffset,VidOffset;
    int    row,col;
  unsigned char far *Video;
VidOffset = (y * 320) + x;
Video = MK_FP(0xA000,VidOffset);
FontOffset = ((ch-32) * 5);
//  Video = ae->ScreenBuffer + VidOffset;
for (row = 0; row < 5; row++)
  {
   memset(Video,TextBGcolor,4);
  if (smFont[FontOffset])
     Video[0] = FontColor;
  if (smFont[FontOffset+1])
     Video[1] = FontColor;
  if (smFont[FontOffset+2])
     Video[2] = FontColor;
  if (smFont[FontOffset+3])
     Video[3] = FontColor;
  Video += 320;
  FontOffset += 294;
  }
}
```

The smWriteChar function is:

```
void smWriteChar(int x,int y,unsigned char ch)
{
    int    FontOffset,VidOffset;
    int    row,col;
  unsigned char far *Video;
```

```
VidOffset = (y * 320) + x;
Video = MK_FP(0xA000,VidOffset);
FontOffset = ((ch-32) * 5);
//   Video = ae->ScreenBuffer + VidOffset;
for (row = 0; row < 5; row++)
  {
   memset(Video,TextBGcolor,4);
  if (smFont[FontOffset])
     Video[0] = FontColor;
  if (smFont[FontOffset+1])
     Video[1] = FontColor;
  if (smFont[FontOffset+2])
     Video[2] = FontColor;
  if (smFont[FontOffset+3])
     Video[3] = FontColor;
  Video += 320;
  FontOffset += 294;
  }
}
```

Both of these functions are responsible for writing the current font to the screen using the current background and foreground colors recorded in the global variables:

```
TextBGcolor = 7,
FontColor = 15;
```

The functions work by locating the appropriate character in the font structure that has been read into the game and is located in the smFont variable. The character bitmap is written to the VGA buffer using the current font color and background color. Now since we will normally be writing different values to the same part of the screen, we will need a way to erase the previous value. We do this by clearing a status line on the overlay. The function to clear the overlay part is:

```
void ClearStatusLine(UCHAR color)
{
 int    rows,cols;
 UCHAR  far *Video;
 rows = (VP_STATUSY * 320) + VP_STATUSX;
 Video = MK_FP(0xA000,rows);
 cols = (VP_STATUSX1 - VP_STATUSX) + 1;
 for (rows = VP_STATUSY; rows < VP_STATUSY1; rows++)
 {
```

```
  memset(Video,color,cols);
  Video += 320;
 }
}
```

You can change the part of the screen that you are writing to by
increasing or decreasing the values in VP_STATUSY, VP_STATUSX,
VP_STATUSY1, and VP_STATUSX1.

Now that we have the font structure loaded and the appropriate functions available, we can look at how to use the functions. To use the functions, we have the initialization code:

```
if (LoadSmallFont())
  {
  AckSetTextmode();
  printf("Error loading font: ErrorCode = %d\n",result);
  AckWrapUp(ae);
  return(1);
  }
```

We put the initialization code after all of the other initialization code in
our main function. You can see precisely where it is put by looking at the
game code in Appendix A. . Once initialized, we can use the code.

In our game, we are going to have bullets for the player. We will want
to display the number of bullets available. We can do this with the code:

```
ClearStatusLine(7);
sprintf (buf, "%d", ammo);
smWriteString(10,181, buf);
```

We start by clearing the part of the screen that will hold the ammo
number. After the screen is cleared, we put the info to be displayed in a
buffer and then call the string writing function to display the buffer.

Adding Items That Players Can Pick Up

The bullets for the player's use are going to be spread out on the floor of
the maze. The player will have to move over to the bullets and pick them
up in order to use them. Since the player doesn't have any arms, we will
just have the player run over the bullets in order to pick them up.

We need an object to hold the bullets—a separate object for each of
the bullet groups that we want the player to pick up. However, we don't
need to read in a bitmap for each of the bullet objects, just one. The
bitmap needs to be put in the global bitmap list. The list is:

```
BMTABLE bmTable[] = {
   1 ,TYPE_WALL      ,"wall.lbm",
   60 ,TYPE_WALL     ,"roman3.lbm",
   61 ,TYPE_WALL     ,"wall.lbm",
   62 ,TYPE_WALL     ,"roman3.lbm",
   1 ,TYPE_OBJECT  ,"man1.lbm",
   2 ,TYPE_OBJECT  ,"man2.lbm",
   3 ,TYPE_OBJECT  ,"man3.lbm",
   4 ,TYPE_OBJECT  ,"man4.lbm",
   5 ,TYPE_OBJECT  ,"mon1.lbm",
   6 ,TYPE_OBJECT  ,"ammocase.lbm",
   7 ,TYPE_OBJECT  ,"bullet.lbm",
   -1 ,-1            ,""          /* End of table */
   };
```

Notice that we have placed the ammo in position 6 and indicated that
the bitmap is an object. If we add the bitmap to the list data structure, it
will automatically be read into the system. We need to manually set up
the three objects that will use the bitmap. From our previous discussions,
we know that all of the objects are set up in the function
AppSetupObjects().

The code for the ammo is:

```
//ammo loads
 bitmaps[0] = 6;
 ae->ObjList[3].Flags = 0;
 ae->ObjList[3].Speed = 0;
 ae->ObjList[3].Dir = 0;
 AckCreateObject (ae, 3, 1, bitmaps);
 bitmaps[0] = 6;
 ae->ObjList[4].Flags = 0;
 ae->ObjList[4].Speed = 0;
 ae->ObjList[4].Dir = 0;
 AckCreateObject (ae, 4, 1, bitmaps);
 bitmaps[0] = 6;
 ae->ObjList[5].Flags = 0;
 ae->ObjList[5].Speed = 0;
 ae->ObjList[5].Dir = 0;
 AckCreateObject (ae, 5, 1, bitmaps);
```

For each of the objects, we have to indicate which of the bitmaps the
object uses. The ammo will use a single bitmap, so we put the bitmap
number in the first position of the bitmaps[] array. Next, we set the Flags,
Speed, and Dir fields of the three separate object fields of the ACK3D

ObjList structure. After all of the fields are set, we make a call to the function AckCreateObject to tell the ACK3D engine to create the objects.

Transmitting Pickup

The ammo has been read into the game, but the bullets do not know when the player runs over them. Actually, the game does know when the player runs over the bullet objects—it just isn't acknowledged. To do this, we need to add some code.

If you look back at the keyboard handling code, we make a call to the function AckMovePOV() when the player presses the Up or Down arrow key. These keys make the player move forward or backward. In the original skeleton program, we just called the function and did not wait for a return result. To determine if the player has hit the bullet objects, we simply wait for a return result from the AckMovePOV() function. The code we are going to add to the Up and Down keys is:

```
result = AckMovePOV(ae,ae->PlayerAngle,16);
if (result == POV_OBJECT)
  check_objects();
```

When the AckMovePOV() function returns, if the result code is POV_OBJECT, we make a call to the function check_objects(). This function is defined as:

```
void check_objects()
{
 int i;
 i = AckGetObjectHit();
 switch (i)
 {
  case 3: if ((com_device == 'n') || (com_device == 'm'))
    {
     com_tx(PORT, 'i');
     com_tx(PORT, 3);
    }
    if (com_device=='e')
    {
     data_packet[20] = 'i';
     data_packet[21] = 3;
     send_pkt (interrupt_number,data_packet, 64);
    }
    if (com_device=='i')
    {
     input_buf[0] = 'i';
```

```
     input_buf[1] = 3;
     sock_write ( &our_socket, input_buf, 2);
    }
    AckDeleteObject (ae, i);
    ammo += 10;
    AckPlaySound(1);
    break;
case 4: if ((com_device == 'n') || (com_device == 'm'))
    {
     com_tx(PORT, 'i');
     com_tx(PORT, 4);
    }
    if (com_device=='e')
    {
     data_packet[20] = 'i';
     data_packet[21] = 4;
     send_pkt (interrupt_number,data_packet, 64);
    }
    if (com_device=='i')
    {
     input_buf[0] = 'i';
     input_buf[1] = 4;
     sock_write ( &our_socket, input_buf, 2);
    }
    AckDeleteObject (ae, i);
    ammo += 10;
    AckPlaySound(1);
    break;
case 5: if ((com_device == 'n') || (com_device == 'm'))
    {
     com_tx(PORT, 'i');
     com_tx(PORT, 5);
    }
    if (com_device=='e')
    {
     data_packet[20] = 'i';
     data_packet[21] = 5;
     send_pkt (interrupt_number,data_packet, 64);
    }
    if (com_device=='i')
    {
     input_buf[0] = 'i';
     input_buf[1] = 5;
```

```
        sock_write ( &our_socket, input_buf, 2);
    }
    AckDeleteObject (ae, i);
    ammo += 10;
    AckPlaySound(1);
    break;
  }
}
```

When we call the function check_objects( ), the first statement we execute is AckGetObjectHit( ). This function returns a number that indicates
the object that the player has collided with. We use this result value in a
SWITCH statement to determine which of the objects was actually collided with. Now we increase the ammo count for the player and remove the
object from the view of the player and any opponent. We do this with the
function AckDeleteObject( ). The parameters to this function are the main
ACK3D variable, **ae**, and the value of the object we want to delete.

In addition to taking care of the player's ammo and deleting the ammo
object from the map, we need to make sure that the object is removed
from the map of the opponent. We always need to inform the opponent
of our actions.

We have reserved the character "i" to indicate that an ammo object is
to be deleted. In addition to the "i" character, we also need to tell the
opponent the object number to delete. If you look in the code above, you
will see that we have to first determine which of the three connections the
players are using. After the determination of the connection, we transmit
an "i" character and the object number of the ammo object to delete.

Now, we also need to make sure that the opponent can receive the "i"
command. *(Put another way, we need to make sure that the player can
receive the "i" command when the opponent picks up ammo.)* This code, like
the code for movement, will be placed in the process_communication( )
function. The code looks like this:

```
case 'i':  if ((com_device == 'n') || (com_device == 'm'))
        ch = com_rx(PORT);
    if (com_device == 'i') ch = input_buf[1];
    if (com_device == 'e') ch = data_packet[21];
    AckDeleteObject (ae, ch);
    break;
```

When a player receives the "i" character from his or her opponent,
the player's game removes the same ammo object from his or her own
map.

Setting the Ammo in the Map

Now that the code is available for picking up the ammo, we need to place the ammo in the map. To do this, we need to first put the ammo objects into the program's resource file. The entries that we are adding to the resource file are:

```
Objects:
 Files:
 1, man1.lbm
 2, man3.lbm
 3, man2.lbm
 4, man4.lbm
 5, mon1.lbm
 6, ammocase.lbm
 EndFiles:
;Other guy figure
Number: 1
Direction: 0
Speed: 1
Bitmaps: 1,2,3,4

Number: 2
Direction:180
Speed: 1
Bitmaps: 5

Number: 3
Direction: 0
Speed: 0
Bitmaps: 6

Number: 4
Direction: 0
Speed: 0
Bitmaps: 6

Number: 5
Direction: 0
Speed: 0
Bitmaps: 6
```

In the AckSetObjects() function, we know that we put the ammo objects in positions 3, 4, and 5 of the ObjList data structure. We need to make sure that we keep these numbers consistent when we put the objects in the resource file.

With the objects placed in the resource file, we use the MEDIT.EXE map editor to place the ammo objects in the map. To do this, just select the Objects icon and change the visible bitmap to number 3, 4, or 5 to show an ammo object. Move the pointer to any of the grid positions and click the mouse to place the object.

When the game is played, the bullets will appear on the map floor. The players can pick them up and the system will acknowledge the pickup.

 # Using the Joystick

As you have probably already noticed, using the keyboard for movement is rather awkward. We need to add code to use the joystick. The joystick is controlled using special hardware in the PC. The actual theory behind the joystick hardware is beyond the scope of this book, but we can present code that will read the current position of the joystick and the joystick buttons:

```
#include <stdlib.h>
#include <dos.h>
#include <bios.h>
int joystick_read(int *x, int *y, int *buttons)
{
 int c, k, jx, jy;
 outportb(0x201, 0xff); /* Trigger joystick */
 c = inportb(0x201);
 *buttons = c;
 for (k = 0; c & 3; k++) /* Get X and Y positions */
 {
  if (c & 1) jx = k;
  if (c & 2) jy = k;
  c = inportb(0x201);
 }
 *x = jx;
 *y = jy;
}
```

As you can see, the code is rather simple. To read the joystick, we simply call the function joystick_read(). Now we need to let ACK3D know about the joystick positions. The code that we are going to use looks like this:

```
if (use_joystick)
  {
  buttons = 0;
  joystick_read (&x, &y, &buttons);
  if ((buttons == 239) && (!is_shooting))
    {
    if (ammo)
      {
      if ((com_device == 'n') || (com_device == 'm'))com_tx(PORT, '1');
      if (com_device=='e')
        {
        data_packet[20] = '1';
        send_pkt (interrupt_number,data_packet, 64);
        }
      if (com_device=='i')
        {
        ch = '1';
        sock_write ( &our_socket, &ch, 1);
        }
      is_shooting = 1;
      ae->ObjList[bullet].x = ae->xPlayer;
      ae->ObjList[bullet].y = ae->yPlayer;
      ae->ObjList[bullet].Dir = ae->PlayerAngle;
      ae->ObjList[bullet].mPos = (ae->ObjList[bullet].y & 0xFFC0) + (ae-
>ObjList[bullet].x >> 6);
      ae->ObjList[bullet].VidRow = 100;
      ae->ObjList[bullet].Active = 1;
      ammo—;
      }
    }
    {
    x = joy_centx - x;
    y = joy_centy - y;
    if ( x>15 ) x -= 15;
    else
      {
      if ( x > -15) x = 0;
      else x += 15;
      }
    if ( y > 15 ) y -= 15;
    else
      {
      if(y>-15) y = 0;
```

```c
      else y+=15;
    }
    if (x!=0)
    {
     ch = x/20;
     if ((com_device == 'n') || (com_device == 'm'))
     {
      com_tx(PORT, 'e');
      com_tx(PORT, ch);
     }
     if (com_device=='e')
     {
      data_packet[20] = 'e';
      data_packet[21] = ch;
      send_pkt (interrupt_number,data_packet, 64);
     }
     if (com_device=='i')
     {
      buf[0] = 'e';
      buf[1] = ch;
      sock_write ( &our_socket, buf, 2);
     }
     ae->PlayerAngle -= ch;
     pan = 1;
    }
    if (y!=0)
    {
     ch = y/20;
     if (y>0)
     {
      if ((com_device == 'n') || (com_device == 'm'))
      {
      com_tx(PORT, 'g');
      com_tx(PORT, ch);
      }
      if (com_device=='e')
      {
      data_packet[20] = 'g';
      data_packet[21] = ch;
      send_pkt (interrupt_number,data_packet, 64);
      }
      if (com_device=='i')
      {
```

```
   buf[0] = 'g';
   buf[1] = ch;
   sock_write ( &our_socket, buf, 2);
    }
   result = AckMovePOV(ae,ae->PlayerAngle,y/20);
   if (result == POV_OBJECT)
  check_objects();
  }
  else
  {
  if ((com_device == 'n') || (com_device == 'm'))
   {
  com_tx(PORT, 'h');
  com_tx(PORT, ch);
   }
   if (com_device=='e')
   {
  data_packet[20] = 'h';
  data_packet[21] = ch;
  send_pkt (interrupt_number,data_packet, 64);
   }
   if (com_device=='i')
   {
  buf[0] = 'h';
  buf[1] = ch;
  sock_write ( &our_socket, buf, 2);
   }
   temp= ae->PlayerAngle + INT_ANGLE_180;
   if (temp >= INT_ANGLE_360)
   temp -= INT_ANGLE_360;
   result = AckMovePOV(ae,temp,-y/20);
   if (result == POV_OBJECT)
   check_objects();
  }
 }
 }
 }
```

The joystick control software starts by reading the current position of
the joystick, which includes the x and y locations as well as the position of
the joystick buttons. In the code, we check to see if the top button of the
joystick is pressed. If the button is pressed, we enable the player to fire a
weapon, which we will discuss in the next section.

Next, the code does a bit of filtering of the joystick data. The joystick is notorious for being noisy, so the filtering tries to take the noise out of the data. After the filtering, the code checks the x joystick value. If the x value is not zero, we need to move the player and the player's representation on the opponent's computer. If you look at the code within the IF statements for the x and y values, you will see that the code is just about the same as the code for the keyboard movements. The only difference is that we need to transmit an actual x and y value to the opponent's computer so that the player's figure on the opponent's computer moves just as much as it does on the player's own computer. We use the character "h" to indicate to the other computer that the player is moving by using the joystick instead of the keyboard. Just as when we used the keyboard, the other computer will need to receive the "h" character and move the graphical character of the opponent.

Adding Firing Capabilities

Being able to move through our map using the keyboard or the joystick is great, but players must also be able to defend themselves. We have already seen that there are ammo objects lying around the map. Let's give the players a way to shoot the bullets.

The first step in allowing a player to shoot is to load a bullet into the system. We do this by adding the name of the bullet bitmap, bullet.lbm, to the global bitmap table, Bmtable. This will allow the bitmap to be automatically read into the game. Now we need to create a bullet object. The bullet is actually created in the AppSetObject() function:

```
//Load bullet
 bitmaps[0] = 7;
 ae->ObjList[6].Flags = 0;
 ae->ObjList[6].Speed = 25;
 ae->ObjList[6].Dir = 0;
 ae->ObjList[bullet].Active = 0;
 AckCreateObject (ae, bullet, 1, bitmaps);
 //Load monster bullet
 bitmaps[0] = 7;
 ae->ObjList[7].Flags = 0;
 ae->ObjList[7].Speed = 25;
 ae->ObjList[7].Dir = 0;
 ae->ObjList[7].Active = 0;
 AckCreateObject (ae, monster_bullet, 1, bitmaps);
 //Load other guy bullet
```

```
bitmaps[0] = 7;
ae->ObjList[8].Flags = 0;
ae->ObjList[8].Speed = 25;
ae->ObjList[8].Dir = 0;
ae->ObjList[8].Active = 0;
AckCreateObject (ae, other_guy_bullet, 1, bitmaps);
```

You will notice that there are three bullets. Since we are already creating the player's bullet, we might as well go ahead and create a bullet for the opponent. Remember that when Player A fires a bullet, the graphical representation of Player A on the opponent's machine will have to fire a bullet as well.

Visualizing a Bullet

With the bullet loaded and ready to go, we need to add some code so that the player can fire the bullet. This code will be added to the joystick and keyboard routines. Let's look at the keyboard code first:

```
case ' ': if (ammo)
          {
          if ((com_device == 'n') || (com_device == 'm'))com_tx(PORT, '1');
          if (com_device=='e')
          {
          data_packet[20] = '1';
          send_pkt (interrupt_number,data_packet, 64);
          }
          if (com_device=='i')
          {
          ch = '1';
          sock_write ( &our_socket, &ch, 1);
          }
          is_shooting = 1;
          ae->ObjList[bullet].x = ae->xPlayer;
          ae->ObjList[bullet].y = ae->yPlayer;
          ae->ObjList[bullet].Dir = ae->PlayerAngle;
          ae->ObjList[bullet].mPos = (ae->ObjList[bullet].y & 0xFFC0) + (ae-
>ObjList[bullet].x >> 6);
          ae->ObjList[bullet].VidRow = 100;
          ae->ObjList[bullet].Active = 1;
          ammo—;
          }
```

When adding keystrokes to our keyboard handling routine, we simply add a case statement. For the bullet routine, we are going to use the spacebar. As you can see from the preceding code, the first thing that we do is let the opponent know that the player is firing a bullet. We do this by sending the character "l" using the appropriate connection routine.

Once the opponent knows that the player is firing a bullet, we set a global variable, is_shooting, equal to 1. This will let other parts of the program know that a bullet is being fired. To actually fire the bullet, we need to put the bullet on the screen directly in front of the player. Then the bullet must be moved forward until it either hits an object or hits a wall. We begin by initializing the bullet by setting the x, y, and angle fields of the object equal to the position of the player. To activate the object so the ACK3D engine will display it, we must set the field Active to 1. Lastly, we decrease the variable **ammo** to reflect that we are using up a variable.

To initialize the bullet when using the joystick, we use the same code in the joystick code and execute it when the player presses the joystick button. Refer to the joystick code listed earlier in this chapter.

Determining a Kill

Once the bullet is initialized, we have to move the bullet forward toward some target. This is something that needs to be done each time through the main loop. At the very top of the main loop code is the statement

```
if (is_shooting) UpdateShoot();
```

Recall that we set the variable is_shooting equal to 1 when we initialized the bullet. Each time the program executes the main loop, this statement will be encountered. The statement makes a call to the function UpdateShoot(). This function is:

```
void UpdateShoot()
{
 int result;
 char ch;
 if ((com_device == 'n') || (com_device == 'm'))
 {
  com_tx(PORT, 'm');
  com_tx(PORT, ((ae->ObjList[bullet].x & 0xFF00)>>8));
  com_tx(PORT, (ae->ObjList[bullet].x & 0x00FF));
  com_tx(PORT, ((ae->ObjList[bullet].y & 0xFF00)>>8));
  com_tx(PORT, (ae->ObjList[bullet].y & 0x00FF));
 }
 if (com_device=='e')
 {
  data_packet[20] = 'm';
```

```
    data_packet[21] = (ae->ObjList[bullet].x & 0xFF00)>>8;
    data_packet[22] = (ae->ObjList[bullet].x & 0x00FF);
    data_packet[23] = (ae->ObjList[bullet].y & 0xFF00)>>8;
    data_packet[24] = ae->ObjList[bullet].y & 0x00FF;
    send_pkt (interrupt_number,data_packet, 64);
  }
  if (com_device=='i')
  {
    input_buf[0] = 'm';
    input_buf[1] = (ae->ObjList[bullet].x & 0xFF00)>>8;
    input_buf[2] = (ae->ObjList[bullet].x & 0x00FF);
    input_buf[3] = (ae->ObjList[bullet].y & 0xFF00)>>8;
    input_buf[4] = ae->ObjList[bullet].y & 0x00FF;
    sock_write ( &our_socket, input_buf, 5);
  }
  result = AckMoveObjectPOV (ae, bullet, ae->ObjList[bullet].Dir, ae-
>ObjList[bullet].Speed);
  if ((result != POV_NOTHING) && (result != POV_PLAYER))
  {
    ae->ObjList[bullet].Active = 0;
    is_shooting = 0;
  if ((com_device == 'n') || (com_device == 'm'))
  {
    com_tx(PORT, 'n');
  }
  if (com_device=='e')
  {
    data_packet[20] = 'n';
    send_pkt (interrupt_number,data_packet, 64);
  }
  if (com_device=='i')
  {
    ch = 'n';
    sock_write ( &our_socket, &ch, 1);
  }
  if (result == POV_OBJECT)
  {
    result = AckGetObjectHit();
    if (result == monster1)
    {
    if ((com_device == 'n') || (com_device == 'm'))
    {
        com_tx(PORT, 'j');
```

```
      com_tx(PORT, monster1);
    }
    if (com_device=='e')
    {
      data_packet[20] = 'j';
      data_packet[21] = monster1;
      send_pkt (interrupt_number, data_packet, 64);
    }
    if (com_device=='i')
    {
      input_buf[0] = 'j';
      input_buf[1] = monster1;
      sock_write ( &our_socket, input_buf, 2);
    }
    AckDeleteObject(ae, monster1);
    AckDeleteObject(ae, monster_bullet);
    }
    else if (result == other_guy)
    {
    if ((com_device == 'n') || (com_device == 'm'))com_tx(PORT, 'w');
    if (com_device=='e')
    {
      data_packet[20] = 'w';
      send_pkt (interrupt_number,data_packet, 64);
    }
    if (com_device=='i')
    {
      ch = 'w';
      sock_write ( &our_socket, &ch, 1);
    }
    AckDeleteObject(ae, other_guy);
    AckDeleteObject(ae, other_guy_bullet);
    }
    }
  }
}
```

The function starts by telling the opponent that we are updating the
location of the bullet. Since the bullet is on a straight line course, we can
simply send the character "m" to the opponent. After the character is
transmitted, we use the function AckMoveObjectPOV to move the bullet
object forward.

```
result = AckMoveObjectPOV (ae, bullet, ae->ObjList[bullet].Dir, ae-
>ObjList[bullet].Speed);
```

We give the function the information about the bullet object. The second parameter in this function is the object number of the object that should be moved. Once this function executes, it returns a value. This value can be used to indicate if the object that just moved has collided with anything. Since we are moving a bullet, we need to check for a collision. The first collision that we check for is general. If the bullet has hit some object—a monster or a wall—it must be removed from the ACK3D screen. This is done by setting the Active field of the object equal to 0. We also send the character "n" to the opponent so that the opponent's computer will remove the bullet from the screen as well.

We now make specific checks to see what the bullet object has hit. We make a check with the code

```
if (result == POV_OBJECT)
```

If this statement is true, then we know that the bullet object has hit some other object. To find which object was hit, we use the code

```
result = AckGetObjectHit();
```

After execution, the variable **result** will hold the number of the object that was hit. The player is concerned with hitting either a monster or his or her opponent, so we check both of these. If either of them was hit by the bullet, we send an indicator character to the other machine and simply remove the appropriate object from the ACK3D screen by using the statement

```
AckDeleteObject()
```

When you design your own game, you don't have to delete the object from the playing field. You can have a secondary bitmap that shows the monster or player lying on the ground as if shot and killed.

Adding Doors

Along with the walls, bullets, and monsters, we can put doors in our map. There are only two types of doors available in an ACK3D game: horizontal and vertical. The doors work by taking an ordinary bitmap and automatically showing different parts of it in a certain order to give the illusion of the door opening. Obviously when the door is closed, you will see all of the bitmap. When the door starts to open, the ACK3D system auto-matically slides the bitmaps so that it looks as if the door is opening. Once fully open, the door will begin to close until fully shut.

Let look at how we add a door. All door bitmaps must be put into the WALL bitmaps array in positions 60 and 62. The bitmap in position 61 is used as frame for the door. This is how the bitmaps are put in the table:

```
BMTABLE bmTable[] = {
    1  ,TYPE_WALL      ,"wall.lbm",
    60 ,TYPE_WALL      ,"roman3.lbm",
    61 ,TYPE_WALL      ,"wall.lbm",
    62 ,TYPE_WALL      ,"roman3.lbm",
    1  ,TYPE_OBJECT    ,"man1.lbm",
    2  ,TYPE_OBJECT    ,"man2.lbm",
    3  ,TYPE_OBJECT    ,"man3.lbm",
    4  ,TYPE_OBJECT    ,"man4.lbm",
    5  ,TYPE_OBJECT    ,"mon1.lbm",
    6  ,TYPE_OBJECT    ,"ammocase.lbm",
    7  ,TYPE_OBJECT    ,"bullet.lbm",
    -1 ,-1             ,""              /* End of table */
```

In addition to the table, you must also put the bitmaps in the resource file. A part of the resource would look like:

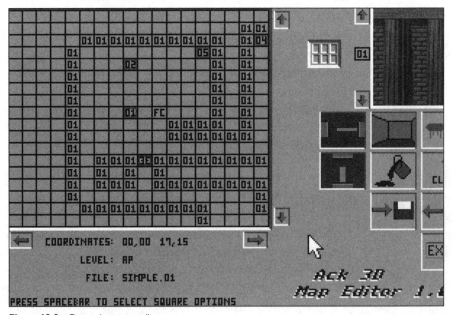

Figure 13.3 Open the map editor.

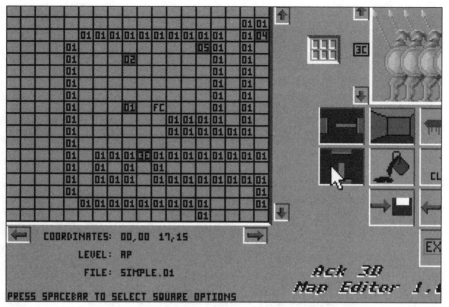

Figure 13.4 The door appears in bitmap space.

```
Walls:
 Files:
 1 , wall.lbm
 60, roman3.lbm
 61, wall.lbm
 62, roman3.lbm
 EndFiles:
EndWalls:
```

With the bitmaps added to the resource file, you can use the map editor to place the doors. To do this, start the map editor using your resource file. Your map should appear in the grid on the left part of the screen as shown in Figure 13.3.

Use the mouse to click on the horizontal door icon or the vertical door icon depending on whether you are placing a horizontal or vertical door. The door bitmap placed in the resource file should appear in the upper right corner as shown in Figure 13.4.

Move the arrow cursor to the appropriate grid location in the map and click the mouse. The door number will appear in the map outlined by a blue line, as shown in Figure 13.5.

Now save the map and you are ready to use doors.

Most of the work for doors is done automatically by the ACK3D engine. All we have to do is call the function AckCheckDoorOpen with the position

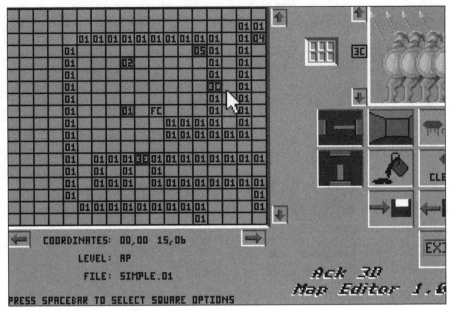

Figure 13.5 The door number appears in the map grid.

and angle of the object that wants to go through the door. In our game, we will want the player to use doors. The code for this would look like:

```
AckCheckDoorOpen(ae->xPlayer, ae->yPlayer, ae->PlayerAngle, ae);
```

If the player is within a certain distance of the door, the ACK3D engine will begin opening the door. Once the door is fully open, the player can walk through. Now remember that each time the player moves, we send a code to the opponent. The figure object that represents the player on the opponent's screen will also move. We need a way of opening the door on the opponent's machine. Thanks to AckCheckDoorOpen, now used with the opponent's object, this is quite easy:

```
AckCheckDoorOpen(ae->ObjList[other_guy].x, ae->ObjList[other_guy].y, ae-
>ObjList[other_guy].Dir, ae);
```

Now if either the player or the opponent gets close enough to a door, it will open and the opponent or player can walk through.

Because of the communication delays involved with the modem and serial port, sometimes the graphical figure object for the opponent will not be able to get through the door fast enough. The door doesn't stay open long enough. To solve this, we are going to check when the doors are fully open and then just prop them open so that the player can get through them easily. The code to do this is in the function check_doors().

We put this function just after the code that checks all of the door open functions. The code is:

```
void check_doors()
{
 if (ae->Door[0].Flags == DOOR_OPENING && (ae->Door[0].ColOffset >= 64))
  ae->Door[0].ColOffset = 0;
 if (ae->Door[1].Flags == DOOR_OPENING && (ae->Door[1].ColOffset >= 64))
  ae->Door[1].ColOffset = 0;
}
```

All of the doors in the ACK3D system are kept in the field Door of the main ACK3D data structure. We can check to see if a door is open by first looking at the door flag and then checking the offset value of the door. If the offset value is greater than or equal to 64 and the door is opening, then we set the offset to 0. This will hold the door open.

Adding Mouse Support

Joystick and keyboard support are usually enough for players. There are times, however, when players will not have access to a joystick and they just don't want to play the game using the keyboard. Typically, the keyboard is a very jerky input device. The solution is to give players the option of using the mouse as an input device. This makes good sense because most computers in use today have a mouse attached.

Normally, we use the mouse as a pointing device. A small arrow appears on the screen and the mouse moves the arrow to some icon that we activate. We are going to use the mouse in a slightly different way. Moving the mouse forward and backward moves the player forward and backward. Moving the mouse to the left or right pans the player left and right. Let's begin our discussion of the mouse by taking a look at the underlying functions necessary to access and read the movements of the mouse.

Mouse Functions

Whether the user has a serial or a bus mouse, a mouse driver is loaded when the computer is first booted. The mouse driver converts the mouse's raw information into something useful for an application. DOS uses software interrupt number 33 to act as an interpreter between the application and the mouse driver. The complete list of interrupt 33 services are given in Table 13.1.

Table 13.1 Mouse interrupt services.

INT 33, 0	Mouse Reset/Get Mouse Installed Flag
INT 33, 1	Show Mouse Cursor
INT 33, 2	Hide Mouse Cursor
INT 33, 3	Get Mouse Position and Button Status
INT 33, 4	Set Mouse Cursor Position
INT 33, 5	Get Mouse Button Press Information
INT 33, 6	Get Mouse Button Release Information
INT 33, 7	Set Mouse Horizontal Min/Max Position
INT 33, 8	Set Mouse Vertical Min/Max Position
INT 33, 9	Set Mouse Graphics Cursor
INT 33, A	Set Mouse Text Cursor
INT 33, B	Read Mouse Motion Counters
INT 33, C	Set Mouse User Defined Subroutine and Input Mask
INT 33, D	Mouse Light Pen Emulation On
INT 33, E	Mouse Light Pen Emulation Off
INT 33, F	Set Mouse Mickey Pixel Ratio
INT 33, 10	Mouse Conditional OFF
INT 33, 13	Set Mouse Double Speed Threshold
INT 33, 14	Swap interrupt subroutines
INT 33, 15	Get mouse driver state and memory requirements
INT 33, 16	Save mouse driver state
INT 33, 17	Restore mouse driver state
INT 33, 18	Set alternate subroutine call mask and address
INT 33, 19	Get user alternate interrupt address
INT 33, 1A	Set mouse sensitivity
INT 33, 1B	Get mouse sensitivity
INT 33, 1C	Set mouse interrupt rate (InPort only)
INT 33, 1D	Set mouse CRT page
INT 33, 1E	Get mouse CRT page
INT 33, 1F	Disable mouse driver
INT 33, 20	Enable mouse driver
INT 33, 21	Reset mouse software
INT 33, 22	Set language for messages
INT 33, 23	Get language number
INT 33, 24	Get driver version, mouse type & IRQ number

The services we will be using are 0, 3, and 11. Before we can use the mouse, we have to determine if a mouse driver has been installed. We do this using service 0. In order to access service 0 of interrupt 33, we must load the CPU's AX register with a value of 00, execute the software interrupt 33, and look for the results of the service in registers AX and BX. The Borland C code to perform this is

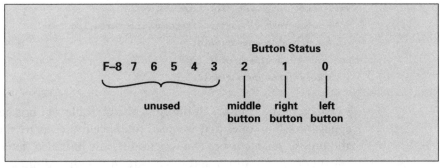

Figure 13.6 BX button bits.

```
union REGS r;
r.x.ax = 0;
int86 (0x33, &r &r);
if (r.x.ax == 0) then no driver installed
else
ax = FFFF (indicating that a driver is present) and
bx = number of buttons on mouse
```

That's all there is to it. Once we have determined that the mouse driver is installed, we are ready to receive data about the mouse's position, which can be completely supplied by interrupt 33 services 3 and 11. Service 3 has two purposes: to report the condition of the buttons on the mouse and to return the current position of the mouse based on a 640 x 480 resolution grid. Upon return from the interrupt, the CX register will contain the current x position of the mouse in units from 0 to 639, whereas the DX register will contain the current y position of the mouse in units from 0 to 199. The BX register will tell us the condition of the buttons. The bits of BX are given the values shown in Figure 13.6. If a button is pressed, the appropriate bit will have a value of 1 instead of 0.

ACKMOUSE

The author of the ACK3D system has included a simple set of functions that we can use to access the mouse in the file ACKMOUSE.C. The functions available are:

```
void mouse_set_mickey_pixel_ratio(int ratrow,int ratcol)
void mouse_set_subroutine(int mflag,void far *func)
void mouse_set_graphics_cursor(int hsrow,int hscol,char far *mask)
void mouse_set_minmax_rows(int minrow,int maxrow)
void mouse_set_minmax_columns(int mincol,int maxcol)
void mouse_release_info(int *bstatus,int *bcount,int *mrow,int *mcol)
void mouse_press_info(int *bstatus,int *bcount,int *mrow,int *mcol)
```

```
void mouse_set_cursor(int mrow,int mcol)
void mouse_read_cursor(int *bstatus,int *mrow,int *mcol)
void mouse_hide_cursor(void)
int mouse_installed(void)
void mouse_show_cursor(void)
```

Many of the routines in the ACKMOUSE file will not be used in our application. The ones that we need to concentrate on are mouse_installed and mouse_read_cursor. The function mouse_installed determines whether a mouse driver and mouse are installed, and mouse_read_cursor determines where the mouse cursor is on the screen.

In order to add mouse support to our game, we need to begin by adding two initialization items to our code. The first is a global variable of type MOUSE. We will add a declaration at the top of our program as

```
MOUSE mouse;
```

This global variable will be used to record position information about the mouse. The second initialization item is a call to the function mouse_installed. The function will be added to the AppInitialize function in our game code. The code to add is:

```
if (mouse_installed() != -1)
 {
  printf("Mouse required to run.\n");
  return(-2);
 }
 mouse_hide_cursor();
```

The code makes a call to the install function to determine if a driver is installed. If the code determines that a mouse driver is not installed, a message is displayed on the screen to alert the user and the program is terminated. If a driver is found, a call is made to the function mouse_ hide_cursor();. This function tells the mouse driver that we are not using the mouse in its traditional sense and that we don't need an arrow cursor displayed on the screen.

At this point, we are ready to use the mouse to control the player. It would seem reasonable to assume that we should read the current state of the mouse each time through our main loop just as we do for the joystick and the keyboard. To do this, we are going to add a function call like

```
checkmouse (&mouse);
```

This function call will make a call to the function checkmouse(), which is defined as

```
void checkmouse(MOUSE *m)
```

```
{
int     dx,dy;
int     x,y,buttons;
mouse_read_cursor(&buttons,&y,&x);
dx = x - 160;
dy = y - 120;
m->mButtons = buttons;
mouse_set_cursor(120,160);
if (abs(dy) > 10 && abs(dx) < 32)
  dx >>= 2;
m->mdx = dx;
m->mdy = dy;
}
```

This function begins by making a call to the ACKMOUSE function mouse_read_cursor(). The mouse_read_cursor() function returns the current position of the mouse based on its screen location. This new position is compared with the mouse's previous position to give a change of position value. The change of position values for both the x and y movements are recorded in the MOUSE variable sent to the checkmouse() function.

After the call to this function we have at our disposal the change of x and y position values. We can use these values to move the player. Let's look at the panning of the player first. The code for panning the player left using the mouse is:

```
checkmouse (&mouse);
if (mouse.mdx < 0)
  {
  ae->PlayerAngle += (-INT_ANGLE_2 * (-mouse.mdx >> 3));
  pan = 1;
  moves++; // Increment our move variable
  }
```

After the call to the function checkmouse(), we make a quick check of the field mouse.mdx. This field is the change of value for the x movement of the mouse. If this value is less than 0, we know that the player has moved the mouse to the left. We will take the change of position value, negate it, and scale it some so that the player is not moving too fast to see what he or she is doing. The scaled value is added to the PlayerAngle field of the ACK3D world variable and we set the other global variable necessary to indicate that a movement has been made.

The code for panning right looks like the left code with a few small differences:

Completing the Game **313**

```
if (mouse.mdx > 0)
  {
  move_val = INT_ANGLE_2 * (mouse.mdx >> 3));
  if (com_device=='i')
    {
    input_buf[0] = '3';
    sock_write ( &our_socket, &input_buf, 1);
    input_buf[1] = mouse.mdx;
    sock_write ( &our_socket, *input_buf, 2);
    }
  ae->PlayerAngle += move_val;
  pan = 1;
  moves++; // Increment our move variable
  }
```

The first difference is that instead of checking to see if the change of value field is less than 0, we check to see if the field is greater than 0. If the field is greater than 0, then we take the current field value, scale it, and assign it to the PlayerAngle field. Notice that we do not negate the change of field type.

You will also see that we have put the Internet code into our code. This will be necessary for all of the mouse movement calls. Check the code on the enclosed CD ROM or in Appendix B & C to see how all of the Internet and other connection code is added.

The code for forward and backward movements looks very similar to the panning code except that it uses the y movement change of value field. The forward movement looks like

```
if (mouse.mdy < 0)
  {
  if (com_device=='i')
    {
    input_buf[0] = '3';
    sock_write ( &our_socket, &input_buf, 1);
    input_buf[1] = -mouse.mdy;
    sock_write ( &our_socket, *input_buf, 2);
    // If Internet connection, let opponent know we are moving forward
    if (com_device=='i')
      {
      ch = '1';
      sock_write ( &our_socket, &ch, 1);
      }
    // Move player forward
    result = AckMovePOV(ae,ae->PlayerAngle,(-mouse.mdy >> 2)+16);
```

```
if (result == POV_OBJECT)
 check_objects();
 moves++;
}
```

The forward movement control for the mouse looks at the field mouse.mdy to determine if movement is necessary. For the forward movement of the player, we have to negate, scale, and call the function AckMovePOV(). For the backward movement of the player, we look at the mdy field to see if it is greater than 0 and then scale and call the AckMovePOV() function.

You will notice that the values we move the player differ from those used for the keyboard and the joystick. For this reason, we will let the opponent know the player's movements using four different character indicators:

> 1=forward
> 2=backward
> 3=left
> 4=right

When the opponent's machine receives any of these values, a call to process_communications() will be made. In the process_communications() function, the code will move the opponent object just as it does for the keyboard and joystick movements, but will use the value sent by the player's machine.

Memory

After all of the additions we have made to our game in this and the previous chapters, we have a program that requires more memory than is available in conventional memory. There are several things that we can do to alleviate this memory problem.

We have already done one thing: We broke our single game into two different files. The first file, MINOSML.c, contains the most basic features we have discussed, with the addition of Internet connections. The second file, MINOTAUR.c, contains connection code for modem/serial port and ethernet as well as additional animation for the opponent's figure and the Minotaur monster.

A second memory solution is to use extended memory. There are many products on the market that allow a conventional program to access extended memory. On the enclosed CD ROM you will find at least one system, ACKGNU.ZIP, that can be used to load many of the bitmaps into additional memory installed in your computer.

A much better solution is to convert the ACK3D system to use a compiling system that puts the computer into protected mode. Protected mode allows a program to take full advantage of all available memory without doing any fancy tricks. One such compiler is called GNU C. This is a freeware package available on the enclosed CD ROM. In addition to the compiler and support systems, you will need to obtain a file called GNUACK.ZIP from the enclosed CD ROM. This file includes source code converted to use the GNU C compiler. With this system, you will be able to use all possible memory in your system. If you use the GNU C package, you will need to convert the modem/serial, ethernet, and the Internet WATTCP package so that it will compile under GNU C. To do this just try to compile the respective files and fix any errors that occur. It should be noted that we have not attempted to convert the communication files to GNU C.

 # Conclusion

There you have it—a complete multi-player 3D Wolfenstein-like arcade computer game. You can use all of the information in this book to create other games of your own or just use parts of it to create network applications. You will find that programming for the network can be very exciting, and allows you to extend your boundaries beyond your own computer.

Installing the Software and Playing Minotaur

Installing the Software

The software for the game we have developed in this book, as well as many other development tools, are available on the enclosed CD ROM. We will look at installing the Minotaur game first and then discuss the other programs available.

Installing Minotaur

The CD ROM contains a directory called \netwario. This is where the minotaur game is located. You can either play the game from the CD ROM or copy it to your hard drive. If you are going to do any development work, you will need to copy the \netwario directory to your hard drive.

Once all of the files are copied, or if you are just going to play the game from the CD ROM, you will find the following executable files in the \netwario directory.

- minotaur—this version allows modem, null modem, and ethernet two-player connection. It allows a single player, as well. This version does not have sound.
- minosml—this version does not allow any two-player connection and does not have sound.
- minosnd—this version has sound and two-player connection as in minotaur above but the player and minotaur monster movements are diminished.
- minointr—this version has no sound and only allows single and two-player internet connection.

A following section will discuss playing the game. Just substitute the appropriate game name that you wish to play.

Other Programs

The CD ROM contains hundreds of packages for game developers. The subdirectories under the directory \game-dev are:

ack	Animation Construction Kit 3D (ACK) related material
ai	Artificial Intelligence related material
art	graphics, music, sound effects, stories
biz	what to do when the program is finished
books	misc book info
convert	file converters, both graphics and music
creative	selectively mirrored files from Creative Tech ftp-site

crypt	data coding, encoding, crypting
demosrc	demos and their source code
docs	documentation and text files, general info
faq	Frequently Asked Questions from internet
fg	Fastgraph graphics library related material
formats	file format specifications
gamesrc	games and their source code
gdm	Game Developers Magazine - official site
gpe	Game Programmers Encyclopedia - official site
hardio	hardware i/o related material - mouse joystick disk cd
libs	programming libraries
math	mathematics related material
memory	memory management related material
microsoft	selectively mirrored files from Microsoft ftp-site
misc	misc material - including 3D world demos
mxcode	music/sound playing/programming/writing source code
mxinfo	music/sound playing/programming/writing information
mxlibs	music/sound playing/programming/writing libraries
mxutil	music/sound playing/programming/writing utilities
net	network programming related material
news	some interesting news articlesw worth saving
ng	Norton Guide databases and related material
packetd	Packet drivers for ethernet communications
pmode	protected mode programming related material
qualitas	Qualitas DPMI libraries
reviews	opinions, summaries, reviews, product infos
rules	rules to games and related info
source	misc source code
specs	technical & official specifications
theory	the theoretical side of things
utils	programming utilities
vla	material from demo group VLA - check 00index.vla
watcom	Watcom (C/C++) compiler related material
wgt	Wordup Graphics Toolkit library related material
windows	MS Windows related material
winsock	Winsock programs
xlib	XLib graphics library related material
vesa	various vesa support libraries
viewers	various GIF, PCX, TIF viewers

Each directory contains many different and interesting libraries, source code, and applications. The majority of the material is from the Internet archive site x2ftp.oulu.fi, a popular game development site.

Playing Minotaur

To play the Minotar game, you will need to have about 610 K of free conventional RAM in a 386 or better IBM PC or compatible. Optional equipment includes a joystick, modem, ethernet card, or Internet connection.

To start the game, type **minotaur**. If you want to use a joystick with the game, add a -j switch like this: **minotaur -j**.

Connection Menu

Once the program loads, you will be given the connection menu shown in Figure A.1.

Single Play

To play the game by yourself, press **S**. The game will then load as single-player only.

Null Modem Serial

To use the null modem connection scheme, you need to have two computers connected via their serial ports and a null modem cable. Press **N** at the connection menu—you will then be asked for the serial port COM number you are using. Next, you will get a selection of baud rates. Press the appropriate value. After all of the selections, you will be asked if this is the originator or the answering machine. Be sure to press the appropriate option. When both machines are at the originator/answering question—press **A** on one machine and then **O** on the other. The machines will establish a connection and you are ready to play.

Modem

You will then be asked for the serial port COM number you are using. Next, you will get a selection of baud rates. Press the appropriate value.

```
   Please select the communication medium that
you would like to use:
  (E)thernet connection
  (I)nternet connection
  (N)ull Modem connection
  (M)odem connection
  (S)ingle User
  :
```

Figure A.1   Connections menu.

After all of the selections, you will be asked if this is the originator or the answering machine. Be sure to only press the appropriate option when both machines are at the originator/answering question.

When both machines are at this question, press **A** on one machine and then **O** on the other. The originating machine will be prompted to enter the phone number of the opponent. The answering machine will just wait for an answer. Once the machine has made a connection, you are ready to play.

Ethernet

If you press the **E** key at the connection menu, you will be using an ethernet connection. To do this you must have an ethernet card installed in your computer as well as a packet driver running as a TSR on your machine. Most ethernet cards now come with packet drivers. If yours does not, you can look in the enclosed CD ROM in the directory \PACKET to find a number of drivers that will work with most cards.

You will be asked if this is the originator or the answering machine. Be sure to only press the appropriate option when both machines are at the originator/answering question: press **A** on one machine and then **O** on the other. The machines will establish a connection and you are ready to play.

If, after pressing the **E** key, you do not get an originating/answering question, then the program was unable to find your packet driver. Check the installation for mistakes and try again.

Internet

Now comes the interesting part. If you pressed the **I** key, then you are going to try for an Internet connection. For this you need have the IP address of the machine that you are going to connect to.

You will be asked if this is the originator or the answering machine. Be sure to only press the appropriate option when both machines are at the originator/answering question: press **A** on one machine and then **O** on the other. On the originating machine you will be asked for the IP address of the answering machine. Enter the address as a hexadecimal number separated by spaces and not periods.

Once a connection has been made with the other machine, you are ready to play.

Game Play

Once the game has loaded, you can use the joystick or the keyboard arrow keys to move. To fire your gun, press the joystick button or the spacebar. You are free to move around the entire map—just be careful of monsters and your opponent.

When you come to a door, it will open automatically.

To quit the game, press the Esc key.

Code Listing for the Internet Version of Minotaur

This is the complete source code for the Internet/single-user version of our game. We have not done any optimizations or pulled the code out of the main() function as would be appropriate for a correct program. The code is presented for the best possible understanding of what is happening in the main_loop.

```c
#include <stdlib.h>
#include <stdio.h>
#include <dos.h>
#include <mem.h>
#include <alloc.h>
#include <io.h>
#include <fcntl.h>
#include <time.h>
#include <string.h>
#include <conio.h>
#include <sys\stat.h>

#include "ack3d.h"
#include "acksnd.h"

#include "simple.h"
#include "tcp.h"
#include "math.h"
#include "joystick.h"

#define HOME        0x4700
#define END         0x4F00
#define PGUP        0x4900
#define PGDN        0x5100
#define LEFT        0x4B00
#define RIGHT       0x4D00
#define UP          0x4800
#define DOWN        0x5000
#define SHLEFT      0x4B01
#define SHRIGHT     0x4D01
#define SHUP        0x4801
#define SHDOWN      0x5001
#define SHPGUP      0x4901
#define SHPGDN      0x5101
#define CTRLLEFT    0x7300
#define CTRLRIGHT   0x7400
#define CTRLHOME    0x7700
#define CTRLEND     0x7500
```

```
#define CTRLPGUP    0x8400
#define CTRLPGDN    0x7600
#define ESC         0x001B


#define other_guy 1                 // Position of opponent in object array
#define monster1  2                 // Position of minotaur in object array
#define bullet    6                 // Position of our bullet in object array
#define monster_bullet 7            // Position of medusa bullet in object
array
#define other_guy_bullet 8          // Position of opponent bullet in object
array
#define medusa 9                    // Position of medusa monster in object
array


//Main ACK3D Variables
extern UCHAR far colordat[];    // Local ACK3D palette array
ACKENG      *ae;                // Main ACK3D 'world' variable
MOUSE       mouse;             // Mouse variable

char        *MapFileName = "simple.MAP";    // Mapfile filename
char        *PalFile    = "simple.PAL";    // Palette filename
char        *PictureFile = "dashboar.lbm"; // Screen overlay filename
UCHAR far   *OverlayPic;                    // Pointer to overlay graphics


// This is the bitmap table for the application.  Each bitmap must include
// information about its bitmap number, bitmap type, and its filename.

BMTABLE bmTable[] = {
    1   ,TYPE_WALL          ,"wall.lbm",
    60  ,TYPE_WALL          ,"roman3.lbm",
    61  ,TYPE_WALL          ,"wall.lbm",
    62  ,TYPE_WALL          ,"roman3.lbm",
    1   ,TYPE_OBJECT        ,"manb1.lbm",
    2   ,TYPE_OBJECT        ,"manf1.lbm",
    3   ,TYPE_OBJECT        ,"manl1.lbm",
    4   ,TYPE_OBJECT        ,"manr2.lbm",
    5   ,TYPE_OBJECT        ,"mino1.lbm",
    6   ,TYPE_OBJECT        ,"ammo.lbm",
    7   ,TYPE_OBJECT        ,"bullet.lbm",
    9   ,TYPE_OBJECT        ,"mino2.lbm",
    11  ,TYPE_OBJECT        ,"minob1.lbm",
```

```
        14 ,TYPE_OBJECT      ,"minol1.lbm",
        16 ,TYPE_OBJECT      ,"minor1.lbm",
        -1 ,-1          ,""               /* End of table */
        };


char far *Sounds[] = { "hitobj1.voc" };
int TOTAL_SOUND = 1;


// This array includes information about the way that our palette is set
// up.
ColorRange  ranges[64] = {
        16,16,
        32,16,
        48,16,
        64,16,
        80,16,
        96,8,
        104,8,
        112,8,
        120,8,
        128,8,
        136,8,
        144,8,
        152,8,
        160,8,
        168,8,
        176,8,
        184,8,
        192,16,
        208,16,
        224,8,
        232,8,
        0,0
        };


//Communication variables
int person = 0,              // What player are we
    com_device = 0,          // What communication device is active
    use_joystick = 0,        // Are we using a joystick
    ammo = 5,                // Current ammo count
```

```
        is_shooting = 0,                // Are we currently shooting
        monster_shooting = 1,           // Is the monster currently shooting
        monster_moves = 0,              // Total monster steps (used for
                                        // animation)
        player_start_x,                 // Starting position and angle of player
        player_start_y,
        player_start_angle,
        opponent_start_x,               // Starting position and angle of opponent
        opponent_start_y,
        opponent_start_angle,
        monster_start_x,                // Starting position and angle of minotaur
        monster_start_y,
        monster_start_angle;


//TCP/IP Variables
tcp_Socket       our_socket;     // Main variable for TCP/IP connection
word             status;         // Status variable for connection
longword         remoteip;       // Resolved IP for receiving machine
char             host[25];       // Input string for receiving IP
unsigned char    input_buf[10];  // Input buffer for incoming data

#define TCP_PORT 23              // TCP/IP port for our connection


//Font variables
UCHAR far *smFont;               // Pointer to our font graphics
int        TextBGcolor = 7,      // Current background color for fonts
           FontColor = 0;        // Current font color


// This is a required function for the WATTCP package.  It is used to
// indicate when an error has occurred in the TCP/IP connection.
void sock_err()
{
 //sock_err:
    switch ( status ) {
        case 1 : cputs("Connection closed");
            break;
        case -1: cputs("REMOTE HOST CLOSED CONNECTION");
            sock_close ( &our_socket );
            sock_wait_closed ( &our_socket, sock_delay, NULL, &status );
            break;
```

```
        }
}


//Forward references for functions defined later
void monster_shoot();
void process_communications(char value);
void hangup();
int select_communication_device();
int setup_com();
int create_link();
void move_monsters();
void check_objects();



//This function loads a font into memory.  The font file is called
//'spfont.bbm'
int LoadSmallFont(void)
{
  int ht,wt,len;

  smFont = AckReadiff("spfont.bbm");
  if (smFont == NULL)
    return(-1);

  ht = (*(int *)smFont);
  wt = (*(int *)&smFont[2]);
  len = ht * wt;
  memmove(smFont,&smFont[4],len);

  return(0);
}



//This function resets all objects and players in our game when either
//player is killed.
void reset_game()
{

  // Reset player
  ae->xPlayer = player_start_x;
  ae->yPlayer = player_start_y;
  ae->PlayerAngle = player_start_angle;
```

```
    // Reset minotaur monster
    ae->ObjList[monster1].x = monster_start_x;
    ae->ObjList[monster1].y = monster_start_y;
    ae->ObjList[monster1].Dir = monster_start_angle;
    ae->ObjList[monster1].mPos = (ae->ObjList[monster1].y & 0xFFC0) + (ae-
>ObjList[monster1].x >> 6);
    ae->ObjList[monster1].Active = 1;


    // Reset opponent monster
    ae->ObjList[other_guy].x = opponent_start_x;
    ae->ObjList[other_guy].y = opponent_start_y;
    ae->ObjList[other_guy].Dir = opponent_start_angle;
    ae->ObjList[other_guy].mPos = (ae->ObjList[other_guy].y & 0xFFC0) + (ae-
>ObjList[other_guy].x >> 6);
    ae->ObjList[other_guy].Active = 1;


    // Put all of the ammo cans back on screen
    ae->ObjList[3].Active = 1;
    ae->ObjList[4].Active = 1;
    ae->ObjList[5].Active = 1;


    // Reset total ammo we are carrying
    ammo = 5;
}



// Displays a character either directly on the video, or into the screen
// buffer depending on whether FontTransparent flag is set.
void smWriteChar(int x,int y,unsigned char ch)
{
    int   FontOffset,VidOffset;
    int   row,col;
    unsigned     char far *Video;

    VidOffset = (y * 320) + x;
    Video = MK_FP(0xA000,VidOffset);

    FontOffset = ((ch-32) * 5);


    for (row = 0; row < 5; row++)
    {
```

```
            memset(Video,TextBGcolor,4);

       if  (smFont[FontOffset])
            Video[0] = FontColor;
       if  (smFont[FontOffset+1])
            Video[1] = FontColor;
       if  (smFont[FontOffset+2])
            Video[2] = FontColor;
       if  (smFont[FontOffset+3])
            Video[3] = FontColor;

     Video += 320;
     FontOffset += 294;
   }
}


// Calls smWriteChar() to display the contents of the passed string. Only
// crude string handling is done in this routine.
int smWriteString(int x,int y,char *s)
{
   int      OrgX;
   char     ch;

   OrgX = x;

   while (*s)
   {
     ch = *s++;

     if (ch == 10)           /* If a linefeed then advance to next row */
         {
     x = OrgX;
     y += 8;
     continue;
         }

     if (ch < ' ')
       continue;

     ch = toupper(ch);
     smWriteChar(x,y,ch);
     x += 5;      /* Advance to next character position */
   }
```

```c
return(y);
}



//This function updates a bullet that has been fired by our player.
void UpdateShoot()
{
  int result;
  char ch;


  // Move bullet forward and check for collision
  result = AckMoveObjectPOV (ae, bullet, ae->ObjList[bullet].Dir, ae-
>ObjList[bullet].Speed);

  // If Internet connection, send new location of our bullet
  if (com_device=='i')
  {
    input_buf[0] = 'm';
    sock_write (&our_socket, input_buf, 1);
    input_buf[1] = (ae->ObjList[bullet].x & 0xFF00)>>8;
    input_buf[2] = (ae->ObjList[bullet].x & 0x00FF);
    input_buf[3] = (ae->ObjList[bullet].y & 0xFF00)>>8;
    input_buf[4] = ae->ObjList[bullet].y & 0x00FF;
    sock_write ( &our_socket, input_buf, 5);
  }


  // Check for bullet collisions
  if ((result != POV_NOTHING) && (result != POV_PLAYER))
  {
    // A collision has occurred, remove bullet from screen
    ae->ObjList[bullet].Active = 0;
    is_shooting = 0;

    //If Internet connection, tell other machine to remove our bullet
    if (com_device=='i')
    {
      ch = 'n';
      sock_write ( &our_socket, &ch, 1);
    }
```

```c
//Check for collision with object
if (result == POV_OBJECT)
{
  result = AckGetObjectHit();

  // Did we hit our minotaur monster
  if (result == monster1)
  {
    // If Internet connection, let other machine know we hit minotaur
    if (com_device=='i')
    {
      input_buf[0] = 'j';
      sock_write(&our_socket, input_buf, 1);
      input_buf[1] = monster1;
      sock_write ( &our_socket, input_buf, 2);
    }
    //Remove monster from screen
    AckDeleteObject(ae, monster1);
    AckDeleteObject(ae, monster_bullet);
  }
  // Check and see if we hit opponent
  else if (result == other_guy)
  {
    // If Internet connection, let other machine know we hit them
    if (com_device=='i')
    {
      ch = 'w';
      sock_write ( &our_socket, &ch, 1);
    }
    //Remove opponent from screen
    AckDeleteObject(ae, other_guy);
    AckDeleteObject(ae, other_guy_bullet);

    // Reset Game
    AckFadeOut(0, 255);
    reset_game();
    AckFadeIn(0, 255, colordat);
  }

}
}
}
```

```c
// This function returns a key from the keyboard
int shifted;
unsigned getkey()
{
  unsigned c;
  union REGS regs;

  regs.h.ah = 2;

  int86(0x16, &regs,&regs );
  shifted = (regs.h.al & 3);

  if ((c=bioskey (0)) & 0xff) c &= 0xff;
  else if ( shifted ) c |= 1;
  return c;
}




//This function checks to see if any of the doors are open.  If they are
//open, they are held permanently open.
void check_doors()
{

  // If a door is open, ColOffset >= 64, then we can hold the door open by
  // setting ColOffset to 0

  if (ae->Door[0].Flags == DOOR_OPENING && (ae->Door[0].ColOffset >= 64))
    ae->Door[0].ColOffset = 0;

  if (ae->Door[1].Flags == DOOR_OPENING && (ae->Door[1].ColOffset >= 64))
    ae->Door[1].ColOffset = 0;
}


// This routine checks the current state of the mouse and fills the MOUSE
// variable with the appropriate information.
void checkmouse(MOUSE *m)
{
    int     dx,dy;
    int     x,y,buttons;
```

```c
    mouse_read_cursor(&buttons,&y,&x);
    dx = x - 160;
    dy = y - 120;
    m->mButtons = buttons;
    mouse_set_cursor(120,160);

    if (abs(dy) > 10 && abs(dx) < 32)
        dx >>= 2;


    m->mdx = dx;
    m->mdy = dy;


}




// This is the main function.  There is far too much stuff here but I have
// left it in so that you can see the progression of the different parts of
// the program.
int main(void)
{
    int         result,
                done=0,             // Main loop control variable
                pan=0,              // Current pan value to player
                i,
                temp,
                packet_length,      // Length of our packets
                x,
                y,
                buttons,            // Joystick button value
                joy_centx,          // Joystick X value
                joy_centy,          // Joystick Y value
                moves=0;
    unsigned    ch_val;
    char        buf[35] = "";       // Buffer to print to screen
    unsigned char ch;


// Start by getting current communicaton device.
    if (select_communication_device())
    {
        printf ( "Error setting up communication device\n");
```

```c
        return(1);
    }


// If we are using a communication device, create the link
    if (com_device != 's')
    if (create_link())
    {
        printf ("Error creating communication link\n");
        return(1);
    }



// Perform an application initialization
    if (result==AppInitialize())
    {
        printf("Error initializing: ErrorCode = %d\n",result);
        return(1);
    }


// Set up the ACK3D engine
    if (result==AppSetupEngine())
    {
        printf("Error setting up ACK engine: ErrorCode = %d\n",result);
        AckWrapUp(ae);
        return(1);
    }


// Load in all of the bitmaps in our global bitmap array
    if (result==AppLoadBitmaps())
    {
        printf("Error loading bitmaps: ErrorCode = %d\n",result);
        AckWrapUp(ae);
        return(1);
    }


// Go to graphics mode
    if (result==AppSetGraphics())
    {
        AckSetTextmode();
        printf("Error loading palette: ErrorCode = %d\n",result);
        AckWrapUp(ae);
        return(1);
    }
```

```
// Read and setup the screen overlay
    if (result == AppSetupOverlay())
    {
      printf("Error loading overlay: ErrorCode = %d\n",result);
      AckWrapUp(ae);
      return(1);
    }


// Load in the fonts for writing to the screen
    if (LoadSmallFont())
    {
      AckSetTextmode();
      printf("Error loading font: ErrorCode = %d\n",result);
      AckWrapUp(ae);
      return(1);
    }


// Create all of our objects
    if (result==AppSetObject())
    {
      AckSetTextmode();
      printf("Error loading palette: ErrorCode = %d\n",result);
      AckWrapUp(ae);
      return(1);
    }


// Set up palette
    AppSetupPalRanges();


/*    if (AckSoundInitialize(DEV_PCSPEAKER))
    {
      AckSetTextmode();
      printf ("Error initializing sound\n");
      AckWrapUp(ae);
      return(1);
    }

    for (i=0;i<TOTAL_SOUND;i++)
    {
      AckLoadSound(i, Sounds[i]);
    }  */
```

```
// Based on the current player value located in the variable PERSON, switch
// locations of the player and opponent for one of the machines.
    if (person)
    {
      temp = ae->ObjList[other_guy].x;
      ae->ObjList[other_guy].x = ae->xPlayer;
      ae->xPlayer = temp;

      temp = ae->ObjList[other_guy].y;
      ae->ObjList[other_guy].y = ae->yPlayer;
      ae->yPlayer = temp;

      ae->ObjList[other_guy].mPos = (ae->ObjList[other_guy].y & 0xFFC0) +
(ae->ObjList[other_guy].x >> 6);

      temp = ae->ObjList[other_guy].Dir;
      ae->ObjList[other_guy].Dir = ae->PlayerAngle;
      ae->PlayerAngle = temp;
    }


// Record the current locations of player, opponent, and minotaur.
    player_start_x = ae->xPlayer;
    player_start_y = ae->yPlayer;
    player_start_angle = ae->PlayerAngle;

    opponent_start_x = ae->ObjList[other_guy].x;
    opponent_start_y = ae->ObjList[other_guy].y;
    opponent_start_angle = ae->ObjList[other_guy].Dir;

    monster_start_x = ae->ObjList[monster1].x;
    monster_start_y = ae->ObjList[monster1].y;
    monster_start_angle = ae->ObjList[monster1].Dir;

// If we are using a joystick, we need to initialize it.
    if (use_joystick)
      joystick_read(&joy_centx, &joy_centy, &buttons);


// Here is the start of the main loop for the program. Note that we need
// to constantly make a check of the Internet connection using the tcp_tick
// function.  We also monitor the variable done.
```

```
        while ((tcp_tick(&our_socket))&&(!done))
        {
// Only player 0 controls the movement of the minotaur monster.
        if (person == 0) move_monsters();


// If we are shooting then we need to update the location of the bullet
// each time through our main loop.
        if (is_shooting) UpdateShoot();


// Each loop iteration should make a call to this function to keep the
// internals of ACK3D happy.
        AckCheckObjectMovement(ae);


// If we have rotated our player, we need to make sure that the angle value
// is not > 360 or < 0.
        if (pan)
        {
          pan = 0;
          if (ae->PlayerAngle >= INT_ANGLE_360)
            ae->PlayerAngle -= INT_ANGLE_360;
          if (ae->PlayerAngle < 0)
            ae->PlayerAngle += INT_ANGLE_360;
        }


// Write the current ammo count to the bottom right part of the screen
        sprintf (buf, "%d\n", ammo);
        smWriteString(280,185, buf);



// Build the new screen - First the walls and objects, then the overlay
        AckBuildView(ae);
        AckDrawOverlay(ae->ScreenBuffer,ae->OverlayBuffer);


// Display our new screen.
        AckDisplayScreen(ae);



// If the Internet connection is active, check to see if any data is
// available. If data is available, it should be read and processed in the
// process_comm unication function.
        if (com_device == 'i')
          if (sock_dataready ( &our_socket ) )
```

```
          {
            sock_read ( &our_socket, &ch, 1);
            process_communications(ch);
          }


// If the player has made more than two moves, we need to sync our machine
// with the opponent.  We do this by sending the current positions of our
// player.  This could be extended to the monsters if we wanted to
     if (moves > 2)
     {
       moves = 0;
       if (com_device=='i')
       {
         input_buf[0] = 'z';
         sock_write (&our_socket, input_buf, 1);

         input_buf[1] = (ae->xPlayer & 0xFF00)>>8;
         input_buf[2] = ae->xPlayer & 0x00FF;
         input_buf[3] = (ae->yPlayer & 0xFF00)>>8;
         input_buf[4] = ae->yPlayer & 0x00FF;
         input_buf[5] = (ae->PlayerAngle & 0xFF00) >> 8;
         input_buf[6] = ae->PlayerAngle & 0x00FF;
         sock_write ( &our_socket, input_buf, 7);
       }
     }

   checkmouse(&mouse);

   // Pan Left with mouse
   if (mouse.mdx < 0)
   {
     if (com_device=='i')
     {
       input_buf[0] = '4';
       sock_write ( &our_socket, &input_buf, 1);
       input_buf[1] = -mouse.mdx;
       sock_write ( &our_socket, &input_buf, 2);
     }
     ae->PlayerAngle += (-INT_ANGLE_2 * (-mouse.mdx >> 3));
     pan = 1;
     moves++;  // Increment our move variable
   }
```

```c
// Pan right with mouse
if (mouse.mdx > 0)
{
  if (com_device=='i')
  {
    input_buf[0] = '3';
    sock_write ( &our_socket, &ch, 1);
    input_buf[1] = mouse.mdx;
    sock_write (&our_socket, &input_buf, 2);
  }
  ae->PlayerAngle += (INT_ANGLE_2 * (mouse.mdx >> 3));
  pan = 1;
  moves++;  // Increment our move variable
}


// Move forward with mouse
if (mouse.mdy < 0)
{
  // If Internet connection, let opponent know we are moving forward
  if (com_device=='i')
  {
    input_buf[0] = '1';
    sock_write ( &our_socket, &ch, 1);
    input_buf[1] = -mouse.mdy;
    sock_write (&our_socket, &input_buf, 2);

  }
  // Move player forward
  result = AckMovePOV(ae,ae->PlayerAngle,(-mouse.mdy >> 2)+16);
  if (result == POV_OBJECT)
    check_objects();
  moves++;
}


// Move backward with mouse
if (mouse.mdy > 0)
{
    // If Internet connection, let opponent know we are moving backward
    if (com_device=='i')
    {
      input_buf[0] = '2';
      sock_write ( &our_socket, &ch, 1);
```

```
          input_buf[1] = mouse.mdy;
          sock_write (&our_socket, &input_buf, 2);
        }
      temp= ae->PlayerAngle + INT_ANGLE_180;
      if (temp >= INT_ANGLE_360) temp -= INT_ANGLE_360;
      if (temp < 0) temp += INT_ANGLE_360;

      result = AckMovePOV(ae,temp,(mouse.mdy>>2)+16);
      if (result == POV_OBJECT)
        check_objects();
      moves++;
    }


// If we are using the joystick, we need to process it.
  if (use_joystick)
  {

    // First read the current state of the joystick
    buttons = 0;
    joystick_read (&x, &y, &buttons);

    // If we are not already shooting and the joystick button is pressed,
    // then fire our gun, but only if we have ammo.
      if ((buttons == 239) && (!is_shooting))
      {
        if (ammo)
        {
    // If Internet connection, let opponent know we are shooting.
    if (com_device=='i')
      {
        ch = 'l';
        sock_write ( &our_socket, &ch, 1);
      }

    // Indicate that we are shooting and place the bullet directly in
// front of us.
      is_shooting = 1;
      ae->ObjList[bullet].x = ae->xPlayer;
      ae->ObjList[bullet].y = ae->yPlayer;
      ae->ObjList[bullet].Dir = ae->PlayerAngle;
      ae->ObjList[bullet].mPos = (ae->ObjList[bullet].y & 0xFFC0) + (ae-
>ObjList[bullet].x >> 6);
      ae->ObjList[bullet].VidRow = 100;
```

```
        ae->ObjList[bullet].Active = 1;
  // Decrease ammo count
     ammo--;
  }
}


// Eliminate some of the noise of the joystick.
{
  x = joy_centx - x;
  y = joy_centy - y;

  if ( x>15 ) x -= 15;
  else
  {
    if ( x > -15) x = 0;
    else x += 15;
  }

  if ( y > 15 ) y -= 15;
  else
  {
    if(y>-15) y = 0;
    else y+=15;
  }


// Process the X value of the joystick
    if (x!=0)
    {
    // Scale the X value substantially
  ch = x/20;

// If Internet connection, transmit X value to opponent
if (com_device=='i')
    {
      buf[0] = 'e';
      buf[1] = ch;
      sock_write ( &our_socket, buf, 2);
    }
// Change the player position
    ae->PlayerAngle -= ch;
    pan = 1;
  }
```

```
// Process the Y value of the joystick
        if (y!=0)
        {
// Scale the Y value substantially
        ch = y/20;

    if (y>0)
{
// If Internet connection, transmit Y value to opponent
if (com_device=='i')
        {
 buf[0] = 'g';
 buf[1] = ch;
 sock_write ( &our_socket, buf, 2);
        }
// Move the player forward
result = AckMovePOV(ae,ae->PlayerAngle,y/20);
// Check to see what we have hit
        if (result == POV_OBJECT)
  check_objects();
        }
        else
// Move the player backward
        {
// If Internet connection, transmit Y value to opponent and
// indicate backward movement
if (com_device=='i')
        {
     buf[0] = 'h';
     buf[1] = ch;
     sock_write ( &our_socket, buf, 2);
        }

// Move the player backward
        temp= ae->PlayerAngle + INT_ANGLE_180;
        if (temp >= INT_ANGLE_360)
    temp -= INT_ANGLE_360;

        result = AckMovePOV(ae,temp,-y/20);
        if (result == POV_OBJECT)
check_objects();
    }
```

```
            }
        }
    }


// Make a call to ACK3D so it will check the status of the doors for both
// the player and the opponent's object.
    AckCheckDoorOpen(ae->xPlayer, ae->yPlayer, ae->PlayerAngle, ae);
    AckCheckDoorOpen(ae->ObjList[other_guy].x, ae->ObjList[other_guy].y,
ae->ObjList[other_guy].Dir, ae);


// Check the doors again to see if they are fully open.
    check_doors();


// Look for a keyboard hit
    if (bioskey(1))
    {
        ch_val = getkey();
        if (ch_val==ESC) break;

        switch(ch_val)
        {
// Pan the player to the left
        case LEFT :
        // If Internet connection, let opponent know we are panning left
                if (com_device=='i')
                {
        ch = 'd';
        sock_write ( &our_socket, &ch, 1);
                }
        // Pan Left
                ae->PlayerAngle += (-INT_ANGLE_2 * 5);
                pan = 1;
        moves++;   // Increment our move variable
                break;


// Pan the player to the right
        case RIGHT:
        // If Internet connection, let opponent know we are panning right
                if (com_device=='i')
                {
        ch = 'c';
        sock_write ( &our_socket, &ch, 1);
```

344 APPENDIX B

```
                    }
            // Pan Right
                        ae->PlayerAngle += INT_ANGLE_2 * 5;
                        pan = 1;
                        moves++;
                        break;


// Move the player forward
        case UP:
        // If Internet connection, let opponent know we are moving forward
                        if (com_device=='i')
                        {
            ch = 'a';
            input_buf[0] = 'a';
            sock_write ( &our_socket, &ch, 1);
                        }
        // Move player forward
                        result = AckMovePOV(ae,ae->PlayerAngle,16);
                        if (result == POV_OBJECT)
             check_objects();
                        moves++;
                        break;


// Move the player backward
        case DOWN:
        // If Internet connection, let opponent know we are moving backward
                        if (com_device=='i')
                        {
            ch = 'b';
            sock_write ( &our_socket, &ch, 1);
                        }
                        temp= ae->PlayerAngle + INT_ANGLE_180;
                        if (temp >= INT_ANGLE_360) temp -= INT_ANGLE_360;
                        if (temp < 0) temp += INT_ANGLE_360;

                        result = AckMovePOV(ae,temp,16);
                        if (result == POV_OBJECT)
             check_objects();
                        moves++;
                        break;


// Fire our gun
case ' ':
```

```c
            if ((ammo)&&(!is_shooting))
            {
                if (com_device=='i')
                {
                ch = 'l';
                sock_write ( &our_socket, &ch, 1);
                }

                    is_shooting = 1;
                    ae->ObjList[bullet].x = ae->xPlayer;
                    ae->ObjList[bullet].y = ae->yPlayer;
                    ae->ObjList[bullet].Dir = ae->PlayerAngle;
                    ae->ObjList[bullet].mPos = (ae->ObjList[bullet].y &
0xFFC0) + (ae->ObjList[bullet].x >> 6);
                    ae->ObjList[bullet].VidRow = 100;
                    ae->ObjList[bullet].Active = 1;
                    ammo--;
                }
        }
    }


    AckWrapUp(ae);
    AckSetTextmode();
    return(0);
}



// This function allocates memory for the ACK3D system.
int AppInitialize(void)
{
    if ((ae=malloc(sizeof(ACKENG))) == NULL)
        return(-1);

    if (mouse_installed() != -1)
    {
        printf("Mouse required to run.\n");
        return(-2);
    }

    mouse_hide_cursor();
```

```c
    memset(ae,0,sizeof(ACKENG));


    return(0);
}


//This function initializes the ACK3D system.
int AppSetupEngine(void)
{
    int result;


// Set size of our viewing window
    ae->WinStartX = VIEW_X;
    ae->WinStartY = VIEW_Y;
    ae->WinEndX   = VIEW_X1;
    ae->WinEndY   = VIEW_Y1;

// Set various variable
    ae->DoorSpeed = DOORSPEED;
    ae->xPlayer = PLAYER_X;
    ae->yPlayer = PLAYER_Y;
    ae->PlayerAngle = INT_ANGLE_180; //PLAYER_ANGLE;

// Initialize the 'world' variable
    if (result==AckInitialize(ae))
        return(result);

// Read Map File
    if (result == AckReadMapFile(ae,MapFileName))
    {
        AckWrapUp(ae);
        return(result);
    }

// Set floor and ceiling options
    ae->TopColor  = CEILING_COLOR;
    ae->BottomColor = FLOOR_COLOR;
    ae->LightFlag = SHADING_OFF;
    if (result == AckBuildBackground(ae))
        return (result);

    return(0);
```

```
}


//This function reads into memory our screen overlay.
int AppSetupOverlay(void)
{
  int result = 0;
  UCHAR far *Video;

  OverlayPic = AckReadiff(PictureFile);

  if (OverlayPic == NULL)
    return(-1);

//Copy the overlay to video memory and let the ACK3D system work on it. After
//ACK3D is finished, we can get rid of the overlay memory.
  Video = MK_FP(0xA000,0);
  memmove(Video,&OverlayPic[4],64000);
  result = AckCreateOverlay(ae,&OverlayPic[4]);
  free(OverlayPic);

  return(result);
}




//This function reads all of our bitmaps into memory
int AppLoadBitmaps(void)
{
 int      result, i=0;

 while (bmTable[i].Number != -1)
 {
  if (result==AckLoadBitmap(ae,bmTable[i].Number,bmTable[i].Type,bmTable[i].Name))
     break;

    i++;
 }

  return(result);
}
```

```c
//This function sets up the graphics screen.
int AppSetGraphics(void)
{
  int result;

  AckSetVGAmode();

  result = AckLoadAndSetPalette(PalFile);
  return(result);
}



//This function reads in our palette and lets the VGA card know about it.
void AppSetupPalRanges(void)
{
  int    i,j,k,found;
  int    rangenos;
  UCHAR  plotcolor;

  for (rangenos = 0; rangenos < 64; rangenos++)
  {
   if (ranges[rangenos].start == 0)
      break;
  }


  for ( i = 0;i<16;i++)
  {
    for (j=0;j<256;j++)
    {
      found = 0;
      for ( k = 0; k < rangenos; k++ )
      {
        if (j >= ranges[k].start && j < ranges[k].start+ranges[k].length)
        {
         found = 1;
         break;
        }
      }

    if (found)
    {
      if (j+i >= ranges[k].start+ranges[k].length)
```

```
         plotcolor = 0;
       else
         plotcolor = j+i;
     }
     else
     {
         plotcolor = j;
     }


   ae->PalTable[j+(i*256)] = plotcolor;
   }
 }
}



// This function takes our bitmaps and creates objects using them
// Each of the objects must have their bitmaps selected, a speed indicated,
// flags set, and a direction indicated.

int AppSetObject(void)
{
   UCHAR bitmaps[3];
   int result;


// Opponent's graphical object
   bitmaps[0] = 1;
   bitmaps[1] = 3;
   bitmaps[2] = 2;
   bitmaps[3] = 4;

   ae->ObjList[other_guy].Speed = 1;
   ae->ObjList[other_guy].Dir = 0;

   AckCreateObject (ae, other_guy, 4, bitmaps);


//Minotaur monster
   bitmaps[0] = 11;
   bitmaps[1] = 14;
   bitmaps[2] = 5;
   bitmaps[3] = 16;
   ae->ObjList[monster1].Speed = 2;
```

```
    ae->ObjList[monster1].Dir = INT_ANGLE_90;


    AckCreateObject (ae, monster1, 4, bitmaps);


// ammo loads
// Ammo 1
    bitmaps[0] = 6;
    ae->ObjList[3].Flags = 0;
    ae->ObjList[3].Speed = 0;
    ae->ObjList[3].Dir = 0;


    AckCreateObject (ae, 3, 1, bitmaps);


// Ammo 2
    bitmaps[0] = 6;
    ae->ObjList[4].Flags = 0;
    ae->ObjList[4].Speed = 0;
    ae->ObjList[4].Dir = 0;


    AckCreateObject (ae, 4, 1, bitmaps);


// Ammo 3
    bitmaps[0] = 6;
    ae->ObjList[5].Flags = 0;
    ae->ObjList[5].Speed = 0;
    ae->ObjList[5].Dir = 0;
    AckCreateObject (ae, 5, 1, bitmaps);



//Load our bullet
    bitmaps[0] = 7;
    ae->ObjList[6].Flags = 0;
    ae->ObjList[6].Speed = 25;
    ae->ObjList[6].Dir = 0;
    ae->ObjList[bullet].Active = 0;
    AckCreateObject (ae, bullet, 1, bitmaps);



//Load other guy bullet
    bitmaps[0] = 7;
    ae->ObjList[8].Flags = 0;
    ae->ObjList[8].Speed = 25;
    ae->ObjList[8].Dir = 0;
```

```c
         ae->ObjList[8].Active = 0;
         AckCreateObject (ae, other_guy_bullet, 1, bitmaps);


    return(0);
    }



//This function is responsible for handling the character values coming from
//our opponent.
void process_communications(char value)
{
   int   temp, num1, num2, num3, num4;
   char ch;


   switch(value)
   {
//Move opponent object forward
     case 'a': AckMoveObjectPOV (ae, other_guy, ae->ObjList[other_guy].Dir, 16);
                     temp = ae->ObjList[other_guy].Dir;


     // Depending on which direction the opponent is facing, we will need to
     // rotate the bitmaps.
                     if ((temp < INT_ANGLE_45) && (temp > INT_ANGLE_315))
                     {
                      ae->ObjList[other_guy].bmNum[0] = 1;
                      ae->ObjList[other_guy].bmNum[1] = 3;
                      ae->ObjList[other_guy].bmNum[2] = 2;
                      ae->ObjList[other_guy].bmNum[3] = 4;
                     }
                     else if ((temp >= INT_ANGLE_45) && (temp < INT_ANGLE_135))
                     {
                      ae->ObjList[other_guy].bmNum[0] = 4;
                      ae->ObjList[other_guy].bmNum[1] = 1;
                      ae->ObjList[other_guy].bmNum[2] = 3;
                      ae->ObjList[other_guy].bmNum[3] = 2;
                     }
                     else if ((temp >= INT_ANGLE_135) && (temp < INT_ANGLE_225))
                     {
                      ae->ObjList[other_guy].bmNum[0] = 2;
                      ae->ObjList[other_guy].bmNum[1] = 4;
                      ae->ObjList[other_guy].bmNum[2] = 1;
                      ae->ObjList[other_guy].bmNum[3] = 3;
                     }
```

```
                    else if ((temp >= INT_ANGLE_225) && (temp < INT_ANGLE_315))
                    {
                     ae->ObjList[other_guy].bmNum[0] = 3;
                     ae->ObjList[other_guy].bmNum[1] = 2;
                     ae->ObjList[other_guy].bmNum[2] = 4;
                     ae->ObjList[other_guy].bmNum[3] = 1;
                    }
                    break;

 case '1':   if (com_device == 'i') ch = input_buf[1];
                    AckMoveObjectPOV (ae, other_guy, ae->ObjList[other_guy].Dir,
                    (ch>>2)+16);
                    temp = ae->ObjList[other_guy].Dir;

// Depending on which direction the opponent is facing, we will need to
// rotate the bitmaps.
                    if ((temp < INT_ANGLE_45) && (temp > INT_ANGLE_315))
                    {
                     ae->ObjList[other_guy].bmNum[0] = 1;
                     ae->ObjList[other_guy].bmNum[1] = 3;
                     ae->ObjList[other_guy].bmNum[2] = 2;
                     ae->ObjList[other_guy].bmNum[3] = 4;
                    }
                    else if ((temp >= INT_ANGLE_45) && (temp < INT_ANGLE_135))
                    {
                     ae->ObjList[other_guy].bmNum[0] = 4;
                     ae->ObjList[other_guy].bmNum[1] = 1;
                     ae->ObjList[other_guy].bmNum[2] = 3;
                     ae->ObjList[other_guy].bmNum[3] = 2;
                    }
                    else if ((temp >= INT_ANGLE_135) && (temp < INT_ANGLE_225))
                    {
                     ae->ObjList[other_guy].bmNum[0] = 2;
                     ae->ObjList[other_guy].bmNum[1] = 4;
                     ae->ObjList[other_guy].bmNum[2] = 1;
                     ae->ObjList[other_guy].bmNum[3] = 3;
                    }
                    else if ((temp >= INT_ANGLE_225) && (temp < INT_ANGLE_315))
                    {
                     ae->ObjList[other_guy].bmNum[0] = 3;
                     ae->ObjList[other_guy].bmNum[1] = 2;
                     ae->ObjList[other_guy].bmNum[2] = 4;
                     ae->ObjList[other_guy].bmNum[3] = 1;
```

```
            }
            break;


// Move the opponent object backward
   case 'b':
        temp = ae->ObjList[other_guy].Dir + INT_ANGLE_180;
            if (temp >= INT_ANGLE_360) temp -= INT_ANGLE_360;
            if (temp < 0) temp += INT_ANGLE_360;


// Save the current position of the bitmaps
            num1=ae->ObjList[other_guy].bmNum[0];
            num2=ae->ObjList[other_guy].bmNum[1];
            num3=ae->ObjList[other_guy].bmNum[2];
            num4=ae->ObjList[other_guy].bmNum[3];


// Turn bitmaps around so that it looks like they are running away from us
            ae->ObjList[other_guy].bmNum[0] = 2;
            ae->ObjList[other_guy].bmNum[1] = 4;
            ae->ObjList[other_guy].bmNum[2] = 1;
            ae->ObjList[other_guy].bmNum[3] = 3;

            AckMoveObjectPOV (ae, other_guy, temp, 16);

            AckBuildView(ae);
            AckDrawOverlay(ae->ScreenBuffer,ae->OverlayBuffer);
            AckDisplayScreen(ae);
            ae->ObjList[other_guy].bmNum[0] = num1;
            ae->ObjList[other_guy].bmNum[1] = num2;
            ae->ObjList[other_guy].bmNum[2] = num3;
            ae->ObjList[other_guy].bmNum[3] = num4;
            break;

   case '2':  if (com_device == 'i') ch = input_buf[1];
            temp = ae->ObjList[other_guy].Dir + INT_ANGLE_180;
             if (temp >= INT_ANGLE_360) temp -= INT_ANGLE_360;
             if (temp < 0) temp += INT_ANGLE_360;


// Save the current position of the bitmaps.
            num1=ae->ObjList[other_guy].bmNum[0];
            num2=ae->ObjList[other_guy].bmNum[1];
            num3=ae->ObjList[other_guy].bmNum[2];
            num4=ae->ObjList[other_guy].bmNum[3];
```

```c
// Turn bitmaps around so that it looks like they are running away from us.
                ae->ObjList[other_guy].bmNum[0] = 2;
                ae->ObjList[other_guy].bmNum[1] = 4;
                ae->ObjList[other_guy].bmNum[2] = 1;
                ae->ObjList[other_guy].bmNum[3] = 3;

                AckMoveObjectPOV (ae, other_guy, temp, (ch>>2)+16);

                AckBuildView(ae);
                AckDrawOverlay(ae->ScreenBuffer,ae->OverlayBuffer);
                AckDisplayScreen(ae);
                ae->ObjList[other_guy].bmNum[0] = num1;
                ae->ObjList[other_guy].bmNum[1] = num2;
                ae->ObjList[other_guy].bmNum[2] = num3;
                ae->ObjList[other_guy].bmNum[3] = num4;
                break;


// Pan the opponent object left
        case 'c': temp = ae->ObjList[other_guy].Dir +( INT_ANGLE_2 * 5);
                if (temp >= INT_ANGLE_360) temp -= INT_ANGLE_360;
                if (temp <= 0) temp += INT_ANGLE_360;
                ae->ObjList[other_guy].Dir = temp;
                break;


        case '3': if (com_device=='i') ch = input_buf[1];
                temp = ae->ObjList[other_guy].Dir +( INT_ANGLE_2 * 5);
                if (temp >= INT_ANGLE_360) temp -= INT_ANGLE_360;
                if (temp <= 0) temp += INT_ANGLE_360;
                ae->ObjList[other_guy].Dir = temp;
                break;



// Pan the opponent object right
        case 'd': temp = ae->ObjList[other_guy].Dir - INT_ANGLE_2 * 5;
                if (temp >= INT_ANGLE_360) temp -= INT_ANGLE_360;
                if (temp <= 0) temp += INT_ANGLE_360;
                ae->ObjList[other_guy].Dir = temp;
                break;


// Joystick pan opponent
        case 'e':
            if (com_device == 'i') ch = input_buf[1];
```

```c
                temp = ae->ObjList[other_guy].Dir - ch;
                if (temp >= INT_ANGLE_360) temp -= INT_ANGLE_360;
                if (temp <= 0) temp += INT_ANGLE_360;
                ae->ObjList[other_guy].Dir = temp;
                break;

// Joystick move opponent forward
        case 'g':
          if (com_device == 'i') ch = input_buf[1];

          AckMoveObjectPOV (ae, other_guy, ae->ObjList[other_guy].Dir, ch);
          temp = ae->ObjList[other_guy].Dir;

          if ((temp < INT_ANGLE_45) && (temp > INT_ANGLE_315))
            {
            ae->ObjList[other_guy].bmNum[0] = 1;
            ae->ObjList[other_guy].bmNum[1] = 3;
            ae->ObjList[other_guy].bmNum[2] = 2;
            ae->ObjList[other_guy].bmNum[3] = 4;
          }
          else if ((temp >= INT_ANGLE_45) && (temp < INT_ANGLE_135))
          {
            ae->ObjList[other_guy].bmNum[0] = 4;
            ae->ObjList[other_guy].bmNum[1] = 1;
            ae->ObjList[other_guy].bmNum[2] = 3;
            ae->ObjList[other_guy].bmNum[3] = 2;
          }
          else if ((temp >= INT_ANGLE_135) && (temp < INT_ANGLE_225))
          {
            ae->ObjList[other_guy].bmNum[0] = 2;
            ae->ObjList[other_guy].bmNum[1] = 4;
            ae->ObjList[other_guy].bmNum[2] = 1;
            ae->ObjList[other_guy].bmNum[3] = 3;
          }
          else if ((temp >= INT_ANGLE_225) && (temp < INT_ANGLE_315))
          {
            ae->ObjList[other_guy].bmNum[0] = 3;
            ae->ObjList[other_guy].bmNum[1] = 2;
            ae->ObjList[other_guy].bmNum[2] = 4;
            ae->ObjList[other_guy].bmNum[3] = 1;
          }
```

```
                    break;

// Joystick move opponent backward
        case 'h':
            if (com_device == 'i') ch = input_buf[1];

            temp = ae->ObjList[other_guy].Dir + INT_ANGLE_180;
            if (temp >= INT_ANGLE_360) temp -= INT_ANGLE_360;
            if (temp <= 0) temp += INT_ANGLE_360;

            num1=ae->ObjList[other_guy].bmNum[0];
            num2=ae->ObjList[other_guy].bmNum[1];
            num3=ae->ObjList[other_guy].bmNum[2];
            num4=ae->ObjList[other_guy].bmNum[3];

            ae->ObjList[other_guy].bmNum[0] = 2;
            ae->ObjList[other_guy].bmNum[1] = 4;
            ae->ObjList[other_guy].bmNum[2] = 1;
            ae->ObjList[other_guy].bmNum[3] = 3;

            AckMoveObjectPOV (ae, other_guy, temp, ch);

// Build the new screen - First the walls and objects, then the overlay.
            AckBuildView(ae);
            AckDrawOverlay(ae->ScreenBuffer,ae->OverlayBuffer);

// Display our new screen.
            AckDisplayScreen(ae);
            ae->ObjList[other_guy].bmNum[0] = num1;
            ae->ObjList[other_guy].bmNum[1] = num2;
            ae->ObjList[other_guy].bmNum[2] = num3;
            ae->ObjList[other_guy].bmNum[3] = num4;
            break;

// Remove ith ammo can from screen - opponent got it
        case 'i':
            if (com_device == 'i') sock_read(&our_socket, input_buf, 2);

            AckDeleteObject (ae, input_buf[2]);
            break;

// Remove minotaur monster from screen - opponent shot it.
        case 'j':
```

```
                       if (com_device == 'i')
                       {
                           sock_read(&our_socket, input_buf, 2);
                       }

                       AckDeleteObject (ae, input_buf[1]);
                       break;

// Remove opponent's object
        case 'k': AckDeleteObject (ae, other_guy);
                  break;


// Place opponent's bullet on screen
        case 'l':
            ae->ObjList[other_guy_bullet].x = ae->ObjList[other_guy].x;
            ae->ObjList[other_guy_bullet].y = ae->ObjList[other_guy].y;
            ae->ObjList[other_guy_bullet].Dir = ae->ObjList[other_guy].Dir;
            ae->ObjList[other_guy_bullet].mPos = (ae->ObjList[other_guy_bullet].y
& 0xFFC0) + (ae->ObjList[other_guy_bullet].x >> 6);
            ae->ObjList[other_guy_bullet].VidRow = 100;
            ae->ObjList[other_guy_bullet].Active = 1;
            break;

// Change location of opponent's bullet
    case 'm':
        if(com_device == 'i')
          {
            sock_read(&our_socket, input_buf, 5);
            ae->ObjList[other_guy_bullet].x = (input_buf[1] << 8)+input_buf[2];
            ae->ObjList[other_guy_bullet].y = (input_buf[3] << 8)+input_buf[4];
          }

            ae->ObjList[other_guy_bullet].mPos = ((ae->ObjList[other_guy_bullet].y
& 0xFFC0) + (ae->ObjList[other_guy_bullet].x >> 6));
        break;

// Remove opponent's bullet from screen.
    case 'n': AckDeleteObject (ae, other_guy_bullet);
              break;


// Opponent has been killed, remove from screen and reset game.
    case 'o': AckDeleteObject(ae, other_guy);
```

```
                AckDeleteObject(ae, other_guy_bullet);
        AckFadeOut(0, 255);
                reset_game();
                AckFadeIn(0, 255, colordat);
                break;


    // We have been killed, reset game.
        case 'w': ammo = 0;
                 AckFadeOut(0, 255);
                reset_game();
                AckFadeIn(0, 255, colordat);
                break;


    // Change location of minotaur monster.
        case 'y':
                if(com_device == 'i')
                {
                    sock_read(&our_socket, input_buf, 5);
                    ae->ObjList[monster1].x = (input_buf[1] << 8)+input_buf[2];
                    ae->ObjList[monster1].y = (input_buf[3] << 8)+input_buf[4];
                }
                if (ae->ObjList[monster1].Active)
                {
                ae->ObjList[monster1].mPos = ((ae->ObjList[monster1].y & 0xFFC0)
+ (ae->ObjList[monster1].x >> 6));
            ae->ObjList[monster1].Active = 1;
            break;


    // Change location of opponent's object.
        case 'z':
                if (com_device == 'i')
                {
                    sock_read(&our_socket, input_buf, 7);
                    ae->ObjList[other_guy].x = (input_buf[1] << 8)+input_buf[2];
                    ae->ObjList[other_guy].y = (input_buf[3] << 8)+input_buf[4];
                    ae->ObjList[other_guy].Dir = (input_buf[5] << 8)+input_buf[6];
                }


            ae->ObjList[other_guy].mPos = (ae->ObjList[other_guy].y & 0xFFC0)
+ (ae->ObjList[other_guy].x >> 6);
                break;
        }
}
```

```c
// This function is called when the user presses the ESC key.   The TCP/IP
// connection is terminated.
void hangup()
{
  if (com_device == 'i')
  {
    sock_close (&our_socket);
    sock_wait_closed(&our_socket, sock_delay, NULL, &status);
  }
}



// This function determines which player is PERSON = 0 and which is
// PERSON = 1.  It works by picking a random number and transmitting the
// number to the opponent.  Each player compares their number with the
// opponent's number.  The lowest number is PERSON 0.
void do_link()
{
  unsigned char ours, theirs, do_again = 1;
  int packet_length;

  randomize();
  while ( do_again )
  {
    do_again = 0;
    randomize();

// Chose our number
    ours = random(50);

// Send our selection
    if (com_device == 'i')
    {
    sock_write (&our_socket, &ours, 1);
    delay(1000);
    }

// Get opponent's number
    if (com_device =='i')
    {
     sock_read (&our_socket, &theirs, 1);
```

```
        }

// Determine who's who
   if (ours<theirs)
    person = 0;
   else
    person = 1;

// If equal numbers, do it again
   if (ours==theirs) do_again = 1;
  }
}


// This function allows the user to select a communication device if they
// wish to do so.
int select_communication_device()
{
  char ch;
  int result;

  while (!com_device)
  {
    clrscr();
    printf ("\n\n\n");
    printf ("Please select the communication medium that you would like to
use:\n\n");
    printf ("(I)nternet connection\n");
    printf ("(S)ingle User\n");

    printf (":");
    ch = getkey();

    printf ("%c\n", ch);

    switch (toupper(ch))
    {
 case 'I': com_device = 'i';
        sock_init();
        result = 0;
        break;
```

Code Listing for the Internet Version of Minotaur **361**

```
    case 'S': com_device = 's';
            result = 0;
            break;
    }
  }
 return(result);
}




//This function is used to establish a link using the selected communication
//device
int create_link()
{

  int got_one = 0, i, packet_length;
  char ch, buffer[40];

  switch(com_device)
    {

// Determine which user will be the originator of the connection and which
// will be the answerer.

    case 'i': while (!got_one)
        {
        clrscr();
        printf ("Is this machine the originating or answering machine?\n");
        printf (":");
        ch = toupper(getkey());
        printf ( "%c\n", ch);

// The answering machine will open the TCP/IP channel and listen for a
// connection by the other machine.  Once a connection is established, a
// call to do_link is made to determine who's who.
            if (ch=='A')
            {
            tcp_listen( &our_socket, TCP_PORT, 0, 0, NULL, 0 );
            sock_mode( &our_socket, TCP_MODE_BINARY );
            sock_wait_established( &our_socket, 0, NULL, &status);
            got_one = 1;
            do_link();
        }
```

```
//The originator will ask for the IP address of the receiving machine. The
//IP address is entered as decimal numbers separated by periods. The originator
//will verify the IP and will try to create the connection.
            else if (ch=='O')
            {
               clrscr();
    printf ("Enter IP Address of answering machine as xxx.xxx.xxx.xxx[.xxx]\n");
            printf ( ":" );
            scanf ("%s", host);

            if (!( remoteip = resolve(host)))
            {
             cprintf("\n\rUnable to resolve '%s'\n\r", host );
             exit( 3 );
            }

            if ( !tcp_open( &our_socket, 0, remoteip, TCP_PORT, NULL ))
            {
             cputs("Unable to open connection.");
             exit( 1 );
            }
    sock_mode( &our_socket, TCP_MODE_BINARY );
            sock_wait_established( &our_socket, sock_delay, NULL, &status);
// Connection has been made
   got_one = 1;
            do_link();
         }
      }
      break;

   }
   return(0);
}



// This function is responsible for moving the minotaur monster.  Refer
// to the text for a description of the algorithm used.
void move_monsters()
{
   int x1, y1, x, y, px, py, dx, dy, angle, result, dx1, dy1;

 if (ae->ObjList[monster1].Active == 1)
```

```
    {
     x = ae->ObjList[monster1].x;
     y = ae->ObjList[monster1].y;


     x1 = ae->ObjList[other_guy].x;
     y1 = ae->ObjList[other_guy].y;



     px = ae->xPlayer;
     py = ae->yPlayer;


     dx = abs(px - x);
     dy = abs(py - y);

// Find out if player or opponent is closest to minotaur.
     if(com_device != 's')
     {
       dx1 = abs(px - x1);
       dy1 = abs(py - y1);

       if (dx1 < dx)
       {
         dx = dx1;
         dy = dy1;

         x = x1;
         y = y1;
       }
     }

     if (dx > dy)
       py = y;

     if (dx < dy)
       px = x;


     if (py == y)
     {
       if (px < x) angle = INT_ANGLE_180;
       if (px > x) angle = 0;
     }
```

```
    if (px == x)
    {
      if (py < y) angle = INT_ANGLE_270;
      if (py > y) angle = INT_ANGLE_90;
    }


    ae->ObjList[monster1].Active = 1;
    ae->ObjList[monster1].Dir = angle;

// Move the monster to a new location.
    result = AckMoveObjectPOV(ae,monster1,ae->ObjList[monster1].Dir,ae-
>ObjList[monster1].Speed);

    // If Internet connection, let opponent know the minotaur has moved.
    if (com_device=='i')
    {
      input_buf[0] = 'y';
      sock_write (&our_socket, input_buf, 1);

      input_buf[1] = (ae->ObjList[monster1].x & 0xFF00)>>8;
      input_buf[2] = (ae->ObjList[monster1].x & 0x00FF);
      input_buf[3] = (ae->ObjList[monster1].y & 0xFF00)>>8;
      input_buf[4] = ae->ObjList[monster1].y & 0x00FF;
      sock_write ( &our_socket, input_buf, 5);
    }


    // Check to see if minotaur has hacked us up.
    if (result == POV_PLAYER)
    {
    // We are dead.  Reset game.
     ammo = 0;

     if (com_device=='i')
     {
       input_buf[0] = 'o';
       sock_write ( &our_socket, input_buf, 1);
     }
    AckFadeOut(0, 255);
    reset_game();
    AckFadeIn(0, 255, colordat);
}
else if (result == POV_OBJECT)
{
```

```
     // Opponent has been killed.  Reset Game.
     AckDeleteObject(ae, other_guy);
     AckDeleteObject(ae, other_guy_bullet);

     // Since Player 0 only moves the minotaur, we need to let the
     // opponent know that they have been killed.
     if (com_device=='i')
     {
       input_buf[0] = 'w';
       sock_write ( &our_socket, input_buf, 1);
     }
     AckFadeOut(0, 255);
     reset_game();
     AckFadeIn(0, 255, colordat);

   }

  }
}

// This function checks to see if any of the ammo cans have been
// collided with by the player.
void check_objects()
{
  int i;

// check for a hit.
  i = AckGetObjectHit();
  switch (i)
  {
    case 3:
        if (com_device=='i')
          {
          input_buf[0] = 'i';
          sock_write(&our_socket, input_buf, 1);
          input_buf[1] = 3;
          sock_write ( &our_socket, input_buf, 2);
        }
        AckDeleteObject (ae, i);
        ammo += 10;
        AckPlaySound(1);
        break;
```

```
case 4:
    if (com_device=='i')
    {
        input_buf[0] = 'i';
        sock_write(&our_socket, input_buf, 1);
        input_buf[1] = 4;
        sock_write ( &our_socket, input_buf, 2);
    }
    AckDeleteObject (ae, i);
    ammo += 10;
    AckPlaySound(1);
    break;

case 5:
    if (com_device=='i')
    {
        input_buf[0] = 'i';
        sock_write (&our_socket, input_buf, 1);
        input_buf[1] = 5;
        sock_write ( &our_socket, input_buf, 2);
    }
    AckDeleteObject (ae, i);
    ammo += 10;
    AckPlaySound(1);
    break;

    }
}
```

CODE LISTING FOR THE MODEM AND ETHERNET VERSION OF MINOTAUR

This is the complete source code for the modem/serial port/ethernet user version of our game. We have not done any optimizations or pulled the code out of the main() function as would be appropriate for a correct program. The code is presented for the best possible understanding of what is happening in the main_loop.

```c
#include <stdlib.h>
#include <stdio.h>
#include <dos.h>
#include <mem.h>
#include <alloc.h>
#include <io.h>
#include <fcntl.h>
#include <time.h>
#include <string.h>
#include <conio.h>
#include <sys\stat.h>

#include "ack3d.h"
#include "acksnd.h"

#include "simple.h"
#include "serial.h"
#include "math.h"
#include "joystick.h"
#include "ruckdac.h"

#define HOME        0x4700
#define END         0x4F00
#define PGUP        0x4900
#define PGDN        0x5100
#define LEFT        0x4B00
#define RIGHT       0x4D00
#define UP          0x4800
#define DOWN        0x5000
#define SHLEFT      0x4B01
#define SHRIGHT     0x4D01
#define SHUP        0x4801
#define SHDOWN      0x5001
#define SHPGUP      0x4901
#define SHPGDN      0x5101
#define CTRLLEFT    0x7300
#define CTRLRIGHT   0x7400
#define CTRLHOME    0x7700
```

```
#define CTRLEND     0x7500
#define CTRLPGUP    0x8400
#define CTRLPGDN    0x7600
#define ESC         0x001B

#define OK                  0
#define CONNECT             1
#define RING                2
#define NOCARRIER           3
#define ERROR               4
#define NODIALTONE          6
#define BUSY                7
#define NOANSWER            8
#define CONNECT300          1
#define CONNECT1200         5
#define CONNECT2400         10
#define CONNECT9600         13
#define CONNECT4800         18
#define CONNECT14400        25
#define CONNECTARQ          14
#define CONNECT300ARQ       14
#define CONNECT1200ARQ      15
#define CONNECT2400ARQ      16
#define CONNECT9600ARQ      17
#define CONNECT4800ARQ      19
#define CONNECT14400ARQ     26


#define other_guy 1             // Position of opponent in object array
#define monster1  2             // Position of minotaur in object array
#define bullet       6          // Position of our bullet in object array
#define monster_bullet 7        // Position of medusa bullet in object array
#define other_guy_bullet 8      // Position of opponent bullet in object array
#define medusa 9                // Position of medusa monster in object array

//Main ACK3D Variables
extern UCHAR far colordat[]; // Local ACK3D palette array
ACKENG      *ae;             // Main ACK3D 'world' variable
MOUSE       mouse;           // Mouse variable

char        *MapFileName = "simple.MAP";    // Mapfile filename
char        *PalFile     = "simple.PAL";    // Palette filename
char        *PictureFile = "dashboar.lbm";  // Screen overlay filename
```

```
UCHAR far    *OverlayPic;                        // Pointer to overlay graphics


    // This is the bitmap table for the application.  Each bitmap must include
    // information about its bitmap number, bitmap type, and its filename.

    BMTABLE bmTable[] = {
        1  ,TYPE_WALL      ,"wall.lbm",
        60 ,TYPE_WALL      ,"roman3.lbm",
        61 ,TYPE_WALL      ,"wall.lbm",
        62 ,TYPE_WALL      ,"roman3.lbm",
        1  ,TYPE_OBJECT    ,"manb1.lbm",
        2  ,TYPE_OBJECT    ,"manf1.lbm",
        3  ,TYPE_OBJECT    ,"manl1.lbm",
        4  ,TYPE_OBJECT    ,"manr2.lbm",
        5  ,TYPE_OBJECT    ,"mino1.lbm",
        6  ,TYPE_OBJECT    ,"ammo.lbm",
        7  ,TYPE_OBJECT    ,"bullet.lbm",
        8  ,TYPE_OBJECT
        9  ,TYPE_OBJECT    ,"mino2.lbm",
        10 ,TYPE_OBJECT    ,"mino3.lbm",
        11 ,TYPE_OBJECT    ,"minob1.lbm",
        12 ,TYPE_OBJECT    ,"minob2.lbm",
        13 ,TYPE_OBJECT    ,"minob3.lbm",
        14 ,TYPE_OBJECT    ,"minol1.lbm",
        15 ,TYPE_OBJECT    ,"minol2.lbm",
        16 ,TYPE_OBJECT    ,"minor1.lbm",
        17 ,TYPE_OBJECT    ,"minor2.lbm",
        18 ,TYPE_OBJECT    ,"medusa.lbm",
        19 ,TYPE_OBJECT    ,"manb2.lbm",
        20 ,TYPE_OBJECT    ,"manf2.lbm",
        21 ,TYPE_OBJECT    ,"manl2.lbm",
        22 ,TYPE_OBJECT    ,"manr1.lbm",
        -1 ,-1            ,""                      /* End of table */
        };


    int play_sound = 0;


    // This array includes information about the way that our palette is set up.
    ColorRange  ranges[64] = { 16,16, 32,16, 48,16, 64,16, 80,16, 96,8,
                104,8, 112,8, 120,8, 128,8, 136,8, 144,8, 152,8, 160,8,
                168,8, 176,8, 184,8, 192,16, 208,16, 224,8, 232,8, 0,0 };
```

```c
//Communication variables
int person = 0, // What player are we
    com_device = 0,         // What communication device is active
    use_joystick = 0,       // Are we using a joystick
    ammo = 5,// Current ammo count
    is_shooting = 0,        // Are we currently shooting
    monster_shooting = 1,   // Is the monster currently shooting
    monster_moves = 0,      // Total monster steps (used for animation)
    player_start_x,         // Starting position and angle of player
    player_start_y,
    player_start_angle,
    opponent_start_x,       // Starting position and angle of opponent
    opponent_start_y,
    opponent_start_angle,
    monster_start_x,        // Starting position and angle of minotaur
    monster_start_y,
    monster_start_angle,
    PORT = 2,// COM port for modem/serial port
    busy = 0,
    null_modem = 0,
    connected = 0,
    num_stored = 0;
long SPEED = 19200;         // Baud rate for modem/serial port


//Ethernet variables
extern unsigned char our_address[6];
extern unsigned char their_address[6];
extern unsigned char interrupt_number;
extern unsigned int  handle;
extern unsigned int  version;
extern unsigned char driver_class;
extern unsigned int  ttype;
extern unsigned char number;
extern unsigned char basic;
extern unsigned int  p_type;
extern unsigned int  main_packet_type;
extern unsigned char ack_packet[64];

// Data areas for incoming and outgoing packet for ethernet connection
unsigned char data_packet[64], get_packet[64];
```

```c
//Font variables
UCHAR far *smFont;              // Pointer to our font graphics
int        TextBGcolor = 7,     // Current background color for fonts
           FontColor = 0;       // Current font color


//SOUND variables
#pragma pack(1)
extern struct DacDataArea pascal DACDATA;
struct SysInfoPack SIP;
struct InitPack IP;
struct XitPack XP;
struct LoadPack LP;
struct SetPack SP;
struct SetProPack SPP;
struct PlaybackPack PBP;
struct GetDataPack GDP;
struct DeallocPack DP;
#pragma pack()

int rez, rez2;
char filename[81];



int their_moves = 0;
void monster_shoot();
void process_communications(char value);
void hangup();
int select_communication_device();
int setup_com();
int create_link();
void move_monsters();
void check_objects();


//This function loads a font into memory.  The font file is called
//'spfont.bbm'.
int LoadSmallFont(void)
{
  int      ht,wt,len;

  smFont = AckReadiff("spfont.bbm");
  if (smFont == NULL)
```

```c
            return(-1);

    ht = (*(int *)smFont);
    wt = (*(int *)&smFont[2]);
    len = ht * wt;
    memmove(smFont,&smFont[4],len);

    return(0);
}


/**************************************************************************
** Displays a character either directly on the video, or into the screen **
** buffer depending on whether FontTransparent flag is set.             **
**                                                                       **
**************************************************************************/
void smWriteChar(int x,int y,unsigned char ch)
{
                int     FontOffset,VidOffset;
                int     row,col;
    unsigned    char far  *Video;


VidOffset = (y * 320) + x;
Video = MK_FP(0xA000,VidOffset);


FontOffset = ((ch-32) * 5);


//    Video = ae->ScreenBuffer + VidOffset;


for (row = 0; row < 5; row++)
    {
      memset(Video,TextBGcolor,4);

    if (smFont[FontOffset])
          Video[0] = FontColor;
    if (smFont[FontOffset+1])
          Video[1] = FontColor;
    if (smFont[FontOffset+2])
          Video[2] = FontColor;
    if (smFont[FontOffset+3])
          Video[3] = FontColor;

    Video += 320;
    FontOffset += 294;
```

```
          }


     }

     /**************************************************************************
     **Calls smWriteChar() to display the contents of the passed string. Only **
     **crude string handling is done in this routine.                         **
     **                                                                       **
     **************************************************************************/
     int smWriteString(int x,int y,char *s)
     {
         int     OrgX;
         char    ch;


OrgX = x;

while (*s)
     {
     ch = *s++;

     if (ch == 10)          /* If a linefeed then advance to next row */
          {
          x = OrgX;
          y += 8;
          continue;
          }

     if (ch < ' ')
          continue;

     ch = toupper(ch);
     smWriteChar(x,y,ch);
     x += 5;     /* Advance to next character position */
     }

return(y);
}



//This function resets all objects and players in our game when either
//player is killed.
void reset_game()
```

```
{

    // Reset player.
    ae->xPlayer = player_start_x;
    ae->yPlayer = player_start_y;
    ae->PlayerAngle = player_start_angle;

    // Reset minotaur monster.
    ae->ObjList[monster1].x = monster_start_x;
    ae->ObjList[monster1].y = monster_start_y;
    ae->ObjList[monster1].Dir = monster_start_angle;
    ae->ObjList[monster1].mPos = (ae->ObjList[monster1].y & 0xFFC0) +
(ae->ObjList[monster1].x >> 6);
    ae->ObjList[monster1].Active = 1;

    // Reset opponent monster.
    ae->ObjList[other_guy].x = opponent_start_x;
    ae->ObjList[other_guy].y = opponent_start_y;
    ae->ObjList[other_guy].Dir = opponent_start_angle;
    ae->ObjList[other_guy].mPos = (ae->ObjList[other_guy].y & 0xFFC0) +
(ae->ObjList[other_guy].x >> 6);
    ae->ObjList[other_guy].Active = 1;

    // Put all of the ammo cans back on screen.
    ae->ObjList[3].Active = 1;
    ae->ObjList[4].Active = 1;
    ae->ObjList[5].Active = 1;

    // Reset total ammo we are carrying.
    ammo = 5;
}



//This function updates a bullet that has been fired by our player.
void UpdateShoot()
{
    int result;
    char ch;

    // Move bullet forward and check for collision.
    result = AckMoveObjectPOV (ae, bullet, ae->ObjList[bullet].Dir, ae-
>ObjList[bullet].Speed);
```

```c
if ((com_device == 'n') || (com_device == 'm'))
{
  com_tx(PORT, 'm');
  com_tx(PORT, ((ae->ObjList[bullet].x & 0xFF00)>>8));
  com_tx(PORT, (ae->ObjList[bullet].x & 0x00FF));

  com_tx(PORT, ((ae->ObjList[bullet].y & 0xFF00)>>8));
  com_tx(PORT, (ae->ObjList[bullet].y & 0x00FF));
}

if (com_device=='e')
{
  data_packet[20] = 'm';
  data_packet[21] = (ae->ObjList[bullet].x & 0xFF00)>>8;
  data_packet[22] = (ae->ObjList[bullet].x & 0x00FF);
  data_packet[23] = (ae->ObjList[bullet].y & 0xFF00)>>8;
  data_packet[24] = ae->ObjList[bullet].y & 0x00FF;
  send_pkt (interrupt_number,data_packet, 64);
}

if ((result != POV_NOTHING) && (result != POV_PLAYER))
{
  ae->ObjList[bullet].Active = 0;
  is_shooting = 0;

if ((com_device == 'n') || (com_device == 'm'))
{
  com_tx(PORT, 'n');
}

if (com_device=='e')
{
  data_packet[20] = 'n';
  send_pkt (interrupt_number,data_packet, 64);
}


  if (result == POV_OBJECT)
  {
    result = AckGetObjectHit();
    if (result == monster1)
    {
```

```c
            if ((com_device == 'n') || (com_device == 'm'))
            {
              com_tx(PORT, 'j');
              com_tx(PORT, monster1);
            }
            if (com_device=='e')
            {
              data_packet[20] = 'j';
              data_packet[21] = monster1;
              send_pkt (interrupt_number, data_packet, 64);
            }
            AckDeleteObject(ae, monster1);
            AckDeleteObject(ae, monster_bullet);
      }
    else if (result == other_guy)
    {
        if ((com_device == 'n') || (com_device == 'm'))com_tx(PORT, 'w');
        if (com_device=='e')
        {
          data_packet[20] = 'w';
          send_pkt (interrupt_number,data_packet, 64);
        }
        AckDeleteObject(ae, other_guy);
        AckDeleteObject(ae, other_guy_bullet);

        AckFadeOut(0, 255);
        reset_game();
        AckFadeIn(0, 255, colordat);
      }


    }

  }
}


int shifted;
unsigned getkey()
{
  unsigned c;
  union REGS regs;

  regs.h.ah = 2;
```

```
      int86(0x16, &regs,&regs );
      shifted = (regs.h.al & 3);

      if ((c=bioskey (0)) & 0xff) c &= 0xff;
      else if ( shifted ) c |= 1;
      return c;
   }



void check_doors()
{
   if (ae->Door[0].Flags == DOOR_OPENING && (ae->Door[0].ColOffset >= 64))
      ae->Door[0].ColOffset = 0;

   if (ae->Door[1].Flags == DOOR_OPENING && (ae->Door[1].ColOffset >= 64))
      ae->Door[1].ColOffset = 0;



}



//This function is used to build an ethernet data packet.  It copies
//the opponent's ethernet address and a data character into the data_packet
//variable.
void build_packet (char ch)
{
   int i;

   data_packet[20] = ch;
   for (i=0;i<6;i++)
   {
      data_packet[i] = their_address[i];
      data_packet[6+i] = our_address[i];
   }
}



// This routine checks the current state of the mouse and fills the MOUSE
// variable with the appropriate information.
void checkmouse(MOUSE *m)
{
```

```
    int       dx,dy;
    int       x,y,buttons;

mouse_read_cursor(&buttons,&y,&x);
dx = x - 160;
dy = y - 120;
m->mButtons = buttons;
mouse_set_cursor(120,160);

if (abs(dy) > 10 && abs(dx) < 32)
    dx >>= 2;

m->mdx = dx;
m->mdy = dy;

}


int pick_device(int *devID, int *XMSflag)
{

  int td=0;
  char nums[9] = {7};

  SIP.Func = SysInfoDac;
  rez = RUCKDAC(&SIP);
  if (rez == 0) {
       printf("\n0. End program");
     printf("\n1. PC speaker at port 42h");
     if (SIP.SD[1].device)
       printf("\n2. LPT-DAC on LPT1, port %xh",SIP.SD[1].Port);
     if (SIP.SD[2].device)
       printf("\n3. Disney Sound Source port %xh",SIP.SD[2].Port);
     if (SIP.SD[3].device)
       printf("\n\n4. AdLib Music Synthesizer Card, port %xh",SIP.SD[3].Port);
     if (SIP.SD[4].device)
       printf("\n5. Sound Blaster, port %xh",SIP.SD[4].Port);
     if (SIP.SD[5].device)
       printf("\n6. Sound Blaster Pro, port %xh",SIP.SD[5].Port);
     if (SIP.SD[4].device)
       printf("\n\n7. Sound Blaster as 5 but use XMS (if applicable)");
     if (SIP.SD[5].device)
       printf("\n8. Sound Blaster Pro as 6 but use XMS (if applicable)\n");
```

```
            printf("\nSelection: ");
               td = atoi(cgets(nums));
            td--;    /* since devices are numbered 0 to 5 */

            if (td > 6) {
               *XMSflag = 1;          /* XMS memory selected with SB */
               td-=2;                 /* map to appropriate device */
            }

            if ((td >=0) && (td <=5)) { /* validate device selected available */
               if (SIP.SD[td].device == 0)
                  td = -1;
            }
            else
               td = -1;
            }

            *devID = td;
            return(rez);
        }


        int init_device(int devID)
        {
            /*
            Initialize RUCKDAC and device and register ExitDac with _atexit
            The IP.port for devices 0 and 3 are set to 0 for low-rez mode,
            or their respective actual ports for hi-rez mode (0x42 and 0x388)
            */

            IP.Func = InitDac;
            IP.DeviceID = devID;
            IP.IOport = SIP.SD[devID].Port;
            IP.IRQline = SIP.SD[devID].IRQ;
            IP.DMAch = SIP.SD[devID].DMA;

            if ((devID == 0) || (devID == 3))   /* use low-rez mode for */
               IP.IOport = 0;                    /* PC speaker and Adlib */

            rez = RUCKDAC(&IP);                  /* Initialize */
            if (rez == 0) {
```

```
                    XP.Func = AtExitDac;
                    rez2 = RUCKDAC(&XP);
                    if (rez2 != 0) {
                        printf("AtExitDac failed, press Enter to continue");
                        getchar();
                    }


        /*
        Increase SB Pro main and vol volumes to max
        */

        if (devID == 5) {
            SPP.Func = SetVolMainSBP;
            SPP.Volume = 0x0F0F;
            rez2 = RUCKDAC(&SPP);
            SPP.Func = SetVolVocSBP;
            SPP.VolVoc = 0x0F0F;
            rez2 = RUCKDAC(&SPP);
        }
    }
    return(rez);
}



void do_sound()
{
    int devID=-1, XMSflag=0;

    rez = pick_device(&devID, &XMSflag);
    if (devID >= 0)
    {

        printf ("Initializing devID %u\n", devID);
        rez = init_device(devID);
        if (rez == 0)
        {
                play_sound = 1;
                /* load file and setup playback parameters */

            LP.Func = LoadDac;
            LP.FilenamePtr = "phaser3.voc";
            LP.StartPos = 0L;                /* start at first byte */
```

```c
            LP.LoadSize = 0L;                    /* autoload entire file */
            LP.XMMflag = XMSflag;
            rez = RUCKDAC(&LP);
            if (rez == 0)
            {

                PBP.Func = PlayDac;
                if (devID >= 4)
                    PBP.Mode = 2;
                else
                {
                    PBP.Mode = 1;
                    if (DACDATA.SampleRate < 11025)
                            SP.IntRate = DACDATA.SampleRate;
                    else
                            SP.IntRate = 8643;

                    SP.Func = SetIntRateDac;
                    rez = RUCKDAC(&SP); /* set the playback rate */
                }

                if (LP.XMMflag == 0)
                {
                    PBP.XMMhandle = 0;
                    PBP.LoadPtr = LP.LoadPtr;
                }
                else
                {
                    PBP.XMMhandle = LP.XMMhandle;
                    PBP.LoadPtr = NULL;
                }
            }
        }
    }
}



int main(void)
{
    int     result,
            done = 0,
            pan = 0,
```

```c
                    i,
                    temp,
                    packet_length,
                    x,
                    y,
                    buttons,
                    joy_centx,
                    joy_centy,
                    moves = 0;
unsigned ch_val;
char buf[35] = "", ch;

do_sound();

if (select_communication_device())
{
  printf ( "Error setting up communication device\n");
  return(1);
}

if (com_device != 's')
  if (create_link())
  {
      printf ("Error creating communication link\n");
      return(1);
  }

if (result==AppInitialize())
{
  printf("Error initializing: ErrorCode = %d\n",result);
  return(1);
}



if (result==AppSetupEngine())
{
  printf("Error setting up ACK engine: ErrorCode = %d\n",result);
  AckWrapUp(ae);
  return(1);
}



if (result==AppLoadBitmaps())
```

```c
  {
    printf("Error loading bitmaps: ErrorCode = %d\n",result);
    AckWrapUp(ae);
    return(1);
  }


  if (result==AppSetGraphics())
  {
    AckSetTextmode();
    printf("Error loading palette: ErrorCode = %d\n",result);
    AckWrapUp(ae);
    return(1);
  }



  if (result == AppSetupOverlay())
  {
    printf("Error loading overlay: ErrorCode = %d\n",result);
    AckWrapUp(ae);
    return(1);
  }


  if (LoadSmallFont())
  {
    AckSetTextmode();
    printf("Error loading font: ErrorCode = %d\n",result);
    AckWrapUp(ae);
    return(1);
  }


  if (result==AppSetObject())
  {
    AckSetTextmode();
    printf("Error loading palette: ErrorCode = %d\n",result);
    AckWrapUp(ae);
    return(1);
  }


  AppSetupPalRanges();



  if (person)
```

```
{
    temp = ae->ObjList[other_guy].x;
    ae->ObjList[other_guy].x = ae->xPlayer;
    ae->xPlayer = temp;

    temp = ae->ObjList[other_guy].y;
    ae->ObjList[other_guy].y = ae->yPlayer;
    ae->yPlayer = temp;

    ae->ObjList[other_guy].mPos = (ae->ObjList[other_guy].y & 0xFFC0) +
(ae->ObjList[other_guy].x >> 6);

    temp = ae->ObjList[other_guy].Dir;
    ae->ObjList[other_guy].Dir = ae->PlayerAngle;
    ae->PlayerAngle = temp;

}

//Get starting positions
player_start_x = ae->xPlayer;
player_start_y = ae->yPlayer;
player_start_angle = ae->PlayerAngle;

opponent_start_x = ae->ObjList[other_guy].x;
opponent_start_y = ae->ObjList[other_guy].y;
opponent_start_angle = ae->ObjList[other_guy].Dir;

monster_start_x = ae->ObjList[monster1].x;
monster_start_y = ae->ObjList[monster1].y;
monster_start_angle = ae->ObjList[monster1].Dir;

//Get initial conditions for joystick
if (use_joystick)
    joystick_read(&joy_centx, &joy_centy, &buttons);

while (!done)
{
    if (person == 0) move_monsters();
    if ((monster_shooting==1) && (person == 0) && (monster_moves > 2))
monster_shoot();
```

```
        if (is_shooting) UpdateShoot();
        AckCheckObjectMovement(ae);

        if (pan)
        {
            pan = 0;
            if (ae->PlayerAngle >= INT_ANGLE_360)
             ae->PlayerAngle -= INT_ANGLE_360;
            if (ae->PlayerAngle < 0)
             ae->PlayerAngle += INT_ANGLE_360;
        }

        sprintf (buf, "%d\n", ammo);
        smWriteString(280,185, buf);

        AckBuildView(ae);
        AckDrawOverlay(ae->ScreenBuffer,ae->OverlayBuffer);
        AckDisplayScreen(ae);

// This code checks to see if we are using a serial connection device.  If
// so, we check first to see if a connection is still available and then
// we check to see if the receive buffer has any data in it.  If data is
// available, we process it.

        if ((com_device == 'n') || (com_device == 'm'))
        {
          if (((!com_carrier(PORT)) && (!null_modem))
          {
            hangup();
            AckSetTextmode();
            printf("Lost communication link");
            AckWrapUp(ae);
            delay(5000);
            exit(1);
          }
          if (!com_rx_empty(PORT))
          {
            process_communications(com_rx(PORT));
          }
        }

// This code checks to see if we are using an ethernet connection.  If we
```

```
// are, we make a call to collect any data in the receive buffer.
      if (com_device == 'e')
      {
          if (get_from_queue(get_packet, &packet_length, 0))
         {
           process_communications(get_packet[20]);
         }
      }


      if (moves > 2)
      {
        moves = 0;
        if ((com_device == 'n') || (com_device == 'm'))
        {
          com_tx(PORT, 'z');
          com_tx(PORT, (ae->xPlayer & 0xFF00) >> 8);
          com_tx(PORT, (ae->xPlayer & 0x00FF));

          com_tx(PORT, (ae->yPlayer & 0xFF00) >> 8);
          com_tx(PORT, (ae->yPlayer & 0x00FF));

          com_tx(PORT, (ae->PlayerAngle & 0xFF00) >> 8);
          com_tx(PORT, (ae->PlayerAngle & 0x00FF));
        }

        if (com_device=='e')
        {
          data_packet[20] = 'z';
          data_packet[21] = (ae->xPlayer & 0xFF00)>>8;
          data_packet[22] = ae->xPlayer & 0x00FF;
          data_packet[23] = (ae->yPlayer & 0xFF00)>>8;
          data_packet[24] = ae->yPlayer & 0x00FF;
          data_packet[25] = (ae->PlayerAngle & 0xFF00) >> 8;
          data_packet[26] = ae->PlayerAngle & 0x00FF;
          send_pkt (interrupt_number,data_packet, 64);
        }
      }


  checkmouse(&mouse);

  // Pan Left with mouse.
```

```c
if (mouse.mdx < 0)
{
  if ((com_device == 'n') || (com_device == 'm'))com_tx(PORT, 'd');
  if (com_device=='e')
  {
    data_packet[20] = 'd';
    send_pkt (interrupt_number,data_packet,64);
  }

  ae->PlayerAngle += (-INT_ANGLE_2 * (-mouse.mdx >> 3));
  pan = 1;
  moves++;  // Increment our move variable
}


// Pan right with mouse.
if (mouse.mdx > 0)
{
  if ((com_device == 'n') || (com_device == 'm'))com_tx(PORT, 'c');
  if (com_device=='e')
  {
    data_packet[20] = 'c';
    send_pkt (interrupt_number,data_packet,64);
  }

  ae->PlayerAngle += (INT_ANGLE_2 * (mouse.mdx >> 3));
  pan = 1;
  moves++;  // Increment our move variable
}


// Move forward with mouse.
if (mouse.mdy < 0)
{
  if ((com_device == 'n') || (com_device == 'm'))com_tx(PORT, 'a');
  if (com_device=='e')
  {
    data_packet[20] = 'a';
    send_pkt (interrupt_number,data_packet,64);
  }

  // Move player forward.
  result = AckMovePOV(ae,ae->PlayerAngle,(-mouse.mdy >> 2)+16);
  if (result == POV_OBJECT)
    check_objects();
```

```
      moves++;
  }


  // Move backward with mouse.
  if (mouse.mdy > 0)
  {
    if ((com_device == 'n') || (com_device == 'm'))com_tx(PORT, 'b');
    if (com_device=='e')
    {
      data_packet[20] = 'b';
      send_pkt (interrupt_number,data_packet,64);
    }


    temp= ae->PlayerAngle + INT_ANGLE_180;
    if (temp >= INT_ANGLE_360) temp -= INT_ANGLE_360;
    if (temp < 0) temp += INT_ANGLE_360;


    result = AckMovePOV(ae,temp,(mouse.mdy>>2)+16);
    if (result == POV_OBJECT)
      check_objects();
    moves++;
  }



if (use_joystick)
{
  buttons = 0;
  joystick_read (&x, &y, &buttons);

  if ((buttons == 239) && (!is_shooting))
  {
    if (ammo)
    {
      if ((com_device == 'n') || (com_device == 'm'))com_tx(PORT, 'l');
      if (com_device=='e')
      {
        data_packet[20] = 'l';
        send_pkt (interrupt_number,data_packet, 64);
      }
      is_shooting = 1;
      ae->ObjList[bullet].x = ae->xPlayer;
      ae->ObjList[bullet].y = ae->yPlayer;
      ae->ObjList[bullet].Dir = ae->PlayerAngle;
```

```c
        ae->ObjList[bullet].mPos = (ae->ObjList[bullet].y & 0xFFC0) + (ae-
>ObjList[bullet].x >> 6);
        ae->ObjList[bullet].VidRow = 100;
        ae->ObjList[bullet].Active = 1;
        ammo--;
    }
}



{
  x = joy_centx - x;
  y = joy_centy - y;

  if ( x>15 ) x -= 15;
  else
  {
    if ( x > -15) x = 0;
    else x += 15;
  }

  if ( y > 15 ) y -= 15;
  else
  {
    if(y>-15) y = 0;
    else y+=15;
  }

  if (x!=0)
  {
    ch = x/20;

    if ((com_device == 'n') || (com_device == 'm'))
    {
      com_tx(PORT, 'e');
      com_tx(PORT, ch);
    }
    if (com_device=='e')
    {
      data_packet[20] = 'e';
      data_packet[21] = ch;
      send_pkt (interrupt_number,data_packet, 64);
    }
```

```
          ae->PlayerAngle -= ch;
        pan = 1;
}


if (y!=0)
{
    ch = y/20;

    if (y>0)
    {
        if ((com_device == 'n') || (com_device == 'm'))
        {
            com_tx(PORT, 'g');
            com_tx(PORT, ch);
        }

        if (com_device=='e')
        {
            data_packet[20] = 'g';
            data_packet[21] = ch;
            send_pkt (interrupt_number,data_packet, 64);
        }

        result = AckMovePOV(ae,ae->PlayerAngle,y/20);
        if (result == POV_OBJECT)
            check_objects();
    }
    else
    {
        if ((com_device == 'n') || (com_device == 'm'))
        {
            com_tx(PORT, 'h');
            com_tx(PORT, ch);
        }

        if (com_device=='e')
        {
            data_packet[20] = 'h';
            data_packet[21] = ch;
            send_pkt (interrupt_number,data_packet, 64);
        }

        temp= ae->PlayerAngle + INT_ANGLE_180;
```

Code Listing for the Modem and Ethernet Version of Minotaur **393**

```
                 if (temp >= INT_ANGLE_360)
                     temp -= INT_ANGLE_360;

                 result = AckMovePOV(ae,temp,-y/20);
                 if (result == POV_OBJECT)
                     check_objects();
              }
          }
        }
      }


  AckCheckDoorOpen(ae->xPlayer, ae->yPlayer, ae->PlayerAngle, ae);
  AckCheckDoorOpen(ae->ObjList[other_guy].x, ae->ObjList[other_guy].y,
ae->ObjList[other_guy].Dir, ae);
  check_doors();

  if (bioskey(1))
   {
          ch_val = getkey();
          if (ch_val==ESC) break;

          switch(ch_val)
          {
  case LEFT : if ((com_device == 'n') || (com_device == 'm'))com_tx(PORT, 'd');
                  if (com_device=='e')
                  {
                          data_packet[20] = 'd';
                          send_pkt (interrupt_number,data_packet,64);
                  }
                  ae->PlayerAngle += (-INT_ANGLE_2 * 5);
                  pan = 1;
                  moves++;
                  break;

  case RIGHT: if ((com_device == 'n') || (com_device == 'm'))com_tx(PORT, 'c');
                  if (com_device=='e')
                  {
                          data_packet[20] = 'c';
                          send_pkt (interrupt_number,data_packet, 64);
                  }
                  ae->PlayerAngle += INT_ANGLE_2 * 5;
                  pan = 1;
                  moves++;
```

```
                break;

    case UP:    if ((com_device == 'n') || (com_device == 'm'))com_tx(PORT, 'a');
                if (com_device=='e')
                {
                        data_packet[20] = 'a';
                        send_pkt (interrupt_number,data_packet, 64);
                }
                result = AckMovePOV(ae,ae->PlayerAngle,16);
                if (result == POV_OBJECT)
                        check_objects();
                moves++;
                break;

    case DOWN:  if ((com_device == 'n') || (com_device == 'm'))com_tx(PORT, 'b');
                if (com_device=='e')
                {
                        data_packet[20] = 'b';
                        send_pkt (interrupt_number,data_packet, 64);
                }
                temp= ae->PlayerAngle + INT_ANGLE_180;
                if (temp >= INT_ANGLE_360) temp -= INT_ANGLE_360;
                if (temp < 0) temp += INT_ANGLE_360;

                result = AckMovePOV(ae,temp,16);
                if (result == POV_OBJECT)
                        check_objects();
                moves++;
                break;


    case ' ':
        if ((ammo) && (!is_shooting))
            {
// Play sound
                rez = RUCKDAC(&PBP);

        if ((com_device == 'n') || (com_device == 'm'))
         com_tx(PORT, 'l');
        if (com_device=='e')
        {
         data_packet[20] = 'l';
         send_pkt (interrupt_number,data_packet, 64);
```

```
            }
          is_shooting = 1;
          ae->ObjList[bullet].x = ae->xPlayer;
          ae->ObjList[bullet].y = ae->yPlayer;
          ae->ObjList[bullet].Dir = ae->PlayerAngle;
          ae->ObjList[bullet].mPos = (ae->ObjList[bullet].y & 0xFFC0) +
(ae->ObjList[bullet].x >> 6);
          ae->ObjList[bullet].VidRow = 100;
          ae->ObjList[bullet].Active = 1;
          ammo--;
          }
        }
      }
    }


  AckWrapUp(ae);
  AckSetTextmode();

  if (com_device == 'e')
  {
    release_type(interrupt_number, handle);
    terminate(interrupt_number, handle);
  }

  return(0);
}


int AppInitialize(void)
{
  if ((ae=malloc(sizeof(ACKENG))) == NULL)
    return(-1);

  if (mouse_installed() != -1)
  {
    printf("Mouse required to run.\n");
    return(-2);
  }


  memset(ae,0,sizeof(ACKENG));
```

```c
    return(0);
}


int AppSetupEngine(void)
{
  int result;

  ae->WinStartX = VIEW_X;
  ae->WinStartY = VIEW_Y;
  ae->WinEndX   = VIEW_X1;
  ae->WinEndY   = VIEW_Y1;

  ae->DoorSpeed = DOORSPEED;
  ae->xPlayer = PLAYER_X;
  ae->yPlayer = PLAYER_Y;
  ae->PlayerAngle = INT_ANGLE_180; //PLAYER_ANGLE;

  if (result==AckInitialize(ae))
    return(result);

  if (result == AckReadMapFile(ae,MapFileName))
  {
    AckWrapUp(ae);
    return(result);
  }

  ae->TopColor   = CEILING_COLOR;
  ae->BottomColor = FLOOR_COLOR;
  ae->LightFlag = SHADING_OFF;
  if (result == AckBuildBackground(ae))
    return (result);

  return(0);
}


int AppSetupOverlay(void)
{
  int result = 0;
  UCHAR far *Video;

  OverlayPic = AckReadiff(PictureFile);
```

```c
  if (OverlayPic == NULL)
    return(-1);


  Video = MK_FP(0xA000,0);
  memmove(Video,&OverlayPic[4],64000);
  result = AckCreateOverlay(ae,&OverlayPic[4]);
  free(OverlayPic);


  return(result);
}




int AppLoadBitmaps(void)
{
  int     result, i=0;

  while (bmTable[i].Number != -1)
  {
    if (result==AckLoadBitmap(ae,bmTable[i].Number,bmTable[i].Type,bmTable[i].Name))
      break;

    i++;
  }

  return(result);
}




int AppSetGraphics(void)
{
  int result;

  AckSetVGAmode();

  result = AckLoadAndSetPalette(PalFile);
  return(result);
}
```

```
void AppSetupPalRanges(void)
{
  int     i,j,k,found;
  int     rangenos;
  UCHAR     plotcolor;

  for (rangenos = 0; rangenos < 64; rangenos++)
  {
    if (ranges[rangenos].start == 0)
      break;
  }


  for ( i = 0;i<16;i++)
  {
    for (j=0;j<256;j++)
    {
      found = 0;
      for ( k = 0; k < rangenos; k++ )
      {
      if (j >= ranges[k].start && j < ranges[k].start+ranges[k].length)
      {
        found = 1;
        break;
      }
    }

    if (found)
    {
      if (j+i >= ranges[k].start+ranges[k].length)
        plotcolor = 0;
      else
        plotcolor = j+i;
    }
    else
    {
      plotcolor = j;
    }

    ae->PalTable[j+(i*256)] = plotcolor;
    }
  }
}
```

```c
void AppShow3D(void)
{
  AckBuildView(ae);

  AckDisplayScreen(ae);
}



int AppSetObject(void)
{
  UCHAR bitmaps[3];
  int result;

  bitmaps[0] = 1;
  bitmaps[1] = 3;
  bitmaps[2] = 2;
  bitmaps[3] = 4;

  ae->ObjList[other_guy].Speed = 1;
  ae->ObjList[other_guy].Dir = 0;

  AckCreateObject (ae, other_guy, 4, bitmaps);


  //Monster Load
  bitmaps[0] = 11;
  bitmaps[1] = 14;
  bitmaps[2] = 5;
  bitmaps[3] = 16;
  ae->ObjList[monster1].Speed = 2;
  ae->ObjList[monster1].Dir = INT_ANGLE_90;

  AckCreateObject (ae, monster1, 4, bitmaps);

  //Ammo loads
  bitmaps[0] = 6;
  ae->ObjList[3].Flags = 0;
  ae->ObjList[3].Speed = 0;
  ae->ObjList[3].Dir = 0;
```

```
AckCreateObject (ae, 3, 1, bitmaps);


bitmaps[0] = 6;
ae->ObjList[4].Flags = 0;
ae->ObjList[4].Speed = 0;
ae->ObjList[4].Dir = 0;


AckCreateObject (ae, 4, 1, bitmaps);

bitmaps[0] = 6;
ae->ObjList[5].Flags = 0;
ae->ObjList[5].Speed = 0;
ae->ObjList[5].Dir = 0;
AckCreateObject (ae, 5, 1, bitmaps);



//Load bullet
bitmaps[0] = 7;
ae->ObjList[6].Flags = 0;
ae->ObjList[6].Speed = 25;
ae->ObjList[6].Dir = 0;
ae->ObjList[bullet].Active = 0;
AckCreateObject (ae, bullet, 1, bitmaps);

//Load monster bullet
bitmaps[0] = 8;
ae->ObjList[7].Flags = 0;
ae->ObjList[7].Speed = 25;
ae->ObjList[7].Dir = 0;
ae->ObjList[7].Active = 0;
AckCreateObject (ae, monster_bullet, 1, bitmaps);

//Load other guy bullet
bitmaps[0] = 7;
ae->ObjList[8].Flags = 0;
ae->ObjList[8].Speed = 25;
ae->ObjList[8].Dir = 0;
ae->ObjList[8].Active = 0;
AckCreateObject (ae, other_guy_bullet, 1, bitmaps);



bitmaps[0] = 18;
ae->ObjList[medusa].Flags = 0;
```

```
                    ae->ObjList[medusa].Speed = 0;
                    ae->ObjList[medusa].Dir = 0;
                    ae->ObjList[medusa].Active = 1;
                    AckCreateObject (ae, medusa, 1, bitmaps);
                    return(0);
        }


        static num1, num2, num3, num4, im_backwards = 0;
        void process_communications(char value)
        {
            int   temp, angle;
            char ch;

            switch(value)
            {
                    case 'a':
                                temp = ae->ObjList[other_guy].Dir;
                                their_moves++;

        // Since the bitmaps of the opponent can get turned around when they
        // run backwards, we first need to see if the previous moves was backward
        // If is was, we replace the current bitmaps with those stored during the
        // backward movements.
                                if(im_backwards)
                                {
                                 im_backwards = 0;
                                 ae->ObjList[other_guy].bmNum[0] = num1;
                                 ae->ObjList[other_guy].bmNum[1] = num2;
                                 ae->ObjList[other_guy].bmNum[2] = num3;
                                 ae->ObjList[other_guy].bmNum[3] = num4;
                                }


        // Both the opponent's object and the minotaur monster have animation
        // when they move.  Every 3 steps will indicate the a different movement
        // is necessary.
                if (their_moves==2) their_moves = 0;



        // Here we display specific bitmaps depending on the angle of the opponent
        // and the value of their_moves.
                if ((temp <= INT_ANGLE_45) && (temp > INT_ANGLE_315))
                {
                   if (their_moves == 0)
```

```
      {
        ae->ObjList[other_guy].bmNum[0] = 1;
        ae->ObjList[other_guy].bmNum[1] = 3;
        ae->ObjList[other_guy].bmNum[2] = 2;
        ae->ObjList[other_guy].bmNum[3] = 4;
      }
      else
      {
        ae->ObjList[other_guy].bmNum[0] = 19;
        ae->ObjList[other_guy].bmNum[1] = 21;
        ae->ObjList[other_guy].bmNum[2] = 20;
        ae->ObjList[other_guy].bmNum[3] = 22;
      }
    }
    else if ((temp >= INT_ANGLE_45) && (temp < INT_ANGLE_135))
    {
      if (their_moves == 0)
      {
        ae->ObjList[other_guy].bmNum[0] = 4;
        ae->ObjList[other_guy].bmNum[1] = 1;
        ae->ObjList[other_guy].bmNum[2] = 3;
        ae->ObjList[other_guy].bmNum[3] = 2;
      }
      else
      {
        ae->ObjList[other_guy].bmNum[0] = 22;
        ae->ObjList[other_guy].bmNum[1] = 19;
        ae->ObjList[other_guy].bmNum[2] = 21;
        ae->ObjList[other_guy].bmNum[3] = 20;
      }
    }
    else if ((temp >= INT_ANGLE_135) && (temp < INT_ANGLE_225))
    {
      if (their_moves == 0)
      {
        ae->ObjList[other_guy].bmNum[0] = 2;
        ae->ObjList[other_guy].bmNum[1] = 4;
        ae->ObjList[other_guy].bmNum[2] = 1;
        ae->ObjList[other_guy].bmNum[3] = 3;
      }
      else
      {
        ae->ObjList[other_guy].bmNum[0] = 20;
```

```c
            ae->ObjList[other_guy].bmNum[1] = 22;
            ae->ObjList[other_guy].bmNum[2] = 19;
            ae->ObjList[other_guy].bmNum[3] = 21;
        }
    }
    else if ((temp >= INT_ANGLE_225) && (temp < INT_ANGLE_315))
    {
        if(their_moves == 0)
        {
            ae->ObjList[other_guy].bmNum[0] = 3;
            ae->ObjList[other_guy].bmNum[1] = 2;
            ae->ObjList[other_guy].bmNum[2] = 4;
            ae->ObjList[other_guy].bmNum[3] = 1;
        }
        else
        {
            ae->ObjList[other_guy].bmNum[0] = 21;
            ae->ObjList[other_guy].bmNum[1] = 20;
            ae->ObjList[other_guy].bmNum[2] = 22;
            ae->ObjList[other_guy].bmNum[3] = 19;
        }
    }
    AckMoveObjectPOV (ae, other_guy, ae->ObjList[other_guy].Dir, 16);
    break;

case 'b': temp = ae->ObjList[other_guy].Dir + INT_ANGLE_180;
    if (temp >= INT_ANGLE_360) temp -= INT_ANGLE_360;
    if (temp < 0) temp += INT_ANGLE_360;
    their_moves++;

    if(their_moves==2)their_moves = 0;
    if(!im_backwards)
    {
        num1=ae->ObjList[other_guy].bmNum[0];
        num2=ae->ObjList[other_guy].bmNum[1];
        num3=ae->ObjList[other_guy].bmNum[2];
        num4=ae->ObjList[other_guy].bmNum[3];
    }

    if(their_moves == 0)
    {
        ae->ObjList[other_guy].bmNum[0] = 2;
        ae->ObjList[other_guy].bmNum[1] = 4;
```

```
          ae->ObjList[other_guy].bmNum[2] = 1;
          ae->ObjList[other_guy].bmNum[3] = 3;
      }
      else
      {
          ae->ObjList[other_guy].bmNum[0] = 20;
          ae->ObjList[other_guy].bmNum[1] = 22;
          ae->ObjList[other_guy].bmNum[2] = 19;
          ae->ObjList[other_guy].bmNum[3] = 21;
      }


      AckMoveObjectPOV (ae, other_guy, temp, 16);

im_backwards = 1;
      break;

  case 'c': temp = ae->ObjList[other_guy].Dir +( INT_ANGLE_2 * 5);
      if (temp >= INT_ANGLE_360) temp -= INT_ANGLE_360;
      if (temp <= 0) temp += INT_ANGLE_360;
      ae->ObjList[other_guy].Dir = temp;
      break;

  case 'd': temp = ae->ObjList[other_guy].Dir - INT_ANGLE_2 * 5;
      if (temp >= INT_ANGLE_360) temp -= INT_ANGLE_360;
      if (temp <= 0) temp += INT_ANGLE_360;
      ae->ObjList[other_guy].Dir = temp;
      break;

  case 'e': if ((com_device == 'n') || (com_device == 'm')) ch = com_rx(PORT);
      if (com_device == 'e') ch = data_packet[21];

      temp = ae->ObjList[other_guy].Dir - ch;
      if (temp >= INT_ANGLE_360) temp -= INT_ANGLE_360;
      if (temp <= 0) temp += INT_ANGLE_360;
      ae->ObjList[other_guy].Dir = temp;
      break;

  case 'g': if ((com_device == 'n') || (com_device == 'm')) ch = com_rx(PORT);
      if (com_device == 'e') ch = data_packet[21];

      AckMoveObjectPOV (ae, other_guy, ae->ObjList[other_guy].Dir, ch);
      temp = ae->ObjList[other_guy].Dir;
```

```
if ((temp < INT_ANGLE_45) && (temp > INT_ANGLE_315))
{
  ae->ObjList[other_guy].bmNum[0] = 1;
  ae->ObjList[other_guy].bmNum[1] = 3;
  ae->ObjList[other_guy].bmNum[2] = 2;
  ae->ObjList[other_guy].bmNum[3] = 4;
}
else if ((temp >= INT_ANGLE_45) && (temp < INT_ANGLE_135))
{
  ae->ObjList[other_guy].bmNum[0] = 4;
  ae->ObjList[other_guy].bmNum[1] = 1;
  ae->ObjList[other_guy].bmNum[2] = 3;
  ae->ObjList[other_guy].bmNum[3] = 2;
}
else if ((temp >= INT_ANGLE_135) && (temp < INT_ANGLE_225))
{
  ae->ObjList[other_guy].bmNum[0] = 2;
  ae->ObjList[other_guy].bmNum[1] = 4;
  ae->ObjList[other_guy].bmNum[2] = 1;
  ae->ObjList[other_guy].bmNum[3] = 3;
}
else if ((temp >= INT_ANGLE_225) && (temp < INT_ANGLE_315))
{
  ae->ObjList[other_guy].bmNum[0] = 3;
  ae->ObjList[other_guy].bmNum[1] = 2;
  ae->ObjList[other_guy].bmNum[2] = 4;
  ae->ObjList[other_guy].bmNum[3] = 1;
}

break;


case 'h': if ((com_device == 'n') || (com_device == 'm')) ch = com_rx(PORT);
          if (com_device == 'e') ch = data_packet[21];

          temp = ae->ObjList[other_guy].Dir + INT_ANGLE_180;
          if (temp >= INT_ANGLE_360) temp -= INT_ANGLE_360;
          if (temp <= 0) temp += INT_ANGLE_360;

          num1=ae->ObjList[other_guy].bmNum[0];
          num2=ae->ObjList[other_guy].bmNum[1];
          num3=ae->ObjList[other_guy].bmNum[2];
          num4=ae->ObjList[other_guy].bmNum[3];
```

```
                    ae->ObjList[other_guy].bmNum[0] = 2;
                    ae->ObjList[other_guy].bmNum[1] = 4;
                    ae->ObjList[other_guy].bmNum[2] = 1;
                    ae->ObjList[other_guy].bmNum[3] = 3;

                    AckMoveObjectPOV (ae, other_guy, temp, ch);

                    AppShow3D();
                    ae->ObjList[other_guy].bmNum[0] = num1;
                    ae->ObjList[other_guy].bmNum[1] = num2;
                    ae->ObjList[other_guy].bmNum[2] = num3;
                    ae->ObjList[other_guy].bmNum[3] = num4;
                    break;

        case 'i': if ((com_device == 'n') || (com_device == 'm')) ch = com_rx(PORT);
                  if (com_device == 'e') ch = data_packet[21];

                    AckDeleteObject (ae, ch);
                    break;

        case 'j': if ((com_device == 'n') || (com_device == 'm')) ch = com_rx(PORT);
                  if (com_device == 'e') ch = data_packet[21];

                    AckDeleteObject (ae, ch);
                    break;

        case 'k': AckDeleteObject (ae, other_guy);
                  break;


        case 'l':
                    ae->ObjList[other_guy_bullet].x = ae->ObjList[other_guy].x;
                    ae->ObjList[other_guy_bullet].y = ae->ObjList[other_guy].y;
                    ae->ObjList[other_guy_bullet].Dir = ae->ObjList[other_guy].Dir;
                    ae->ObjList[other_guy_bullet].mPos = (ae->ObjList[other_guy_bullet].y
& 0xFFC0) + (ae->ObjList[other_guy_bullet].x >> 6);
                    ae->ObjList[other_guy_bullet].VidRow = 100;
                    ae->ObjList[other_guy_bullet].Active = 1;
                    break;

        case 'm': if ((com_device == 'm') || (com_device == 'n'))
                  {
```

```c
            ae->ObjList[other_guy_bullet].x = (com_rx(PORT)<<8)+(com_rx(PORT));
            ae->ObjList[other_guy_bullet].y = (com_rx(PORT)<<8)+(com_rx(PORT));
        }


        if(com_device == 'e')
        {
          ae->ObjList[other_guy_bullet].x = (get_packet[21] << 8)+get_packet[22];
          ae->ObjList[other_guy_bullet].y = (get_packet[23] << 8)+get_packet[24];
        }


        ae->ObjList[other_guy_bullet].mPos = ((ae->ObjList[other_guy_bullet].y
& 0xFFC0) + (ae->ObjList[other_guy_bullet].x >> 6));
        break;

    case 'n': AckDeleteObject (ae, other_guy_bullet);
        break;

    case 'o': AckDeleteObject(ae, other_guy);
        AckDeleteObject(ae, other_guy_bullet);

        AckFadeOut(0, 255);
        reset_game();
        AckFadeIn(0, 255, colordat);
        break;

    case 'w': ammo = 0;
        AckFadeOut(0, 255);
        reset_game();
        AckFadeIn(0, 255, colordat);
        break;

    case 'x': if ((com_device == 'm') || (com_device == 'n'))
        {
           ae->ObjList[monster_bullet].x = (com_rx(PORT)<<8)+(com_rx(PORT));
           ae->ObjList[monster_bullet].y = (com_rx(PORT)<<8)+(com_rx(PORT));
        }

        if(com_device == 'e')
        {
        ae->ObjList[monster_bullet].x = (get_packet[21] << 8)+get_packet[22];
        ae->ObjList[monster_bullet].y = (get_packet[23] << 8)+get_packet[24];
        }
```

```
          ae->ObjList[monster_bullet].mPos = ((ae->ObjList[monster_bullet].y &
0xFFC0) + (ae->ObjList[monster_bullet].x >> 6));
          ae->ObjList[monster_bullet].VidRow = 100;
          ae->ObjList[monster_bullet].Active = 1;
          break;

   case 'y': if ((com_device == 'm') || (com_device == 'n'))
        {
          ae->ObjList[monster1].x = (com_rx(PORT)<<8)+(com_rx(PORT));
          ae->ObjList[monster1].y = (com_rx(PORT)<<8)+(com_rx(PORT));
          ae->ObjList[monster1].Dir = (com_rx(PORT)<<8)+(com_rx(PORT));
        }
        if (com_device=='e')
        {
          ae->ObjList[monster1].x = (get_packet[21] << 8)+get_packet[22];
          ae->ObjList[monster1].y = (get_packet[23] << 8)+get_packet[24];
          ae->ObjList[monster1].Dir = (get_packet[25] << 8)+get_packet[26];
        }


        angle = ae->ObjList[monster1].Dir;
        {
          if (ae->ObjList[monster1].Active)
          {
                }
                }
// Just as in the case of the opponent, the minotaur monster has animation
// in its movements.  We have to change the bitmaps accordingly.
          if (++monster_moves == 7) monster_moves = 0;
          if (angle == 0)
          {
            if (monster_moves == 3)
            {
              ae->ObjList[monster1].bmNum[0] = 11;
              ae->ObjList[monster1].bmNum[1] = 14;
              ae->ObjList[monster1].bmNum[2] = 5;
              ae->ObjList[monster1].bmNum[3] = 16;
            }
            else if (monster_moves == 6)
            {
              ae->ObjList[monster1].bmNum[0] = 13;
              ae->ObjList[monster1].bmNum[1] = 15;
              ae->ObjList[monster1].bmNum[2] = 10;
              ae->ObjList[monster1].bmNum[3] = 17;
            }
```

```
        }
            else if (angle == INT_ANGLE_90)
    {
      if (monster_moves == 3)
      {
        ae->ObjList[monster1].bmNum[0] = 16;
        ae->ObjList[monster1].bmNum[1] = 11;
        ae->ObjList[monster1].bmNum[2] = 14;
        ae->ObjList[monster1].bmNum[3] = 5;
      }
      else if (monster_moves == 6)
      {
        ae->ObjList[monster1].bmNum[0] = 17;
        ae->ObjList[monster1].bmNum[1] = 13;
        ae->ObjList[monster1].bmNum[2] = 15;
        ae->ObjList[monster1].bmNum[3] = 10;
      }
    }
    else if (angle == INT_ANGLE_180)
    {
      if (monster_moves == 3)
      {
        ae->ObjList[monster1].bmNum[0] = 5;
        ae->ObjList[monster1].bmNum[1] = 16;
        ae->ObjList[monster1].bmNum[2] = 11;
        ae->ObjList[monster1].bmNum[3] = 14;
      }
      else if (monster_moves == 6)
      {
        ae->ObjList[monster1].bmNum[0] = 10;
        ae->ObjList[monster1].bmNum[1] = 17;
        ae->ObjList[monster1].bmNum[2] = 13;
        ae->ObjList[monster1].bmNum[3] = 15;
      }
    }
    else
    {
      if (monster_moves == 3)
      {
        ae->ObjList[monster1].bmNum[0] = 14;
        ae->ObjList[monster1].bmNum[1] = 5;
        ae->ObjList[monster1].bmNum[2] = 16;
        ae->ObjList[monster1].bmNum[3] = 11;
```

```
        }
      else if (monster_moves == 6)
      {
        ae->ObjList[monster1].bmNum[0] = 15;
        ae->ObjList[monster1].bmNum[1] = 10;
        ae->ObjList[monster1].bmNum[2] = 17;
        ae->ObjList[monster1].bmNum[3] = 13;
      }
  }
        ae->ObjList[monster1].mPos = ((ae->ObjList[monster1].y & 0xFFC0) +
(ae->ObjList[monster1].x >> 6));
        ae->ObjList[monster1].Active = 1;
    {
        break;

    case 'z': if ((com_device == 'm') || (com_device == 'n'))
        {
          ae->ObjList[other_guy].x = (com_rx(PORT) << 8)+com_rx(PORT);
          ae->ObjList[other_guy].y = (com_rx(PORT) << 8)+com_rx(PORT);
          ae->ObjList[other_guy].Dir = (com_rx(PORT) << 8)+com_rx(PORT);
        }
        if (com_device == 'e')
        {
          ae->ObjList[other_guy].x = (get_packet[21] << 8)+get_packet[22];
          ae->ObjList[other_guy].y = (get_packet[23] << 8)+get_packet[24];
          ae->ObjList[other_guy].Dir = (get_packet[25] << 8)+get_packet[26];
        }

        ae->ObjList[other_guy].mPos = (ae->ObjList[other_guy].y & 0xFFC0) +
(ae->ObjList[other_guy].x >> 6);
        break;
    }
}


void hangup()
{
  if (com_device == 'm')
  {
    com_lower_dtr(PORT);
    delay(1100);
    if (com_carrier(PORT))
    {
```

```
          com_tx_string_with_delay(PORT, "+++", 10, 10);
          delay(1100);
          com_tx(PORT, 13); delay(10);
          com_tx_string_with_delay(PORT, "ATH", 10, 10);
          com_tx(PORT, 13); delay(10);
      }
      com_flush_rx(PORT);
      com_flush_tx(PORT);
      busy = num_stored = null_modem = connected = 0;
   }
}


void do_link()
{
   char ours, theirs, do_again = 1;
   int packet_length;

   randomize();
   while ( do_again )
   {
     do_again = 0;
     randomize();
     ours = random(50);

         if ((com_device == 'n') || (com_device == 'm'))
           com_tx(PORT, ours);

         if (com_device=='e')
         {
           data_packet[20] = ours;
           send_pkt (interrupt_number, data_packet, 64);
         }

         if ((com_device == 'n') || (com_device == 'm'))
           theirs=com_rx(PORT);

         if (com_device=='e')
         {
           while (!get_from_queue(get_packet, &packet_length, 0)) ;

           theirs = get_packet[20];
         }
```

```
          if (ours<theirs)
            person = 0;
          else
            person = 1;

          if (ours==theirs) do_again = 1;
    }
}


// This routine handles the answering of the modem when using a modem
// connection.
void answer()
{

  char a, b, d, result;

  clrscr();
  if (!connected)
  {
    com_raise_dtr(PORT);
    com_flush_rx(PORT);
    delay(1100);
    com_tx_string_with_delay(PORT, "ATE0X4V0AS0=1", 10, 10 );
    com_tx(PORT, 13); delay(10);

    printf ( "Waiting to answer modem...\n\n");
    delay(3500);

    a=b=d=0;
    while((!bioskey(1))&&(a==0)&&(!com_carrier(PORT)))
      if(!com_rx_empty(PORT))
      {
        a = com_rx(PORT);
        if ( a == 50 )
        {
          b = com_rx(PORT);
          if (b==13)
          {
            a = com_rx(PORT);
            b = 0;
          }
        }
```

```
    }

delay(2000);

if (!bioskey(1))
{
   if(b==0)   b = com_rx(PORT);
   if(b!=13)  d = com_rx(PORT);
}

if ( b == 13 ) result = a - 48;
else if ( d == 13 ) result = (a-48)*10 + (b-48);

if (bioskey(1))
{
   getkey();
   if (!com_carrier(PORT))
           com_tx(PORT,13);
   else
           hangup();
   return;
}

if ((com_carrier(PORT))&&(result!=ERROR)&&(result!=
NODIALTONE)&&(result!=NOCARRIER))
   {
     printf ("Waiting to connect...\n\n");
     com_flush_rx(PORT);
     connected = 1;
     delay(5000);
     do_link();
   }
   else if ( result == NODIALTONE )
   {
     busy = 1;
     printf ( "No Dial Tone...\n");
     delay(5000);
   }
   else if ( result == NOCARRIER )
   {
     busy = 1;
     printf ( "No Carrier...\n\n");
     delay(5000);
```

```
    }
    else
    {
      hangup();
      printf ( "Unable to connect.  Please Try Again...\n");
      delay(5000);
      busy = 1;
    }
  }
}


// This function handles the dialing of the modem when using a modem
// connection.
void dial()
{
  char a, b, d, result, inbuff[15];


  clrscr();
  if (!connected)
  {
    if ( busy && num_stored )
    {
      printf ("Redial previous number? (y/n)");
      a = getkey();
      while ( (a!='y') && (a!='n'))
      a = getkey();

      if ( a == 'y' )
      {
            com_raise_dtr(PORT);
            com_flush_rx(PORT);
            delay(1100);
            com_tx_string_with_delay(PORT, "A/", 10, 10);
            com_tx(PORT,13);
      }
    }

    if ( (!busy) || (a == 'n') )
    {
      printf ("Number: ");
      scanf ("%s", inbuff);
```

```
          com_flush_rx(PORT);
          com_raise_dtr(PORT);
          printf ("Dialing...\n\n");
          num_stored = 1;

          delay(1100);
          com_tx_string_with_delay(PORT, "ATE0X4V0DT", 10, 10 );
          com_tx_string_with_delay(PORT, inbuff, 10, 10);
          com_tx(PORT, 13);
      }

      delay(3500);
      a=0;

      while (((!bioskey(1))&&(!com_carrier(PORT)&&(a==0)))
        if(!com_rx_empty(PORT)) a = com_rx(PORT);

      delay(2000);

      if (!bioskey(1))
      {
        b = com_rx(PORT);
        if(b!=13) d = com_rx(PORT);
      }

      if ( b == 13 ) result = a - 48;
      else if ( d == 13 ) result = (a-48)*10 + (b-48);

      if (bioskey(1))
      {
        getkey();
        if (!com_carrier(PORT))
            com_tx(PORT,13);
        else
            hangup();
        return;
      }

      if
((com_carrier(PORT))&&(result!=ERROR)&&(result!=NODIALTONE)&&(result!=NOCARR
IER)&&(result!=BUSY))
        {
          busy = num_stored = 0;
```

416 APPENDIX C

```c
        printf ("Waiting to connect...\n\n");
        com_flush_rx(PORT);
        connected = busy = 1;
        delay(5000);
        do_link();
    }
    else if ( result == NODIALTONE )
    {
        busy = 1;
        printf ( "No Dialtone...\n\n");
        delay(5000);
    }
    else if ( result == BUSY )
    {
        busy = 1;
        printf ( "Busy...\n\n");
        delay(5000);
    }
    else if ( result == NOCARRIER )
    {
        busy = 1;
        printf ( "No carrier...\n\n");
        delay(5000);
    }
    else
    {
        hangup();
        printf ("Unable to connect..Please try again...\n\n");
        delay(5000);
        busy = 1;
    }
  }
}


// This function handles the 'dialing' of the serial port during a
// null modem connection.
void null_dial()
{

  clrscr();
  printf ("This machine will begin the NULL modem communication
link.\n\n");
```

```
        printf ("Be sure that the cable connects both of the machines.\n\n\n\n");

        printf ("Initializing serial port for link...\n");
        com_flush_rx(PORT);
        com_flush_tx(PORT);
        com_raise_dtr(PORT);
        delay(3500);

        null_modem = connected = 1;

        printf ("Exchanging initial data...\n");
        delay(3500);
        do_link();
}


// This function handles the answering of the serial port during a
// null-modem connection.
void null_answer()
{
    clrscr();
    printf ("This machine will receive the NULL modem communication
link.\n\n");
    printf ("Be sure that the cable connects both of the machines.\n\n\n\n");

        printf ("Initializing serial port for link...\n");
        com_flush_rx(PORT);
        com_flush_tx(PORT);
        com_raise_dtr(PORT);
        delay(3500);

        null_modem = connected = 1;

        printf ( "Exchanging initial data...\n");
        delay(3500);
        do_link();
}

// This function tries to communicate with a modem.
int check_port()
{
    char a,b;
    long test;
```

```
        com_raise_dtr(PORT);
        com_flush_rx(PORT);
        delay(1100);
        com_tx_string_with_delay(PORT, "ATE0V0", 10, 10 );
        com_tx(PORT, 13); delay(10);
        delay(3500);

        a=b=test=0;
        while((com_rx_empty(PORT))&&(test<1500000))
          test++;

        if (!com_rx_empty(PORT)) a = com_rx(PORT);
        if (!com_rx_empty(PORT)) b = com_rx(PORT);
        com_lower_dtr(PORT);

        if (a == 48 ) return 1;
        else return 0;


}


// This function handles setting up a modem or null modem connection.
// Appropriate control software is installed and the COM port is checked
int setup_com()
{
    int com, ok = 0;
    char ch;


    // Get COM port of serial device.
    clrscr();
    printf ( "\n");
    printf ( "Select the COM port to which your modem or NULL modem
connection."); printf ( "\n");
    printf ( "is attached.");printf ( "\n\n");
    printf ( "Enter COM port number ( 1,2,3, or 4):");
    ch = getkey();
    while ( (ch<49) || (ch>52))
    {
      printf ( "\n");
      printf ( "Enter COM port number ( 1,2,3, or 4):");
```

```c
        ch = getkey();
    }
PORT = ch-48;

if ((com = com_install(PORT)))
{
    printf ( "Unable to install COM driver\n");
    exit(1);
}

SPEED=0;
while (!SPEED)
{
    clrscr();
    printf ( "\n");
    printf ("Please select the appropriate baud rate\n\n");
    printf ("(A)  2400\n");
    printf ("(B)  4800\n");
    printf ("(C)  9600\n");
    printf ("(D)  14400\n");
    printf ("(E)  28800\n");
    ch = toupper(getkey());
    switch(ch)
    {
        case 'A': SPEED = 2400; break;
        case 'B': SPEED = 4800; break;
        case 'C': SPEED = 9600; break;
        case 'D': SPEED = 19200; break;
        case 'E': SPEED = 38400; break;
    }
}

com_set_speed(PORT, SPEED );
com_set_parity(PORT, COM_NONE, 1);
com_lower_dtr(PORT);
com_raise_dtr(PORT);
com_lower_dtr(PORT);

if (com_device=='m')
{
    printf ( "\n");

    printf ( "\nChecking Modem at COM Port %d...\n", PORT );
```

```
    if (check_port())
    {
        com_raise_dtr(PORT);
        com_tx_string ( PORT, "ATV0E0S0=0");
        com_tx(PORT,13);
        com_lower_dtr(PORT);
        ok = 1;
    }

    if ((!ok)&&check_port())
    {
        com_raise_dtr(PORT);
        com_tx_string ( PORT, "ATV0E0S0=0");
        com_tx(PORT,13);
        com_lower_dtr(PORT);
        ok = 1;
    }

    if ((!ok)&&check_port())
    {
        com_raise_dtr(PORT);
        com_tx_string ( PORT, "ATV0E0S0=0");
        com_tx(PORT,13);
        com_lower_dtr(PORT);
        ok = 1;
    }
}

if (!ok)
{
    clrscr();
    printf ( "\n\n\nThe system was unable to locate a modem at the COM
port specified" );
    printf ( "\n\nPlease check the connection and COM port.  It is
imperative that" );
    printf ( "\nThe modem has a dedicated IRQ line.  Check the following
chart to");
    printf ( "\nDetermine if you have a possible conflict");
    printf ( "\n\n\n");
    printf ( "            Modem COM Port          COM Ports Not to Use");
    printf ( "\n\n");
    printf ( "            COM Port 1              Ports - 3\n");
    printf ( "            COM Port 2              Ports - 4\n");
```

```
                printf ( "              COM Port 3                Ports - 1\n");
                printf ( "              COM Port 4                Ports - 2\n");
                printf ( "\n\n\n\n\n\n\n");
            exit(1);
        }
    }
    else
    {
        printf ( "\n\nBypassing Modem setup...\n");
        delay(1000);
    }


    return(0);
}


// This function does the low level build of the ethernet packets.
void build_packets()
{
    int i;

    for (i=6;i<12;i++)
    {
        ack_packet[i] = our_address[i-6];
        data_packet[i] = our_address[i-6];
        get_packet[i] = our_address[i-6];
    }


    for (i=0;i<6;i++)
    {
        ack_packet[i] = their_address[i];
        data_packet[i] = their_address[i];
        get_packet[i] = their_address[i];
    }

    ack_packet[12] = (0xFF00 & main_packet_type) >> 8;
    ack_packet[13] = (unsigned char)(0x00FF & main_packet_type);

    get_packet[12] = data_packet[12] = ack_packet[12];
    get_packet[13] = data_packet[13] = ack_packet[13];

    ack_packet[14] = 'a';
    ack_packet[15] = 'c';
    ack_packet[16] = 'k';
```

422 APPENDIX C

```c
        }

int select_communication_device()
{
  char ch;
  int result;

  while (!com_device)
  {
    clrscr();
    printf ("\n\n\n");
    printf ("Please select the communication medium that you would like to
use:\n\n");
    printf ("(E)thernet connection\n");
    printf ("(N)ull Modem connection\n");
    printf ("(M)odem connection\n");
    printf ("(S)ingle User\n");

    printf (":");
    ch = getkey();

    printf ("%c\n", ch);

    switch (toupper(ch))
    {
      case 'E': com_device = 'e';
                p_type = 0x1234;

                set_type (p_type);
                find_driver(&interrupt_number);
                driver_info(interrupt_number, &handle, &version,
&driver_class, &ttype, &number, &basic );
                access_type (interrupt_number, &handle, driver_class,
ttype, number, p_type, 2);
                get_address (interrupt_number, handle);
                result = 0;
                break;

      case 'N': com_device = 'n';
                result = setup_com();
                break;

      case 'M': com_device = 'm';
```

```
                        result = setup_com();
                        break;

            case 'S': com_device = 's';
                        result = 0;
                        break;
        }
    }
    return(result);
}




int create_link()
{

    int got_one = 0, i, packet_length;
    char ch, buffer[40];

    switch(com_device)
    {

        case 'e': clrscr();
                printf ("Are we the (O)riginator or (A)nswerer?\n");
                printf (":");
                ch = toupper(getkey());
                printf ("%c\n", ch);

                if (ch == 'O')
                {
                    for (i=0;i<6;i++)
                        their_address[i] = 0xff; //0;

                    build_packets();
                    data_packet[20] = 'x';

                    send_pkt(interrupt_number, data_packet, 64);

                    while (!get_from_queue(get_packet, &packet_length, 0))
                        { if (kbhit()) exit(1); }

                    if (get_packet[20] == 'y')
```

```
            {
              for(i=0;i<6;i++)
                their_address[i] = get_packet[6+i];

              build_packets();
              do_link();
            }
        }
      else
      {

          build_packets();
          while (!get_from_queue(get_packet, &packet_length, 0))
          { if (kbhit()) exit(1); }

          if (get_packet[20] == 'x')
          {
            data_packet[20] = 'y';
            for (i=0;i<6;i++)
            {
              data_packet[i] = get_packet[6+i];
              their_address[i] = get_packet[i];
            }

            for (i=0;i<6;i++)
             data_packet[i+6] = our_address[i];

            send_pkt(interrupt_number, data_packet, 64);
            build_packets();
            do_link();
          }
        }
        break;

case 'n': while (!got_one)
      {
      clrscr();
      printf ("Is this machine the originating or answering machine?\n");
      printf (":");

      ch = toupper(getkey());
      printf ("%c\n", ch);

      if (ch == 'O')
```

```
              {
                 null_dial();
                 return(0);
              }

              if (ch == 'A')
              {
                 null_answer();
                 return(0);
              }
           }
        return(1);

   case 'm': while (!got_one)
       {
           clrscr();
           printf ("Is this machine the originating or answering machine?\n");
           printf (":");

           ch = toupper(getkey());
           printf ("%c\n", ch);

           if (ch == 'O')
           {
              dial();
              return(0);
           }

           if (ch == 'A')
           {
              answer();
              return(0);

           }
        }
            return(1);
     }
   return(0);
}


void move_monsters()
{
```

```
       int x1, y1, x, y, px, py, dx, dy, angle, result, dx1, dy1;

monster_moves++;

if (ae->ObjList[monster1].Active == 1)
{
 x = ae->ObjList[monster1].x;
 y = ae->ObjList[monster1].y;

 x1 = ae->ObjList[other_guy].x;
 y1 = ae->ObjList[other_guy].y;


 px = ae->xPlayer;
 py = ae->yPlayer;

 dx = abs(px - x);
 dy = abs(py - y);

 if(com_device != 's')
 {
   dx1 = abs(px - x1);
   dy1 = abs(py - y1);

   if (dx1 < dx)
   {
     dx = dx1;
     dy = dy1;

     x = x1;
     y = y1;
   }
 }

 if (dx > dy)
   py = y;

 if (dx < dy)
   px = x;


 if (py == y)
 {
```

```
          if (px < x) angle = INT_ANGLE_180;
          if (px > x) angle = 0;
       }


       if (px == x)
       {
          if (py < y) angle = INT_ANGLE_270;
          if (py > y) angle = INT_ANGLE_90;
       }



       if (monster_moves == 7) monster_moves = 0;
       if (angle == 0)
       {
          if (monster_moves == 3)
          {
             ae->ObjList[monster1].bmNum[0] = 11;
             ae->ObjList[monster1].bmNum[1] = 14;
             ae->ObjList[monster1].bmNum[2] = 5;
             ae->ObjList[monster1].bmNum[3] = 16;
          }
          else if (monster_moves == 6)
          {
             ae->ObjList[monster1].bmNum[0] = 13;
             ae->ObjList[monster1].bmNum[1] = 15;
             ae->ObjList[monster1].bmNum[2] = 10;
             ae->ObjList[monster1].bmNum[3] = 17;
          }
       }
       else if (angle == INT_ANGLE_90)
       {
          if (monster_moves == 3)
          {
             ae->ObjList[monster1].bmNum[0] = 16;
             ae->ObjList[monster1].bmNum[1] = 11;
             ae->ObjList[monster1].bmNum[2] = 14;
             ae->ObjList[monster1].bmNum[3] = 5;
          }
          else if (monster_moves == 6)
          {
             ae->ObjList[monster1].bmNum[0] = 17;
             ae->ObjList[monster1].bmNum[1] = 13;
             ae->ObjList[monster1].bmNum[2] = 15;
```

```
        ae->ObjList[monster1].bmNum[3] = 10;
    }
}
else if (angle == INT_ANGLE_180)
{
    if (monster_moves == 3)
    {
        ae->ObjList[monster1].bmNum[0] = 5;
        ae->ObjList[monster1].bmNum[1] = 16;
        ae->ObjList[monster1].bmNum[2] = 11;
        ae->ObjList[monster1].bmNum[3] = 14;
    }
    else if (monster_moves == 6)
    {
        ae->ObjList[monster1].bmNum[0] = 10;
        ae->ObjList[monster1].bmNum[1] = 17;
        ae->ObjList[monster1].bmNum[2] = 13;
        ae->ObjList[monster1].bmNum[3] = 15;
    }
}
else
{
    if (monster_moves == 3)
    {
        ae->ObjList[monster1].bmNum[0] = 14;
        ae->ObjList[monster1].bmNum[1] = 5;
        ae->ObjList[monster1].bmNum[2] = 16;
        ae->ObjList[monster1].bmNum[3] = 11;
    }
    else if (monster_moves == 6)
    {
        ae->ObjList[monster1].bmNum[0] = 15;
        ae->ObjList[monster1].bmNum[1] = 10;
        ae->ObjList[monster1].bmNum[2] = 17;
        ae->ObjList[monster1].bmNum[3] = 13;
    }
}


ae->ObjList[monster1].Active = 1;
ae->ObjList[monster1].Dir = angle;

result = AckMoveObjectPOV(ae,monster1,ae->ObjList[monster1].Dir,ae-
```

```
     >ObjList[monster1].Speed);
       if ((com_device == 'n') || (com_device == 'm'))
       {
         com_tx(PORT, 'y');
         com_tx(PORT, ((ae->ObjList[monster1].x & 0xFF00)>>8));
         com_tx(PORT, (ae->ObjList[monster1].x & 0x00FF));

         com_tx(PORT, ((ae->ObjList[monster1].y & 0xFF00)>>8));
         com_tx(PORT, (ae->ObjList[monster1].y & 0x00FF));

         com_tx(PORT, ((ae->ObjList[monster1].Dir & 0xFF00)>>8));
         com_tx(PORT, (ae->ObjList[monster1].Dir & 0x00FF));
       }

       if (com_device=='e')
       {
         data_packet[20] = 'y';
         data_packet[21] = (ae->ObjList[monster1].x & 0xFF00)>>8;
         data_packet[22] = (ae->ObjList[monster1].x & 0x00FF);
         data_packet[23] = (ae->ObjList[monster1].y & 0xFF00)>>8;
         data_packet[24] = ae->ObjList[monster1].y & 0x00FF;
         data_packet[25] = (ae->ObjList[monster1].Dir & 0xFF00)>>8;
         data_packet[26] = ae->ObjList[monster1].Dir & 0x00FF;
         send_pkt (interrupt_number,data_packet, 64);
       }

       if (result == POV_PLAYER)
       {
         ammo = 0;
         if ((com_device == 'n') || (com_device == 'm')) com_tx(PORT, 'o');
         if (com_device=='e')
         {
           data_packet[20] = 'o';
           send_pkt (interrupt_number,data_packet, 64);
         }

         AckFadeOut(0, 255);
         reset_game();
         AckFadeIn(0, 255, colordat);

         AckDeleteObject(ae, other_guy);
         AckDeleteObject(ae, other_guy_bullet);
       }
```

```
    else if (result == POV_OBJECT)
    {
      AckDeleteObject(ae, other_guy);
      AckDeleteObject(ae, other_guy_bullet);
      AckFadeOut(0, 255);
      reset_game();
      AckFadeIn(0, 255, colordat);


      if ((com_device == 'n') || (com_device == 'm')) com_tx(PORT, 'w');
      if (com_device=='e')
      {
        data_packet[20] = 'w';
        send_pkt (interrupt_number,data_packet, 64);
      }
    }


  }
}


void check_objects()
{
  int i;

  i = AckGetObjectHit();
  switch (i)
  {

    case 3: if ((com_device == 'n') || (com_device == 'm'))
      {
        com_tx(PORT, 'i');
        com_tx(PORT, 3);
      }
      if (com_device=='e')
      {
        data_packet[20] = 'i';
        data_packet[21] = 3;
        send_pkt (interrupt_number,data_packet, 64);
      }

      AckDeleteObject (ae, i);
      ammo += 10;
```

```
                    AckPlaySound(1);
                    break;

                case 4: if ((com_device == 'n') || (com_device == 'm'))
                    {
                        com_tx(PORT, 'i');
                        com_tx(PORT, 4);
                    }
                    if (com_device=='e')
                    {
                        data_packet[20] = 'i';
                        data_packet[21] = 4;
                        send_pkt (interrupt_number,data_packet, 64);
                    }

                    AckDeleteObject (ae, i);
                    ammo += 10;
                    AckPlaySound(1);
                    break;

                case 5: if ((com_device == 'n') || (com_device == 'm'))
                    {
                        com_tx(PORT, 'i');
                        com_tx(PORT, 5);
                    }
                    if (com_device=='e')
                    {
                        data_packet[20] = 'i';
                        data_packet[21] = 5;
                        send_pkt (interrupt_number,data_packet, 64);
                    }

                    AckDeleteObject (ae, i);
                    ammo += 10;
                    AckPlaySound(1);
                    break;

            }
        }



// This function handles the shooting of the medusa head monster.    If works
// just like the shooting of the player's bullet.
```

```
void monster_shoot()
{
    int result;

    result = AckMoveObjectPOV(ae, monster_bullet, ae-
>ObjList[monster_bullet].Dir, ae->ObjList[monster_bullet].Speed);

    if ((com_device == 'n') || (com_device == 'm'))
    {
        com_tx(PORT, 'x');
        com_tx(PORT, ((ae->ObjList[monster_bullet].x & 0xFF00)>>8));
        com_tx(PORT, (ae->ObjList[monster_bullet].x & 0x00FF));

        com_tx(PORT, ((ae->ObjList[monster_bullet].y & 0xFF00)>>8));
        com_tx(PORT, (ae->ObjList[monster_bullet].y & 0x00FF));
    }

    if (com_device=='e')
    {
        data_packet[20] = 'x';
        data_packet[21] = (ae->ObjList[monster_bullet].x & 0xFF00)>>8;
        data_packet[22] = (ae->ObjList[monster_bullet].x & 0x00FF);
        data_packet[23] = (ae->ObjList[monster_bullet].y & 0xFF00)>>8;
        data_packet[24] = ae->ObjList[monster_bullet].y & 0x00FF;
        send_pkt (interrupt_number,data_packet, 64);
    }

    if (result != POV_NOTHING)
    {
        ae->ObjList[monster_bullet].Active = 0;
        monster_shooting = 0;

        result = AckGetObjectHit();
        if (result == POV_PLAYER)
        {
            ammo = 0;
            if ((com_device == 'n') || (com_device == 'm')) com_tx(PORT, 'o');

            AckFadeOut(0, 255);
            reset_game();
            AckFadeIn(0, 255, colordat);

            AckDeleteObject(ae, other_guy);
```

```
          AckDeleteObject(ae, other_guy_bullet);
      }

      if (com_device=='e')
      {
        data_packet[20] = 'o';
        send_pkt (interrupt_number,data_packet, 64);
      }


    }
    else if (result == POV_OBJECT)
    {
      ae->ObjList[other_guy].Active = 0;
      if ((com_device == 'n') || (com_device == 'm')) com_tx(PORT, 'w');

      if (com_device=='e')
      {
        data_packet[20] = 'w';
        send_pkt (interrupt_number,data_packet, 64);
      }
      AckFadeOut(0, 255);
      reset_game();
      AckFadeIn(0, 255, colordat);
    }

    if (monster_shooting == 0)
    {
      monster_shooting = 1;
      ae->ObjList[monster_bullet].x = ae->ObjList[medusa].x;
      ae->ObjList[monster_bullet].y = ae->ObjList[medusa].y;
      ae->ObjList[monster_bullet].Dir = random (INT_ANGLE_360);
      ae->ObjList[monster_bullet].mPos = (ae->ObjList[monster_bullet].y &
  0xFFC0) + (ae->ObjList[monster_bullet].x >> 6);
      ae->ObjList[monster_bullet].VidRow = 100;
      ae->ObjList[monster_bullet].Active = 1;
    }
}
```

Index